The reader's construction of narrative

to Dorle

The reader's construction of narrative

HORST RUTHROF

ROUTLEDGE & KEGAN PAUL
London, Boston and Henley

First published in 1981
by Routledge & Kegan Paul Ltd
39 Store Street,
London WC1E 7DD,
9 Park Street,
Boston, Mass. 02108, USA, and
Broadway House,
Newtown Road,
Henley-on-Thames,
Oxon RG9 1EN
Printed in Great Britain by
Thomson Litho Ltd, East Kilbride

British Library Cataloguing in Publication Data

Ruthrof, Horst
The reader's construction of narrative.
1. Narration
2. Hermeneutics
I. Title
809'.923   PN12   80-41950

ISBN 0-7100-0662-4

Contents

Preface

Following an invitation by Roman Jakobson, Edmund Husserl gave a paper on 18 November 1935 entitled Phenomenology and the Science of Language before the Prague Linguistic Circle. Since then phenomenology and structuralism have on the whole developed separately with occasional points of convergence in Poland, France and Germany. In recent years the two methods have again moved closer to one another with the growing structuralist interest in how meaning is established during the 'activity of reading' (J. Culler, 'Structuralist Poetics', Routledge & Kegan Paul, London, 1975, p. viii) and the incorporation by phenomenology of structuralist findings into its holistic approach to the literary work of art (e.g., Wolfgang Iser, 'The Implied Reader', Johns Hopkins University Press, Baltimore, 1974 and 'The Act of Reading', Routledge & Kegan Paul, London, 1979; or Rainer Warning's important collection of essays in 'Rezeptionsaesthetik', Wilhelm Fink, Munich, 1975, which combines representatives of both schools. (1)

Though leaning in its method towards Husserl and his successors, the present study borrows as well as modifies both phenomenological and structuralist conceptions. The application, for example, of Husserl's distinction between acts of experiencing ('noesis') and that which is experienced ('noema') to 'discours' and 'histoire' produced a radical reassessment of the relations between the narrative speech act and its fictive projections (for such other items as reductions, appresentation, formalization, deformalization, intentionality, polythetic–synthetic–monothetic experience, protentions, retentions, intersubjectivity, horizon, or adumbrational aspects, see the Index).

Apart from my general acceptance of Alfred Schutz's view of the social life-world, I have borrowed from his works such concepts as stock-of-knowledge-at-hand, biographical situation, three different kinds of relevance and typifications of everyday experience. For the purposes of this study I have split the last concept into general typifications and specifically literary typifications, or the reader's typified sense of intertextuality.

My greatest and most obvious debt is to Roman Ingarden, whose dynamic view of the interplay of strata and the forward reading dimension I have adapted to the reading of narrative – as against generally literary texts. Of equal importance to my project is his distinction between artistic and aesthetic object, between potential and realized literary structure. On the other hand, I have left aside two important issues: his theory of language (which I am planning to discuss in a separate study) and his theory of how value qualities constitute a work's overall value (which has invited much adverse criticism). However, his notion of a 'polyphony of aesthetic value qualities' as realized in the reading performance has been retained as useful. Other phenomenological influences have been the works of Mikel Dufrenne, Nicolai Hartmann, Wolfgang Iser, Michael Murray, Maurice Natanson, George Poulet, and Paul Ricoeur, as well as the applications of phenomenological theory to specific texts by Peter Berger, Paul Brodtkorb and R. Swaeringen. (2)

From the linguistic structuralist camp the concept of sign as signifier and signified has been borrowed to demonstrate that, with certain exceptions, narrative surface texts are sets of signs coding at the same time two ontologically different sets of signifieds: presentational process and presented world. At various points the Saussurean-Jakobsonean distinction between metonymy and metaphor helped to consolidate the argument, while Jakobson's doubts about linguistic solutions at the level of 'part-whole' relationships crystallized one of the concerns of this study. Such other items as the reader's transformation of surface into deep structures, the grammar of action sequences, or the notion of narrative modality are critically absorbed into my conception of the performance of narrative in the act of reading.

As to deep structure transformation, I have found especially promising (though requiring a comprehensive, interdisciplinary debate) Roger Fowler's suggestions of how

transformational operations can be central to the reading,
for example, of the novel. Three problems, however, must
be noted here. First, the emphasis on transformations
tends to undermine the significance of the surface text;
second, other kinds of transformations, such as various
forms of concretization, tend to be negated; and third, the
hierarchy of transformations from operations on the narrative surface text to final summary propositions is wholly
reductive.

In order to balance this purely propositional conception
of reading I am proposing that a different kind of transformation must also be allowed for: Roman Ingarden's concept
of concretization, a special case of the Husserlian appresentation. Both the successors of Ingarden and those of
the Prague Linguistic Circle (as, for example, Felix V.
Vodička) have put the term to their various special uses. (3)
In 'The Act of Reading' (IV, A, 2) Wolfgang Iser subjects
Ingarden's usage of concretization to a brilliant analysis,
concluding that in the reading performance it plays a much
less significant role than the Polish philosopher would have
us believe. My own view on the matter is somewhat closer
to Ingarden's, except that I distinguish between two kinds
of concretization: linguistic concretization, or the reader's
refinement of the given linguistic mesh (when something is
named of which we have available in our stock of knowledge
a detailed definition and at the same time the context
encourages a filling aesthetic construction), and imaginative
concretization (when during the act of reading we put ourselves in the position of, for instance, a quasi-movie
producer). Both forms of filling should be sub-divided into
'pairing', or compulsory concretization (without which we
are unable to grasp what is being presented) and general
concretization (of various degrees of deformalization).
Wolfgang Iser's example of the advert (footnote 26 in 'The
Act of Reading', IV, A, 2), 'Come along with me / Have a
Genessee' which is shortened later to read 'Come along with
me / ...' is a case of pairing, the special case of compulsory concretization. Concretization as a refining linguistic response operates, for instance, when we read Robert
Coover's versions of fairy stories against our verbal background knowledge of the genuine article; as imaginative
concretization, for example, when a text presents a highly
schematic view of a building in Tudor style. Depending on
our linguistic competence as well as on the speed and
intensity of our reading, we 'understand' by activating to a

certain degree the text schema with the help of propositional
and imaginational subsidiary categorization.

A more serious disagreement exists between my own
position and the widespread structuralist equation of the
grammar of action sequences with a grammar of stories.
Structuralism has found it difficult to go beyond Vladimir
Propp's then brilliant protocol.   Roland Barthes's concept
of 'narrative transgression' (cf. chapter 2 below), Tzvetan
Todorov's claim that only referential sentences allow a
construction, (4) or Gerald Prince's insistence that his own
summary is identical with Perrault's 'Little Red Riding
Hood' except in style and tone all testify to the high degree
of identification of action sequence with narrative.
Prince's book is indeed an excellent grammar of action
sequences, but not a 'Grammar of Stories' as its title
suggests.   What is not covered, and not coverable by the
method, is called style and tone, an embarrassing and un-
wieldy extra not essential to narrative structure. (5)   The
corrective, though, is now being developed in the same
camp.   Lubomír Doležel's 'Narrative Modalities' marks, I
think, the change of direction with its promise to apply
modal systems to narrative action. (6)   Earlier in Poland,
the structuralist Janusz Slavinski published a paper entitled
'Semantyka wypowiedzi narracyjnej' (1967), now available
in German as 'Die Semantik der narrativen Äusserung', in
which a programme for an integration of all aspects of
narrative is tentatively proposed. (7)

But since the study of narrative modality is still in its
infancy, I have had to rely on my own description of what
happens when we read a narrative text.   The central
contention is that unlike pragmatic discourse where modality
is either available as a set of non-linguistic signs or is
defined as stable by a pragmatic horizon of expectations (as
is the case in technical instructions, scientific reports,
legal documents, etc.), fictive narrative modality is a set
of signifieds which must be constructed by the reader
through, prior to, or apart from the presented world.   As
a complex semantic unit it interacts dynamically with the
presented world in the reading consciousness at each point
of the forward reading process.   This semantic interaction
replaces both the relation between propositional content and
illocutionary force (Austin, Searle) (8) and the conception
of style and tone as an adjunct to action sequence.

Style is understood strictly as an aspect of the surface
text – language style – with its own polyphony of aesthetic

value qualities affecting both presentational process and
presented world at the semantic level. Tone, by contrast,
must be constructed by the reader (a) as a speaker's
attitude pertaining to presentational speech acts and (b) as
attitudes pertaining to presented speech acts. As such,
tone is not an aspect of the surface text, although coded in
it, but of other strata.

Stating the case of narrative modality extremely, without
I think overstating it, one could say that in the quasi-
judgmental phrase 'standing on the shaky ladder' the very
preposition 'on' implies two semantic realms: the presented
world and the presentational process, both with their
aspects of space, time, personae, acts, etc. In this case,
the presented world is foregrounded, with the presentational realm as a secondary construction on the part of the
reader. In narrative, this 'standard' situation undergoes
a number of transformations. But one can make the general
observation that the surface text is capable of carrying this
double signification simultaneously, while in the act of
reading we cannot construct both realms of meaning at the
same time. Depending on their specific coding, one of the
two is always a primary, the other a secondary consideration. But having experienced them separately by means of
a radical reorientation of consciousness, we must
dynamically interrelate them to establish narrative meaning.

In 'The Act of Reading' (I, B, 2) Wolfgang Iser discusses
a catalogue of readers in order to isolate his own 'implied
reader' as a distinct concept. There are the ideal reader,
the 'informed' (Fish), 'intended' (Wolff), or 'created'
reader (Booth), the 'archilecteur' (Riffaterre), or the
actual historical reader. (9) My own distinction between
'stated' and implied or 'stipulated' reader refers to a
difference in degree between control through linguistic
coding and the relative independence of reader construction.
I am suggesting further that the only kind of identification
possible between actual reader and work is his construction
of the implied reader, adequate or inadequate, and not
between reader and fictive personae.

Ultimately, Rainer Warning is certainly right in demanding
that literary theory focus on the historical convention of
the constitution and integration of 'histoire' and 'discours'
instead of on autonomous, universally conceived models of
narrativity. (10) Except for chapter 6, the historical
perspective is indeed missing. The present study is an
investigation which needs to be balanced by historical

enquiries. Another conspicuous lack is my scarce use of
Marxist theory. The reason is that I have found it
fascinating and persuasive as far as speculation at a high
level of abstraction is concerned, but not at all helpful in
the specific question of how the reader constructs a work
ideology from the surface text through the two sets of
signifieds, presentational process and presented world. A
case in point is Terry Eagleton's 'Criticism and Ideology:
A Study in Marxist Literary Theory'. Though generally
stimulating, it leaves us guessing as to how precisely the
reader proceeds from decoding the surface text to his
establishment of ideology, the 'signification of history'. (11)

Finally, a word about the arrangement of chapters. They
are conceived as selected adumbrational aspects of a narrative theory. As such they do not stand in a cogently causal
relation to one another, nor are they meant to be exhaustive.
Some chapters are designed more as grids for further more
detailed research than as solutions to a problem. Each
chapter therefore returns to the starting point of the theory
before pursuing its special goal. Chapter 1, What Happens
When We Read a Narrative Text? discusses modality, two
sets of signifieds, concretization and deep structure transformations, and projects two poles of narrative structure:
foregrounded presented world and foregrounded presentational process. Chapter 2 attacks Roland Barthes's notion
of 'narrative transgression' from the perspective of the
first chapter. Chapter 3, Narrative Language, suggests
the modification of word-fixated theories by means of a
holistic model of narrative structure as it is constituted in
the reading consciousness. Chapter 4, Narrative Stratification and the Dialectic of Reading, adapts Ingarden's
theory of strata to meet the requirements of narrative and
its typical reading performance. Chapter 5, Ladders of
Fictionality, resumes an old debate by proposing a ladder
of fictionality and its corresponding acts of reading in
relation to our typified experience of the world-out-there.
In so doing the chapter becomes a sort of balancing act
between mimetic and non-mimetic theories. In chapter 6,
Bracketed World and Reader Construction in the Modern
Short Story, the reduction, in addition to linguistic
restrictions, of presentational process and presented world
is seen as the characteristic feature of a particular story
type. Chapter 7, Narrative Strands: Presented and
Presentational, applies the view of a double set of
signifieds to a macro-structural phenomenon, suggesting

that the concept of strands should refer to both multi-
strand world and multi-strand discourse. Chapter 8, Acts
of Narrating: Transformations of Presentational Control,
projects a graded scale of narrative structures arranged
according to the changing relations of control between
narrator, signified world, and implied reader; from
authoritarian control by the narrator over the presented
world and full dependence of the implied reader to the
reverse position of the narrator's dependence on the world
he himself presents and the reader's relative authority.
Chapter 9, Parodic Narrative, proposes a schematic
definition by sketching the kind and degree of parodic distortion with the tools developed in other chapters.
Chapter 10, Narrative and the Form-Content Metaphor,
systematically applies the concept of interaction between
process and world to the form-content trope to highlight the
critical confusion which the pair is bound to cause in the
discussion of narrative. Chapter 11, Translating Narrative, is meant to contribute to translation theory by pointing
out a few consequences for the translator of narrative,
emerging from an emphasis on the double set of signifieds,
process and world and their realization in the reading
consciousness. Lastly, chapter 12, Fictional Modality:
A Challenge to Linguistics, sums up the main points about
narrative structure if viewed from the holistic perspective
of 'doing' narrative. At the same time the chapter is a
summary invitation to other theories, especially linguistic
structuralism, to supply tools capable of handling aspects
of fictional modality more adequately than the present state
of the discipline allows.

The literary texts quoted are examples to support the
argument. In choosing them I have been guided solely by
their value in underlining a theoretical point. Despite
its shortcomings I hope that this study will be able to play
a modest role in the debate between phenomenology and
structuralism instanced forcefully by Edmund Husserl and
Roman Jakobson almost half a century ago, and re-emerging
today.

I should like to acknowledge gratefully the detailed
criticism of David George and Volker Schulz and thank
Thomas Szlezák for introducing me to Ingarden's work many
years ago. For encouragement and stimulating comments I
wish to express my gratitude to Bob Hodge, Didier Coste,
Mel Faber, Roger Fowler, John Frow, Mike Haliday, Nick
Visser, Maurice Natanson and Rainer Warning. I am

grateful also to the publishers of 'Language and Style' for
permission to include Narrative Language as part of chapter
3, to the Human Sciences Research Council for a Senior
Bursary allowing me to do research towards chapters 3, 4
and 5 in 1973-4, to the DAAD for a visiting fellowship, and
to Murdoch University for the sabbatical leave in 1978
during which I completed the first draft.

Chapter 1

What happens when we read a narrative text?

Attempts at defining or describing narrative have tended to proceed 'empirically' by deducing the properties of the object from a large number of examples of what one generally agrees to be narratives, (1) or by describing its characteristic features by means of the tools applicable to a larger set (e.g., the tools of logic, semiotics, or linguistics) of which narrative texts are regarded as a sub-set. (2) Satisfactory as such approaches are in many respects, the former makes the unclarified assumption that narrative is an object, while the latter certainly runs the danger of discovering in the sub-set what in general terms is already known about the large set, while overlooking aspects characteristic only of the historically rooted item to be described. And although it cannot be a foregone conclusion that there are such specific characteristics, the possibility of their existence should not be denied.

For the purposes of this study I wish to describe narra-tive structure primarily in terms of its reception, using eclectically what help from other areas the explanations of the reading performance demand. My starting point suggests itself through the observation that our knowledge of things is intimately linked with the way in which we are able to encounter and use them. This applies most obviously to items which are not homogeneous ontologically, as are material objects such as pens or tables or non-material phenomena such as mathematical and other defini-tions, but ontologically heterogeneous, i.e. existing at the same time at different levels of materiality, ideality, etc. (3) A poem, for example, exists at the same time as a physical object inasmuch as it is print or sound and as a multiple, non-material construct in its linguistic relation-

ships, propositional meanings, constructable image world,
or interpretable, abstract overall, aesthetic, philosophical
meaning.

What do we do then when we read a novel or story? Let
me start with the trivial and then advance to the more complex aspects of the reading act. Let us assume that we
take the physical object 'book' from the shelf, our minds
wide open to the possible nature of its contents. As we
recognize the text as that of a novel (because it is either
called a novel or we know the title or we suppose that it is
a novel since it is fairly long, with chapter headings, etc.)
our 'horizon of expectations' is suddenly narrowed down to
a more or less loose set of generic features. (4) It is
during our reading that this set is then transformed into a
cumulative list of aspects which, by the end of our first
reading, make up our understanding of the work as a generic
entity.

Let us further assume that we come across sentences of
the following kind:

1.1 I shall only add that this character of male chastity,
though doubtless as desirable and becoming in one
part of the human species as in the other, is almost
the only virtue which the great apologist hath not
given himself for the sake of giving the example to
his readers. (Joseph Andrews, B.I., Ch. 1)

or

1.2 No, no, there's nothing to be gained by burdening
our fabrications with impieties. (Robert Coover,
The Magic Poker)

2 I suppose he was plotting to get Paul out in the boat
and play some joke on him, like pushing him in the
water. (Ring Lardner, Haircut)

3 And now our case was very dismal indeed; for all
saw plainly, that the sea went so high that the boat
could not live, and that we should be inevitably
drowned. (Daniel Defoe, 'Robinson Crusoe')

4 O I'm not going to think myself into glooms about
that any more   I wonder why he wouldn't stay the
night I felt all the time it was somebody strange he

brought in instead of roving around the city meeting
God knows who nightwalkers and pickpockets
(James Joyce, 'Ulysses')

5   Already while that fever-fit of holiness lay upon him
     he had encountered but out of chastity had declined
     to penetrate disillusioning forces. (James Joyce,
     'Stephen Hero')

6   'What should we drink?' the girl asked.   She had
     taken off her hat and put it on the table. (Ernest
     Hemingway, Hills Like White Elephants)

7   From what had it proceeded?   From his aunt's
     supper, from his own foolish speech (James Joyce,
     The Dead)

8   You've been had, haven't you, Jocko?   You sad sour
     stew-faced sonofabitch.   Really, did you read this
     far? (William H. Gass, Willie Master's Lonesome
     Wife)

TWO SETS OF SIGNIFIEDS

As we attempt to describe what happens when we read these
sentences, we note an obvious and crucial difference
between our acts of consciousness directed at unmediated
phenomena and those directed at the phenomena of discourse.
The way in which we experience our everyday reality can be
argued to be determined to a large extent by the total sedimented stock of typified knowledge which we have available
at any given moment.   This stock-of-knowledge-at-hand
(Schutz) we may assume to be structured in terms of a quasi-
spatio-temporal matrix with typified aspects of personae,
acts, events, tonal and atmospheric qualities, etc., and
above all an ever-changing ideological pattern which acts as
an interpretative filter and umbrella giving weight and value
to specific items in the matrix. (5)   These observations are
highly schematic and perhaps trivial.   But they become
increasingly complex when we apply them to our experience
of discourse and especially fictional discourse.
    When we read or hear a piece of discourse, the same
general principles as outlined above appear to operate.
But in addition they must be available 'in duplicate' if we are

to understand fully the meaning of any speech. This means
that we must be able to grasp the aspects of space, time,
acts, personae, etc., and the ideological position of both
the presented items and the presentational speech act. In
the discourse-situations of everyday life where we grasp
intuitively the social context and the way it modifies propositional meanings this usually poses no problem. In written
discourse, and especially in fictional narrative where the
total speech situation is highly artificial, the reader is
called upon to perform complex tasks of interpretative
construction before narrative meaning can be adequately
established. Even in isolation, sentence 5 – 'Already while
that fever-fit of holiness lay upon him he had encountered
but out of chastity had declined to penetrate disillusioning
forces' – makes sense fully only if we construct a double
reality, the presented world of Stephen, his mental development and the presentational process with an authorial
narrator in total control of his spatial and temporal position
in relation to his protagonist, and a sympathetically omniscient and probing attitude. This has often been dealt with
under such labels as 'post of observation' (James), point of
view, 'narrative situation', mediation, or 'narrative transmission'. (6) Apart from the sophistication of Stanzel's
and Chatman's approaches, the majority of the discussions
either take over traditional terms such as point of view and,
without subjecting them to any careful scrutiny, endow them
with a new rationale and/or simply do not distinguish precisely enough between the multiple aspects of modality
which are activated in the reading process. The term
point of view, for example, tacitly assumes that the condition
of spatio-temporal unity which we attach to our everyday
reality must also apply to fictive narrative. But what
really happens when we read a narrative text is that often
only the spatial locus of the act of telling is schematically
determined while its temporal side remains an undetermined
lacuna, or vice versa.

While in example 5 the temporal and spatial locus of narrating remains vague, it becomes increasingly well defined as
we read the total work. Then we are able to construct,
beyond the shifting, quasi-physical position of the speaker,
a narrating persona or at least a voice with specific acts of
telling, foreshadowing, pre-interpreting, concealing and
revealing, a persona that is dependent on certain events
(authorial arrangements beyond his control), with tonal and
atmospheric qualities and, most important, a partly stated
and, by way of transformations, largely inferred ideological
characterization. If this is so, it suggests that the grid of

expectations which we must have available in order to be
able to activate fully the potential of narrative discourse
can be schematized as shown in Table 1.1.

TABLE 1.1

	Presentational process	Presented world
Time	temporal locus of narrating	presented world's temporal matrix
Space	spatial locus of narrating	world's spatial matrix
Personae	kinds of narrators, narrator 'personality'	personae 'characters'
Acts	acts of telling, lying, describing, reporting, foreshadowing, etc.	physical and mental acts: movement, discourse, thought
Events	author's arrangements beyond the narrator's control	non-human events
Tonal aspects	narrator's attitude to reader and presented world (benevolent, cynical)	personae's attitudes to themselves and one another and to rest of presented world
Atmospheric aspects	qualities we attach to narrator and acts of telling	e.g., gloomy, idyllic etc.
Ideological patterns	narrator's overall abstractable ideological stance and commitment	ideological identification of total world presented

All references to reader, whether stated or implied, should
be seen as part of the presentational process, since they all
foreground the acts of mediation rather than items of the
projected world. A column closely attached to presentational process and listing the potential properties of stated
and implied readers could certainly improve the grid. (7)

Whenever we encounter discourse, this double schema
acts as a formally empty horizon of expectations within
which the experience of any specific discourse is possible.
The basic assertion here is that reading narrative is the
construction of first a twofold set of propositional meanings
and through them the construction of a double vision: on the
one hand, the vision of what could be seen, heard, imagined
or, in terms of the filmic medium, what could be projected
and enacted on a screen; and, on the other, that vision
which allows the former to come into existence, the quasi-
reality of the presentational process. Two asides must be
made here which will be given more attention later. In
staged drama one side of the scheme, the process, is transformed into material aspects such as curtains or movement
on the stage, or the actual production of such items of the
dramatic sub-text as 'enthusiastically', or 'with sword drawn'.
By contrast, in what one tends to describe as highly lyrical
poetry the two sides of process and world appear to be
deliberately fused into one homogeneous expression of a
state of mind. Narrative, no matter which side is emphasized, lives from the distinction of and interplay between
presentational process and presented world.

(a) Examples 1 to 4: first-person statements

1.1   In the first example a quasi-author narrator who is
      standing outside the presented world is telling us that
      he is giving us further information, linking aspects of
      the world with his own personality.
1.2   Here the same type of narrator apologizes or pretends
      to apologize for information which slipped in, but
      should not have been provided. By referring to the
      story as to 'our fabrications' he makes the reader an
      accomplice to the blasphemy or prank, depending on
      whether we construct the narrator's attitude as sincere
      or ironical.
2   In this case the first-person narrator is part of the
      presented world. The phrase 'I suppose' charac-
      terizes him as a peripheral narrator with limited
      access to vital information, while such further clues
      as 'some joke' and 'like pushing him' urge the reader
      to envisage a narrator who is not merely at a spatio-
      temporal disadvantage, but one whose interpretative
      faculties are similarly restricted. In this case the

time gap indicated by the past tense cannot be said to
mark the difference between the 'narrating self' (the
barber telling the story to a customer) and the
'experiencing self', since the narrator could not himself have observed the world he presents. (8)

3   In example 3 the phrases 'our case ... we should be
... drowned' identifies the narrator as being inside
the presented world and at the heart of the recorded
events. By contrast with example 2, the past tense
establishes the time gap between the narrating self
(the old Crusoe) and the experiencing self (the young
Crusoe on the ship). Little more can be said without
speculation about the presentational process except
that we are aware that the narrator must have survived
to tell the tale and that the reader can tentatively infer
a personality of rich experience; further perhaps,
that the kind of personality the narrator must be is the
result to a large extent of the very experiences to
which the reader is giving imaginative shape as he is
reading on. As a result, the cumulative view of the
total narrative process assumes a complexity towards
the end of the novel not unlike the complexity of the
reader's vision of the presented world.

4   The discourse in this example is not the discourse
which I term process: it is the thought discourse of a
presented persona and as such an aspect of the presented world. Although there is a speech act in the
first person, interior monologue makes sense best if
understood as one instance of discourse within the presented world next to monologue, dialogue, free indirect
style, diary entries, or letters. By contrast with
examples 2 and 3, there is no significant continuous
time gap between the level of experiencing and that of
the experienced items except for brief flashbacks of
memory which, however, are all incorporated in the
stream of consciousness of Molly's now. This almost
compulsive flux of thoughts is her most immediate way
of grasping reality: all of it.

(b) Examples 5 to 7: third-person statements

5   The quasi-author narrator of example 5 suppresses his
'I-origo' and in comparison with examples 1, 2 and 3,
taxes more strongly the inferential imagination of the

reader who is to construct the compound predicate of
the narrator 'personality'. (9)   In this sentence the
narrator knows not only what the protagonist himself
experiences or his state of mind ('fever-fit of holiness
... encountered ... [and] declined to penetrate
disillusioning forces'), but also the motive for
Stephen's inaction ('but out of chastity'), a motive of
which the Hero, we must assume, is not meant to be
aware at the time.   Perhaps the narrator could
adequately be described as a highly sympathetic,
indeed fascinated, omniscient quasi-observer who
keeps in close, though unilateral, touch with his
protégé.

6   Example 6 displays a syntactical arrangement typical
of Hemingway's short fiction: a piece of discourse
within the presented world, a brief process marker,
and the recorded physical act of the fictive persona.
Even without the process marker, 'the girl asked', the
modality of the two statements can be construed, at
least in general terms.   From a fairly close spatial
locus (close enough to understand what the girl is
saying) and the temporal locus of 'contemporary' (who
at some later, unspecified time remembers and dis-
closes the action) a keen observer presents us with
statements about what could have been heard or seen
by any other observant bystander.   If we wish to
comment further on the narrator's attitudes and philosophical stance, we must place the excerpt in its
context.   This does not mean that no information as to
such aspects is provided; it only means that in isolation they would have to remain highly speculative.
Cumulatively, they do make persuasive sense.   An
adequate inference of the narrator's overall attitude
could be to say that he is sympathetic to the young
woman to whom a prospective abortion is an extremely
weighty decision and who is shocked by the man's
insensitivity as well as her own sudden realization
that their relationship was in fact much more shallow
than she had thought.   The narrator's quasi-authorial
philosophical position could be described perhaps by
way of negative inference.   By refusing to comment
on or colour with personal evaluations what can be
observed, he is rejecting the pre-interpretation and
thus falsification of a presented world which, as raw
factuality, should be coherent and powerful enough in

itself for the reader to grasp its existential message. The fact that such inferences cannot be binding does not make their drawing illegitimate or useless. Just as we concretize a presented world from an often flimsy set of signifiers, so too must we concretize the quasi-reality of the presentational process if we are to experience narrative in its total structure.

7   Except that it is in the third person, example 7 is related to example 4 in that we have unmediated thought discourse as part of the presented world, with the narrative process suspended for the time being. The main difference is that the present example is in free indirect style: the thinking consciousness refers to himself and items of presented world in the third person. A more subtle difference, to my mind, affects the reader's interpretation of the protagonist's understanding of himself: the use of the third-person pronoun has a slight distancing effect; it introduces a separation between consciousness and the items to which it pays attention. In The Dead the reader realizes this gap by portraying Gabriel toward the end of the story as distancing himself from himself.

(c) Example 8: second-person statements

8   This example illustrates the possibility of a quasi-author narrator addressing the reader directly without reference to the presented world. While in example 1.1 the signified 'character of male chastity' and in 1.2 'our fabrications' link reader and narrator via an inter-subjectively shared fiction, example 8 establishes merely the narrator's trickery and the reader's pedantic and unintelligent performance of the text; it is a pure process marker. (10)

In terms of our double set of operational features, those of the presentational process and those of the presented world, narrative statements occur in four possible combinations:

(a) Process statements with reference to presented world.
(b) 'World' statements with reference to process.
(c) Process statements without reference to presented world (pure process markers).

(d) 'World' statements without specific reference to
process but always allowing its construction.

When Roger Fowler observes that 'syntactically "un-
marked" modality is still modality, still implies a specific
kind of personal involvement in the act of speech', he is
certainly right. (11) However, to make the observation
useful specifically for the description of narrative statements one should add that, conversely, syntactically pure
modality, pure process markers, such as example 8, do not
allow the reader's construction of any portion of the presented world.

The dynamic inter-relations in narrative between presentational process and presented world are underlined when
we consider the distinction drawn by Jurij M. Lotman between
verbal and non-verbal narrative. In Bemerkungen zur
Struktur des narrativen Textes, Lotman notes that verbal
narrative is characterized by an additive structure of signs,
while non-verbal, e.g., iconic, narrative relies on the
transformation of an initial configuration. (12) In the
light of my earlier remarks I would like to suggest that in
reading narrative we transform an additive structure of
signs containing the double set of signifiers, presentational
process and presented world, into a concretized world seen
from a specific quasi-physical and ideological angle. In
non-verbal narrative, on the contrary, we make sense of a
given figure and its transformation by lending them a silent
text signifying at the same time presentational process and
presented world.

My focus on the interaction between the two poles of
narrative, transmission and world (not teller and tale:
teller is only part of the whole process, while tale then is
only one element of the whole story) sets these observations
apart in degree from the followers of Propp, especially
A.J. Greimas with his emphasis on the structural abstraction of a total plot repertoire; (13) Tzvetan Todorov, whose
interest is mainly in action sequences defined in such terms
as 'mode indicatif', 'mode de la volonté', and 'mode de
l'hypothèse'; (14) or the groups of scholars around Teun
van Dijk whose ambitiously accurate descriptions rest on
assumptions like 'a first such condition [for narrative] is
that events are causally linked'. (15) Even a cursory
reading of the fictive narrative of Beckett, Barth, Borges,
Coover, Gass and many others makes clear that what is
going to be defined as narrative is a certain kind of narrative only, namely, causally linked action sequences.

In his refreshing little book 'Linguistics and the Novel' Roger Fowler demonstrates that linguistic categories can be applied to the study of the novel by the common reader who is willing to accept a few basic definitions. I am quite sure that his eclectic linguistic method will become a manageable and fruitful approach to the discussion of literary texts. It is because of this reason of appreciation that I wish to make a series of critical observations which the starting point and course of my own approach demand to be made.

My first suggestion is that if there are two distinct sets of signifiers operative in narrative (Fowler's modality/ discourse v. proposition/content) and assuming that we proceed from reading a surface structure to constructing deep structures or propositional meaning, then Fowler's scheme: (16)

SENTENCE	PROSE FICTION
surface structure	text
modality	discourse
proposition	content

should be replaced by the following arrangement:

	Text (as physical phenomenon)	
Surface	Text (as linguistic code)	
	T R A N S F O R M A T I O N I	
Deep	Presentational	Presented
structure	process (discourse)	world (content)

Further, it is not enough to say that both presentational process and presented world, or discourse and content in Fowler's terminology, have a deep structure. When we read a narrative text, we not only transform the surface text into propositional meanings establishing process and world. For a novel or story to make sense to us we perform further transformations. First, a transformation to derive a set of ideological abstractions from both pre-sentational process and presented world, and a final transformation in which we abstract an overall aesthetic-ideological meaning from previous, usually conflicting, deep structures. The above scheme could be complemented then to look like this:

	Text (as physical phenomenon)	
Surface	Text (as linguistic code)	
	T R A N S F O R M A T I O N I	
Deep	Presentational	Presented
structure 1	process	world
	T R A N S F O R M A T I O N II	
Deep	Ideology of	Ideology of
structure 2	process	world
	T R A N S F O R M A T I O N III	
Deep	Overall aesthetic–ideological meaning	
structure 3		

For simplicity's sake process and world are realized here
at one level. In chapters 4 and 5 I shall argue for the
reader's construction of the two components to be ontologically separate acts. Unlike modality and meaning in
everyday speech, process and world cannot be concretized
simultaneously; although in the act of reading they are
realized spontaneously and fast, one always precedes the
other; one is always the necessary condition for the other.

A third contention concerns Fowler's use of the term
'content'. Admittedly, he is not altogether happy with it
himself; and, as far as I can see, there is no reason why
one should restrict the term – if one is to use it at all – to
one level of interpretation only. However, if we use it, as
Fowler does, in the sense of our presented world and at the
same time 'theme' (another confused item) which at least
partly covers what I call overall aesthetic–ideological
meaning (the work's content?), we are faced with a fundamental contradiction. On the one hand, content is merely
one aspect of a narrative, the presented world, and, on the
other, an abstraction from the whole (i.e. world and process). There is not much point in continuing the critical
debate with traditionally woolly nomenclature, and I suggest
dropping the term content altogether in the description of
narrative.

A more radical query refers to the fact that what
linguists call transformations in Chomsky's sense can
account for only one, though essential, kind of response to
fictional narrative. I suspect that much of literary critics'
unhappiness with the application of transformational
linguistics to literary texts – leaving aside the unfortunate,
outright unwillingness to acknowledge the linguist's achieve-
ment for literary criticism – stems from this restriction,
which, though perhaps necessary for linguistics, would make
the reading of novels a fairly sterile exercise.

TWO KINDS OF TRANSFORMATION

To my mind two fundamentally different transformations are
performed when we read a fictional text. The one, a
propositional transformation which is analytical and inter-
subjective, producing meanings not unlike those of
definitions: lexical or denotative meanings; the other, a
concretizing transformation which is inter-subjective to a
degree, but to a certain extent also personal. The former
is necessary for us to make sense of a novel as a shared
code, the latter allows us to understand the novel in terms
of shared coded experience. The former, though more
readily communicable, is reductive; it narrows a number of
similar surface expressions down to a more general
propositional meaning; the latter, though less easily
communicable, is expansive, activating as it does the
reader's propositional understanding of the linguistic
surface by means of his/her typified stock of literary and
lived experience.

The surface text signifying an act of planting a 'eucalyptus
tetragona' can be transformed merely propositionally by a
reader who, for lack of experience, has to look up the terms
in the relevant dictionary, whereas the reader who has in
fact planted and watered the tree and enjoyed its growth and
beauty will be able to add to the propositional transformation
a concretizing transformation in which, as it were, the
words come to life. One may argue that this is highly
personal and has nothing to do with the structure of narrative. But indeed it has. The concretizing reader, too, is
always a member of a group with a shared, typified socio-
cultural experience, so that his experience must, to a
considerable degree, be inter-subjective. The problem of
how concretizations can be communicated cannot be the aim
of this study.

Our realization of the functions of the two kinds of transformation, propositional deep structure and concretization,
assists us in understanding how such different texts as
scientific report or argument and fictive narrative are
read. It is true, as Roger Fowler notes, that 'an article
on the classification of "Lepidoptera" has a semantic
content just as "Lolita" does, though it is logical rather
than chronological in structure'. (17) However, the
important difference between the scientific article and the
novel does not seem to me to be that the one is logically, the
other chronologically arranged. There are both fictional

accounts which are not chronological and scientific reports
which are strictly chronological (when for instance the
precise temporal sequence of an experiment is to be
recorded). The difference lies in the way in which the
stipulated reader's response is coded in each case. In the
scientific piece we are presented primarily with definitions
and linking propositions which invite propositional response
and undermine concretizations; they operate much like the
definition of a square of which our drawing or imagined
drawing is always a falsification, however helpful. By
contrast, the fictional text invites both propositional reduction to an analytical meaning and concretizing expansion by
means of the reader's typified experience of other texts as
well as of his everyday life.

GENESIS AND THE MAGIC POKER

To read a story is to construct the double vision of presentational process and presented world, not as technical discovery but as perceptive performance of any narrative text.
This double vision can rarely be said to be balanced, with
process and world having equal weight; in any given text
the one or the other of the compound aspects of world and
process will have to be granted prominence by the reader
according to the cues in the guiding system of the textual
surface. But the fact that the double set is operative in
any text to which we intuitively attach the name narrative
can best be shown with the help of two, in certain respects
extreme, examples. As an illustration, I have chosen the
opening section from the biblical Genesis and a piece of
metafiction by Robert Coover, The Magic Poker. (18)
   Few pairs of stories could be less alike as to their
language, presentational process, presented world, or
ideological commitment. Indeed, as far as implied
authorial attitude is concerned they form the opposing poles
of a spectrum. And yet, it is between these poles of unquerying, unquestionable authority of telling, on the one
hand, and, on the other, of querying authority inviting
query that narrative exists.
   Both accounts of the Creation in Genesis begin with an
authorial summary statement: (a) 'in the beginning God
created the heaven and the earth'; (b) 'These are the
generations of the heavens and of the earth when they were
created, in the day that the Lord God made the earth and the

heavens.' In each case there follows a catalogue listing
the various acts of creation in highly formulaic language.
In the first version there are seven distinct formulae and
their variants: (a) 'And God said, let there be light
[firmament, lights], or 'let [the waters be gathered
together, the earth bring forth grass]'; (b) 'and there was
light [and it was so]'; (c) 'And God made [divided, set,
created]'; (d) 'And God saw that it was good'; (e) 'And God
called the light Day [the firmament Heaven, the dry land
Earth]'; (f) 'And God blessed ... living creatures [man and
woman]'; (g) 'And the evening and the morning were the
first [second, third] day'.

In the second version of the myth there are only two
formulae, one referring to acts of creation, the other to
verbal acts: (a) 'And the Lord God made [formed, planted,
took, caused]' and (b) 'And the Lord God commanded [said,
gave names]'.

When we look at the relationship between presentational
process and presented world both versions display very
similar characteristics. They both start with an authorial
reference to world (i.e. God and his Creation) as an
occurrence beyond question, and throughout the text all
statements function to establish further what in fact
happened. Even the sophisticated reader feels strongly
discouraged from asking any questions. This sense of the
establishment of undoubted, undoubtable factuality is contrasted. with, but at the same time strengthened by the total
absence of attempts at legitimizing the acts of telling.
Neither spatial nor temporal locus of narrating is acknowledged (though they are vaguely reconstructable: where
must the speaker have been standing when it all happened?),
no orientation or ideological identification is supplied or
indeed necessary. As a result, no relativization is
possible: God's act of Creation cannot be understood in
relation to anything else, but only as such. This attempted
negation of the presentational process discourages also the
sense of dialogue in which the reader is a partner. The
story negates itself as 'merely a story' by affirming itself
as verbal reflection of a factual occurrence: it negates its
own inter-textuality. That the biblical Genesis does
nevertheless function inter-textually is evident to anybody
who has read other creation myths. Above all, this
exclusively authorial, one could even go as far as to say
authoritarian, presentation of world at the expense of
process stipulates a very special reader: a child who does

not yet know, or has forgotten and needs reminding, or a prelogical, a mythic mind, in short: a reverently accepting, unquerying consciousness.

In comparison with Genesis, Robert Coover's The Magic Poker is at least as much an exercise in the art of story telling as a traditional story. To give a plot summary would be as unsatisfactory as to abstract the presented world from 'Tristram Shandy'. To make sense, any abbreviated version of The Magic Poker would likewise have to include also a summary of the presentational process. Self-conscious as Coover's fiction is and in order to spare the readers and critics the labour, The Magic Poker includes a paragraph which, cum grano salis, could pass as a plot summary, focusing as it does on a possible core action around which the narrator has twined his tale.

> Once upon a time, two sisters visited a desolate island.
> They walked its paths with their proclivities and scruples,
> dreaming their dreams and sorrowing their sorrows.
> They scared a snake and probably a bird or two, broke a
> few windows (there were few left to break), and gazed
> meditatively out upon the lake from the terrace of the main
> house. They wrote their names above the stone fireplace
> in the hexagonal loggia and shat in the soundbox of an old
> green piano. One of them did anyway; the other one
> couldn't get her pants down. On the island, they found a
> beautiful iron poker, and when they went home, they took
> it with them.

Apart from the inclusion of summary versions of the story within the text Coover employs a number of strategies all of which point to the literariness of the construct rather than to its referential meanings.

1 Coover fuses the quasi-authorial level of telling, the level of the narrating I, with different levels of the presented world. As an opening, the narrator appears as a figure in the setting and at the same time as its creator. He introduces himself as authority over and manipulator of the world he is going to present, while at the same time suggesting that his creation is somewhat out of control, for 'anything can happen'.

> I wander the island, inventing it. I make a sun for it,

and trees – pines and birch and dogwood and firs – and
cause the water to lap the pebbles of its abandoned shores.
This, and more: I deposit shadows and dampness, spin
webs, and scatter ruins. Yes: ruins. A mansion and
guest cabins and boat houses and docks. Terraces, too,
and bath houses and even an observation tower. All
gutted and window-busted and autographed and shat upon.
I impose a hot midday silence, a profound and heavy
silence. But anything can happen.

In paragraph 36 the narrator takes the reader by surprise
when he identifies himself with the story's two opposing
male personae, the primeval caretaker's son and the
'tall slender man, dressed in slacks, white turtleneck
shirt, and navy-blue jacket smoking a pipe': 'It is one
thing to discover the shag of hair between my buttocks,
quite another to find myself tugging the tight gold pants
off Karen's sister.'
2 There is a fusion also of the autorial level proper, of
the person who is writing the manuscript (Coover), and
the level of the presented world when, for instance, the
narrator wonders, 'but the caretaker's son? To tell the
truth, I sometimes wonder if it was not he who invented
me' (paragraph 21).
3 There also occurs a mixing of elements of the presented
world which one normally expects to be kept separate.
When the girl in the gold pants sketches the handsome
tall man, she achieves what the narrator calls a 'reasonable likeness, except that his legs are stubby (perhaps
she failed to center her drawing properly, and ran out
of space at the bottom of the paper) and his buttocks are
bare and shaggy' (paragraph 38).
4 Further, Coover intertwines the different levels of time
of the presented world. In paragraph 72, for example,
we have a grandmother watch her grandchildren playing
'Chopsticks' on the green piano – a scene from an earlier
level of time – encounter the caretaker's hairy son as
well as the girl in gold pants, both personae of the
narrated present.
5 Not unlike many other stories, The Magic Poker has
three strands of action (the girls, the caretaker's son,
and the tall handsome man). But unlike traditional
narrative, the strands are not stable but alter their
structure and function in accordance with other modifications of world and process.

6 The narrator introduces a number of alternative 'worlds', while not changing significantly his quasi-physical position or mental disposition. For example, paragraph 13 receives alternative versions in paragraphs 14, 16 and 19.

7 Some of the alternative presented worlds display at the same time radically different ways of handling the presentational process. Not only is the presented world of paragraph 50 that of the 'Märchen' – there is the initial situation of the Princess's pants not coming down, the almost impossible task to remove them, the king's challenge and promise, a series of unsuccessful suitors, the unexpected victor, the magic object, a metamorphosis, and a mangled but recognizable version of the reward – there is also the formulaic language which, even without reference to the specific action portrayed, signifies the 'Märchen' structure ('Once upon a time ... and they huffed and they puffed and they grunted and they groaned, but ...'). But at the same time it is self-evident that the paragraph is anything but a 'Märchen': it is a multiple parody of the given versions of The Magic Poker as well as of 'Märchen' structures. Especially in its parodic aspects Coover's story is a funny and complex exercise in inter-textuality. It demonstrates that the whole body of literature is available, at least potentially, when a new literary artefact is being encoded by a writer and decoded by a reader.

8 As in many traditional stories there is a central symbolic object: the magic poker. But like the story's narrative strands and multiple world it is stable neither in appearance nor in function. According to the requirements of rapidly changing process and presented world the poker can be a realistically portrayed rusted piece of furniture or a magic wand in a fairy tale.

9 Throughout the story Coover has made his quasi-authorial narrator remind us of the fictionality of the presented world. An instance of foreshadowing the main points of the action in paragraph 10 ('Though the two girls will not come here for a while – first they have the guest cabin to explore, the poker to find ...') is combined with a reference to the narrator's act of creation ('I have been busy. In the loggia, I have placed a green piano ...') and a brief self-characterization ('I am nothing if not thorough, a real stickler for detail').

10 Finally, there is the salient prominence of the presenta-

tional process. As mentioned before, even where the presented world appears to stand on its own without process markers, the presentational process is always constructable with a certain degree of probability and adequacy. Coover adds an abundance of phrases and paragraphs specifically signifying narrative process.

A love letter! Wait a minute, this is getting out of hand! What happened to that poker, I was doing much better with the poker, I had something going there, archetypal and even maybe beautiful, a blend of eros and wisdom, sex and sensibility, music and myth. But what am I going to do with shit in a rusty tea-kettle? No, no, there's nothing to be gained by burdening our fabrications with impieties. Enough that the skin of the world is littered with our contentious artifice, lepered with the stigmata of human aggression and despair, without suffering our songs to be flatted by savagery. Back to the poker. I am disappearing. You have no doubt noticed. Yes, and by some no doubt calculable formula of event and pagination. But before we drift apart to a distance beyond the reach of confessions (though I warn you: like Zeno's turtle, I am with you always), listen: it's just as I feared, my invented island is really taking its place in world geography. Why, this island sounds very much like the old Dahlberg place on Jackfish Island up on Rainy Lake, people say, and I wonder: can it be happening? Someone tells me: I understand somebody bought the place recently and plans to fix it up, maybe put a resort there or something. On my island? Extraordinary! – and yet it seems possible. I look on a map: yes, there's Rainy Lake, there's Jackfish Island. Who invented this map? Well, I must have, surely. And the Dahlbergs, too, of course, and the people who told me about them. Yes, and perhaps tomorrow I will invent Chicago and Jesus Christ and the history of the moon. Just as I have invented you, dear reader, while lying here in the afternoon sun, bedded deeply in the bluegreen grass like an old iron poker.

(Compare also paragraphs 1, 6, 10, 15, 21 or 36.)

If inter-textuality as 'a dependence on multiple codes' and an 'indirect link with other texts that draw on the same codes' is undermined by the modality of the kind of text we activate in Genesis, Coover's story certainly grants it a leading role. (19)   Foregrounding as it does process, alternatives of telling, distinct levels of reality and quasi-reality, or a variety of codes, The Magic Poker invites query and fantasying, refers us to story telling and reading as dialogue and game, and defines the reader as an equal partner who participates in an act of fiction making, as a grown-up, as secular and irreverent as the narrator him-self.

The detailed construction of the presentational process by the reader is crucial not only in metafiction, but in any narrative.   The presentational process is the manner in which the presented world can be seen; any alternative manner of seeing produces a different world.   The per-spective and focus offered in a literary work, Jurij M. Lotman observes, is 'active only as long as its anti-system, the diametrically opposed perspective, operates.'   This applies to any single work as well as to the larger horizon of literary history where 'the volume of information is increased since the systems of representation are given alternatives in subsequent periods'.   Consequently, as Lotman interprets the development of narrative, we now encounter that 'complex "polyphonic" structure of perspec-tives which forms the basis of modern artistic narrative.' (20)

Lotman's 'systems of representation' incorporate presen-tational process and presented world.   But if we wish to emphasize our two poles of process and world, we would have to rephrase Lotman's statement by saying that the volume of information in a text is increased as the presen-tational processes with their quasi-physical locus, activi-ties of telling, or ideological commitment are provided with alternatives.   For although we often first construct aspects of a world and then, by inference, aspects of pro-cess, it is process which makes world possible or, to utilize an everyday truism for the technical description of narrative, new ways of viewing produce new world views. In this sense metafiction with its polyphonic treatment of presentational process and presented world highlights the absence of such polyphony in texts which foreground action sequences.

Another way of looking at the problem of narrative is to use Saussure's and Jakobson's distinctions between syntag-matic and associative, contiguity and similarity, metonymic and metaphoric.   Refining Saussure's seminal discovery,

Jakobson attributes to poetry the associative, selective, or metaphoric, to prose the metonymic mode. Metaphoric linking of language items leads to similarity or dissimilarity, metonymic linking to contiguity. 'The principle of similarity underlies poetry.... Prose, on the contrary, is forwarded by contiguity. Thus, for poetry, metaphor, and for prose, metonymy is the line of least resistance.' (21)

When we introduce this distinction to the discussion of narrative structure, we note that both presentational process and presented world can be treated in a predominantly metonymic or predominantly metaphoric manner. An author's emphasis on one or the other, on metonymy or metaphor, produces one or the other extreme of story telling on our scale, with infinite possibilities in between. If an author proceeds like Laurence Sterne in 'Tristram Shandy' or Robert Coover in The Magic Poker he acts very much in the way in which Jakobson sees the writer of poetry treat language. 'Similarity superimposed on contiguity imparts to poetry its thorough-going symbolic, multiplex, polysemantic essence.... In poetry where similarity is superimposed upon contiguity, any metonymy is slightly metaphorical and any metaphor has a metonymic tint.' (22) Without wishing to claim that metafiction is more poetic than narrative stressing action sequence, Jakobson's distinction can certainly be adduced to support the view that there are two distinct structural poles in narrative each of which, if emphasized, results in a distinct type of story.

Using Jakobson's terms, a definition of the two poles of narrative with which we are here concerned could read thus. The one pole of narrative, represented for example by metafiction, is characterized by texts in which both presentational process and presented world are metaphoric at the expense of their metonymic potential: alternatives of process as well as alternatives of world are signified. The other pole can be recognized in texts in which not only presentational process and presented world are metonymic at the expense of their metaphoric potential, but where the contiguity of the presented world is foregrounded, while the metonymic presentational process is left largely to the reader's imaginative inferential construction.

Chapter 2

Presentational process and 'narrative transgression'

Once upon a time there was a beautiful young Princess in
tight gold pants, so very tight in fact that no one could
remove them from her. Knights came from far and wide,
and they huffed and they puffed, and they grunted and they
groaned, but the pants would not come down. (From
Robert Coover, The Magic Poker)

You've been had, haven't you, Jocko? You sad sour
stew-faced sonofabitch. Really, did you read this far?
Puzzle your head?... But honestly, you skipped a lot.
(From William H. Gass, Willie Master's Lonesome Wife)

Such passages do not exactly fulfil the expectations raised
by the study of classical narratives or the popular stories
of their modern epigones. Nevertheless, we quickly
adjust our reading responses to the unfamiliar patterns,
and little doubt remains that we are in fact dealing with
narrative structures. In the first excerpt there is a
parodic discrepancy between formulaic exordium and
'Märchen' motif, on the one hand, and a deflated world on
the other. As a result, the narrator-reader relationship
undergoes an analogous modification.

In the second quotation, the life world of the story is
recognizable only by way of inference. The narrator, at
an ironically formal distance from his narrated world in
Coover's passage, is completely foregrounded here, so that
there is no room for any items of a presented world.

The question of whether the primacy of the act of communication over the message negates narrative structure must
remind us of assumptions earlier this century that the novel
was dead since it had lost its 'plot'. It is quite obvious

that what had been lost was merely plot in the narrow sense
of causal nexus as derived from realist narrative and
formalized by 'The King died and then the Queen died of
grief'. A return to Aristotle's definition by the Russian
Formalists secured the more general and more useful
notion of plot as the artistic arrangement of the incidents,
so that a range of texts no longer have to be seen as
deviations from the sacred norm of causality.

It appears now that the judgment of deviation has again
been made. Roland Barthes, in demonstrating the
significance of action-sequences for our understanding of
narrative, arrives at the conclusion that an insistence on
the foregrounding of the communicative act itself reveals
the 'anti-nature' of narrative and 'the limits of narrative,
beyond which begins a new art - that of narrative transgression'. (1)

In contradistinction, the purpose of this chapter is to
show that, far from alienating narrative from itself, the
active presence of the communicative act and indeed its
dynamic interaction with the 'message' must be recognized
as vital aspects of all artistic narrative structure.

What possibly are the reasons for Barthes's conclusion?
Let me attempt a few brief speculations. It is not that a
number of false observations are responsible. On the
contrary, his description of the shift from traditional narrative to narrative dominated by 'presentational process' is
highly accurate. 'Today', Roland Barthes says in 'An
Introduction to the Structural Analysis of Narrative',
'writing is not "telling"; rather it signifies that one is
telling, thereby making the whole referent ("What is being
said") contingent upon this illocutionary act ... "logos"
being reduced - or expanded - to a "lexis".' (2) Rather,
Barthes's judgment appears to be an interpretative leap
encouraged by a number of aspects of the methodology of
linguistic structuralist enquiry as applied to artificial
narrative.

1 Classical narrative and its modern popular derivatives
  are taken as a norm. But since many of the linguistic
  functions of a traditional narrative have entered 'langue'
  and survive in it, there do not seem to be any obvious
  contradictions when the tools of general linguistics are
  applied. However, the 'parole' of experimental present-
  day narrative must be expected to be a significant deviation from 'langue'. Experimental narrative juggles with

'langue' and thus renders the application of extrinsic tools at least problematic.

2 A similar danger lies in proceeding from 'natural narrative' to 'artificial narrative'. (3) Natural narrative is characterized by a subordination of its communicative acts to the message, so that its study tends to focus on 'proairetic patterns', 'simple rapports' (4) or categories of characterization, as does, for instance, Greimas and Courtès's schema of the cognitive positions 'true, false, secret, delusion'. (5) Although highly useful investigations, they must not conceal the fact that they all operate on one side of narrative: the story's quasi-life-world. Likewise, the transference of 'pragmatic norms' from the discussion of natural to that of artificial narrative sometimes yields unsatisfactory results. 'Artificial narrative', van Dijk observes, 'does not respect the pragmatic conditions of natural narrative;' (6) or 'one of the characteristic pragmatic (or perhaps pragmatico-semantic) properties of artificial narration is that the narrator is not obliged to tell the truth.' (7) From the perspective of linguistics this is an accurate and a fruitful statement; from the viewpoint of poetics it is not only trivial but reveals a distorting perspective. Not only is the narrator not obliged to tell the truth in literary artefacts, but the whole apparatus of telling becomes part of an artistic play giving rise in its overall interaction to what Ingarden calls a 'polyphony of aesthetically valent qualities'. (8) Pragmatic constraints are largely replaced by artistic-aesthetic ones.

3 Because artificial narrative operates within a different system of constraints, the linguistic assumption that 'there is nothing in discourse that is not matched in the sentence' (9) may not be adequate if applied to narrative artefacts. It certainly cannot be taken for granted.

Perhaps it is useful to review a traditional concept of narrative in order to arrive at a more balanced description of artistic narrative constructs. The well-known starting point taken by Scholes and Kellogg in 'The Nature of Narrative' sees narrative as characterized by 'the presence of a story and a story teller'. (10) But although their insistence on 'a teller and a tale' allows for the fundamental distinction between aspects pertaining to narrating and aspects pertaining to that which is narrated, 'teller' and 'tale' need much refining to pass muster. As the terms stand, we are not sure whether 'teller' refers to author, narrator or voice, and 'tale' to the whole work including title and communicative acts, or is restricted to the quasi-life-world which the narrator portrays.

No doubt much refining has taken place in recent years. As to the 'presented world', there are a number of studies on spatial features, (11) aspects of time, (12) fictional personnel, (13) acts, events, phases and strands of action, (14) or work ideology. (15) Likewise, as far as the aspects of the presentational process are concerned, such as spatial and temporal locus of mediation, narrative situation, kinds of narrator, free indirect style, thought report, or interior monologue, some impressive work is now available. (16) The third fundamental element of any communicative act, the recipient of the message, has also recently been paid critical attention, especially within the framework of the aesthetics of literary response (Rezeptionsästhetik) rooted largely in the seminal work of Roman Ingarden and the Prague Linguistic Circle. (17)

One of the less satisfying features of structuralist and formalist research, however, is the fact that concepts such as 'narrator' have been accepted as summary explanations of the realm of the presentational process. Bronzwaer's insight that 'on a purely logical level' the narrator is merely a 'perspective from which the story is presented' (18) must be pressed further. 'Perspective', however, is still a composite of a number of aspects each of which may play a significant artistic function in contributing to the 'polyphony of aesthetically valent qualities'. Even the carefully argued theory of 'narrative situations' by Stanzel does not pay enough attention to the dynamics operating between presented world and presentational process; it is characterized by a sense of stasis. In spite of its brilliance, it is a freeze-frame imposed on the motion of experienced narrative. (19)

My own position is founded on Ingarden's ontology and cognition of the literary work of art as characterized by the potential 'polyphony of aesthetically valent qualities' which arises from the work's complex inter-relationship between the forward reading dimensions and its depth stratification. The constraints of artificial narrative are understood as a modification of those of the literary work of art by what I see as the essence of general narrative structure. This modification can be shown by changing Ingarden's schema of strata to read:

1   Print/Sound
2   Linguistic formation
3.1 Presented world
3.2 Presentational process
3.3 Implied reader
4   Work ideology

whereby 3.1, and 3.2/3.3 are separate ontological realms
within the stratum of 'portrayed objectivities' and 3.1 and
3.2 must be called essential characteristics.   Each realm
(or system) displays the general aspects of space, time,
personae, acts, events, tonal and atmospheric qualities,
and ideology in a distinct manner.   Further, in the reading
process any one of the three systems may be foregrounded,
with the other two in the 'background'.   One could also say
that if the presented world and the presentational process
(with the implied reader as part of process) are ontologically distinct, they could logically be conceived of as
separate strata.   This point is made in chapters 4 and 5.
    The observation that the general aspects of space, time,
etc. each perform specific and potentially crucial functions
certainly in the two central features of narrative, presented
world and presentational process,has to my knowledge not
been paid any serious attention.   It is important to stress
that the spatial, temporal and other analogies do not lead to
a mimetic concept of the literary work of art as long as we
keep in mind that all three systems or realms have a purely
eidetic relationship with the world-out-there, with actual
sets of narrating and with actual, i.e. historical, readers:
we intuit the essences of presented world, presentational
process, and implied reader by activating linguistic
formulae with the help of typifications derived from
literary as well as life experience.
    As indicated earlier, the implied reader is of secondary
importance for the discussion of the essential features of
narrative: implied audiences do play a role also in the
highly lyrical construct as well as in read or staged drama.
It is the simultaneous active presence in narrative of both
presented world and presentational process which suggests
the defining distinction.   While in the lyrical mode the two
signified cores tend to fuse into one 'existential expression',
staged drama converts all aspects of the presentational process into the material aspects of stage, curtain, and
wings, and dramatic narrators into 'acteurs' of the presented world.

TABLE 2.1

Realm/System	Space	Time	Personae	Acts	Events	Tonal quality	Atmospheric quality	Work ideology
3.1 Presented	Spatial detail and spatial relationships matrix	temporal detail and matrix	Acteurs	doing thinking speaking	non-human occurrences	fictional personae's attitudes to their 'world'	e.g. idyllic	presented World's overall system of values seen as ideologically organized
3.2 Presentational process	Spatial locus of mediation	tense; temporal locus of mediation; place	voice, narrator	mediating telling deploreing commenting etc.	occurrences outside narrator's control; e.g., replacement of narrator	narrator tone: ironical, cynical, adoring, etc.	atmosphere evoked by manner of narrating: e.g., a leisurely atmosphere	Set of values inferred from all other aspects of presentational process
3.3 Stated and implied reader	Spatial distance of implied reader to presented world and presentational process	temporal position of implied reader to presented world and process as reader against that of the actual historical reader	the stipulated personality of the implied reader	manner of reading and responding	?	stipulated reader attitude	atmosphere of reading situation	stipulated reader ideology as derived from all other reader signals

In the reading process the three different ontological realms which are signified in the one linguistic stratum are concretized in a number of combinations. The following simple schema (Table 2.2) and selected quotations will illustrate the point.

TABLE 2.2

3.1 Presented world	1	2	(3)	1	2	(3)
3.2 Presentational process	2	3	1	3	1	2
3.3 Stated and/or implied reader	3	1	2	2	3	1
Type of combination	I	II	III	IV	V	VI

I indicates a high degree of foregrounding, whereas 3 means that a system leans heavily on the inferential participation of the reader. Also, the reader's concretization of the more or less foregrounded systems occurs in two distinct ways: first, in the linear direction of the forward reading dimension, or word for word.

> 'No, thank you. No, no, don't do that,' I said. Such attentions always get to me, and it seemed a dreadfully long time since anyone had done me any intimate kindness like this. There are days when one wants to go to the barber, not for a haircut (there's not much hair to cut) but just for the sake of the touch. (Saul Bellow, 'Humboldt's Gift')

Here, the reader's ray of attention is guided from items of the presented world (speech) to the emotional state of the narrator, then to a more general observation which the reader is invited to share ('one wants'), interrupted by a parenthetic, more specific, self-reflective comment on the narrator's physical appearance.

Second, concretization occurs also in the direction of the language's depth stratification, often in a single word. Consider for instance the phrase 'pale, convalescent houses'. Here we experience first an aspect of an imaginable world, then, by inference and conjecture, a speaker's attitude and, by further and more cautious concretization, the implied reader's stipulated attitude to the presented item.

Type I   An example of the first type of combination is the opening of 'Sir Gawain and the Green Knight'.

> The siege and the assault being ceased at Troy,
> The citadel smashed and mouldering in its
> ashes, (The treacherous trickster whose
> treason ...),

in which the narrative ray is first on aspects of a
fictional ruined Troy before a parenthetic 'aside'
focuses on the cause of the smouldering ashes,
thus revealing a narrator's presence as well as a
sense of communion between narrative voice and
reader.

A similar presentational aside operates in 'Spät
um Mitternacht – es mochte im Herbste des Jahres
1690 sein ...' in E.T.A. Hoffmann's 'Das Fräu-
lein von Scuderi'.

Type II   Who, faced with this tree, is going to talk to me
           about falling leaves and the white death.
           (Ingeborg Bachmann, Youth in an Austrian
           Town)

This appears to be a fairly rare combination with
the foregrounded implied reader suggesting the
inference of a narrative act (the act of asking the
question) and followed by the item 'tree' of the
presented world.

Type III   Type III is essential to our discussion.   With its
           foregrounded narrative process it would appear to
           be restricted mainly to metafiction; and it
           certainly looms large there.

> I am disappearing.   You have no doubt noticed.
> (Robert Coover, The Magic Poker)

or

> The narrator gathers that his audience no
> longer cherishes him.   And conversely.
> (John Barth, Title)

But the type can be found in 'Don Quixote' as well
as in 'Tom Jones' and cannot be regarded as a
form of transgression.

> After this short introduction, the reader will be pleased to remember, that the parson had concluded his speech with a triumphant question. (Henry Fielding, 'Tom Jones', Book III, ch. 3)

Type IV   Here the reader is given in sequence: first, aspects of the presented world, then a reader allusion and, last, references to the presentational manipulation.

> She [i.e. Sophia] now first felt a sensation to which she had been before a stranger, and which, when she had leisure to reflect on it, began to acquaint her with some secret, which the reader, if he does not already guess them, will know in due time. ('Tom Jones', Book IV, ch. 5)

Type V   The opening sentences of Ovid's 'Metamorphoses',

> My purpose is to tell of bodies which are transformed into shapes of a different kind. You heavenly powers ... look favourably on my attempts

illustrate a combination in which the reader must proceed from understanding signals about presentational process, in this case artistic intention, to summary signals about the world to be projected, and, third, to the invoked audience of the gods. If we compare the exordium with the conclusion, we notice a secularization of the initially stated readership and a defiance of divine interference, a shift which highlights the rhetorical nature of the proemial invocation.

Type VI   Finally, a favourite combination among metafiction writers in which the foregrounded reader is followed by words signalling the mediating acts, often with the presented world altogether absent.

> The reader! You dogged, uninsultable print-oriented bastard, it's you I'm addressing, who else. (John Barth, Life Story)

Transformations of one combination to another take place in all narratives. The more self-conscious the narrative, the more frequent and varied the changes. Also, certain modes within recognizable narrative situations favour specific combinations. Authorial omniscient narration, for example, tends towards Types I, II and, though less frequently, also III. In authorial 'objective' narration the presented world is powerfully foregrounded, so that the other two systems can be experienced only by relying on heavily inferential concretization, as in Types I and IV. In first-person narrative, characterized by the interaction of the narrating and experiencing selves (unlike, e.g., 'Joseph Andrews' or 'Vanity Fair' in which the authorial narrator also appears as I, but not as experiencing self), Types V, III, and I are prominent. In the special case of fusion of experiencing and narrating selves, indicated by the present tense and progressive form, Types I and V are intertwined. In the following example both presented world and presentational process are thus simultaneously and powerfully present, while the reader can only be stipulated as a distanced witness.

> twirling around on my piano stool my head begins to swim my head begins to swim twirling around on my piano stool (Donald Barthelme, Alice)

In figural narrative situation we usually meet with a transformation of an authorial situation of Type I into a figural reduction of the narrative structure to the presented world and Type IV. The self-presenting consciousness can then be witnessed directly by a distanced reader, with the overall mediation of the narrative suspended for the time being.

> Gabriel, leaning on his elbow, looked for a few moments unresentfully on her tangled hair and half open mouth, listening to her deep-drawn breath. So she had had that romance in her life: a man had died for her sake. (James Joyce, The Dead)

So far we have dealt with transformations of combinations in the forward reading dimension. Briefly, a few more comments on the potential, simultaneous presence of more than one of the ontological realms: presented world, presentational process, and implied reader. It seems that

we can distinguish between narrative units belonging
primarily to the realm of the presented world, and carrying
three signified cores: world, process and reader; those
pertaining to the realm of stated and implied reader which
carry two signified cores: reader and process ('print-
oriented bastard'); and those of the realm of the presentational process which carry two or three signified cores:
(a) process and reader, or (b) process, world, and reader.
(E.g., (a) 'This is getting out of hand', and (b) 'I am
inventing the island as I go along'.)

The debate about the interaction of the three signified
systems, presented world, presentational process, and
stated and/or implied reader, adds significantly to the
'structural theory of content in prose fiction'. Isolating
actual bits of information in narrative texts, Lubomír
Doležel separates 'motif texture' (as it presents itself)
from 'motif paraphrase' (as the reader sums up motif texture)
and concludes that the structural analysis of both motif
texture and motif paraphrase are a necessary precondition
for metastructural interpretation. (20)

This is certainly useful. However, in the light of our
previous observations it appears that linguistic structuralist
research again tends to emphasize that which is narrated,
our presented world, at the expense of the activities of
narrating, its spatio-temporal matrix and its ideological
implications. Instead, any metastructural interpretation
ought to be rooted in paraphrases of these three: motif
texture, texture of the presentational process, and texture
of the stated and implied reader.

'Narrative transgression' appears possible at both ends
of the spectrum: as reduction to a minimum of the presentational process in 'natural' narrative or as reduction of the
presented world to a few items in the freeplay of experimental fiction. Positively seen, these are merely the two
antithetic regions of all narrative of which the inexhaustible
dialectic interplay always results in the synthesis of a
specific, i.e. historical, narrative structure. From
different philosophical angles Ingarden and Baxtin saw this
in the late 1920s. 'One of the essential peculiarities of
prose fiction,' Baxtin says, 'is the possibility it allows of
using different types of discourse, with their distinct
expressiveness intact, on the plane of a single work without
reduction to a common denominator.' (21)

Insistence on the simultaneity and interaction of different
kinds of discourse embedded in the same linguistic stratum

also makes sense if applied diachronically to the development of artificial narration. Just as Erich Kahler discovers an 'Inward Turn of Narrative', a gradual foregrounding of consciousness from cosmogonies to the presentation first of external action and then to the activities of the mind, so too could one fruitfully trace the history of the relationship between the distinct ontological realms of presented world and presentational process in terms of their aspects of space, time, personae, acts, events, tonal and atmospheric qualities, and ideological structure, from myth to meta-fiction. (22)

Chapter 3

Narrative language

THE CONCRETE DATUM

'Narrative,' Michel Butor tells us, 'is a phenomenon which
extends considerably beyond the scope of literature; it is
one of the essential constituents of our understanding of
reality. From the time we begin to understand language
until our death, we are perpetually surrounded by narratives, first of all in our family, then at school, then through
our encounter with people and reading.' (1) An even wider
conception of narrative is offered by Barbara Hardy in
'Towards a Poetics of Fiction: An Approach Through Narrative', the focus of which is on 'the qualities which
fictional narrative shares with the inner and outer story
telling that plays a major role in our sleeping and waking
lives.' And her paper makes the further claim that 'we
dream in narrative, daydream in narrative, remember,
anticipate, hope, despair, believe, doubt, plan, revise,
criticize, construct, gossip, learn, hate, and love by narrative.' (2)

This widens the discussion about narrative considerably,
and I would like to specify some of these issues by first
distinguishing 'narrative' as a non-literary or literary unit,
a closed form, from 'narrative mode' as the predominant
mode of presentation in narratives as well as in the non-
formal inner and outer streams of story telling. As a
second qualification, I should point out that there are also
non-narrative modes in our mental lives. Do we not sometimes slip into the role of a second self in order to defeat
the opponent of a past real verbal contest by employing a
superior strategy a posteriori? An inner drama is acted

out in which we not simply sympathize or try to identify with one of the contestants but are the protagonist. Or, our stream of thought may take on an attitude of praying, total admiration, fear, triumph, or resignation in which the chanting I, the addressed object and the process of addressing appear to melt into one homogeneous whole. This, in accordance with a long-standing literary tradition, I wish to regard as a lyrical mode.

The question which now remains is what precisely in such pre-literary modes - or, better, non-literary modes, since only a very small portion of these phenomena is actually ever moulded into literary forms - allows us to identify them as, for instance, narrative modes. As in the previous chapters, I propose to refer to them as narrative if the processes of telling and that which is told are predominant interacting features. (3)   In this sense the 'novel merely heightens, isolates, and analyses the narrative motions of human consciousness.' (4)   But, one ought to add, so do the parable, 'Märchen', folk tale, medieval saint's legend, mythical legend, fable, fabliau, novella, tale, modern short story, and also the narrative documentary forms.   In fact, it is the necessary consideration of the novelistic documentary or non-fiction novel which questions the terminology of many a poetics of fiction.   Käte Hamburger's distinction between lyrical poetry as 'Wirklichkeit' on the one hand and, on the other, narrative and dramatic writing as 'Fiktion' or 'Nicht-Wirklichkeit' in her study 'Die Logik der Dichtung', for instance, stumbles over such documentary forms which resist identification as non-fiction by the way in which they present the story of actual life. (5)   One also wonders why David Lodge's analysis of the language of a novel should be restricted to fictional narratives.   Since his emphasis is so strongly on the concrete features of the novel's medium I fail to see why it should not yield results if applied to, let us say, 'In Cold Blood' or 'Armies of the Night'. (6)

But before we can discuss some aspect of Lodge's work we must consider briefly the opposing positions of traditional poetics and linguistics, somewhere between which his approach through language can be found. (7)   The debate between linguists and literary critics has concentrated largely on matters of competence and the delineation of spheres of interest, and it is therefore immaterial, for the moment, whether the bone of contention is actually narrative language or literary language in general.   My impression is that so far much of the discussion has been fruitless, for

the reason that neither side has been able to develop a
critical framework allowing for both close linguistic
analysis of literary language and those looser but nevertheless important inferences at a fairly high level of abstraction with which poetics has traditionally been concerned. (8)

Roger Fowler, who appears to be making a genuine attempt
in 'The Languages of Literature' at sorting out the controv-
ersy between Mrs Vendler and his own standpoint, sees a
'meaningless opposition of linguistic and literary
studies', (9) but, I think, brings about only a partial
reconciliation. An outright schismatic position is F.W.
Bateson's; he doubts any fruitful co-operation between the
two disciplines.   It is therefore somewhat unexpected to
find him exclaim at the prospect of removing the text, 'what
is left? Blank pages!' (10)   Unfortunately, Bateson refuses
to follow up this promising insight and, instead, presents
us with an adaptation of Socratic wit by 'crowning these
linguistic invaders of literature with garlands of wool and
annointing them with myrrh – and sending them away to
another city.' (11)   Helpful indeed.   If we fail to link, in
some meaningful way, the 'concrete datum' (12) of all
literature, its text, with the world which it presents, our
interpretative inferences are at best highly persuasive
speculation.

On the other hand, many prominent linguists have
expressed their dissatisfaction with the way in which
linguistics has been tackling literary language.   There is
indeed not much one can hold against Roman Jakobson's
general view that 'a linguist deaf to the poetic function of
language and a literary scholar indifferent to linguistic
problems and unconversant with linguistic methods are
equally flagrant anachronisms'. (13)   And, turning
specifically to his own colleagues, he deplores the
'frequent limitation' of treating the 'sentence as the highest
linguistic unit,' (14) instead of putting more emphasis on
'superior wholes', such as 'utterances' ('higher integers of
sentences') or 'discourse' ('exchange of utterances'). (15)
He also notes that 'the primacy of successivity in language
has sometimes been misinterpreted as linearity', a 'dogma
which prompts its adherents to ... overlook the hierarchical arrangement of any syntactic construction.' (16)
Regrettably, Jakobson has to admit that the problems central
to our discussion, the hierarchical features and the 'multi-
form whole–part relations' and their exact investigation
'broadly extends the scope of our science.' (17)   Our

hopes, then, to receive assistance from this side of
linguistics in the area of the relationship between word,
sentences, and the total discourse of the narrative text
appear dashed.

However, a promising pointer is inherent in Jakobson's
clarification of the essential difference between sender and
receiver of verbal messages. The listener moves through
distinctive elements such as phonemes to 'grammatical form
and understanding of meanings', a process in which probability plays a decisive role. 'Certain unities are succeeded
by certain other units with greater or lesser probability,'
while 'some are excluded a priori,' so that the receiver,
unconsciously at least, has a 'statistical attitude'. For
the speaker, Jakobson argues, 'the sequence is reversed.
His course moves from the sentence through the hierarchy
of immediate elements and, finally, through the morphologi-
cal unit' to their sound form. In speech discourse both
orders exist simultaneously, and their mutual relation is
based ... on the principle of complementariness.' (18)

This allows us to delineate the areas which can be
explored auspiciously by linguists and literary scholars.
First, there is the field of pre-predicative experience in
the author's consciousness prior to language formation, a
section of the creative process studied by psychologists and
psychoanalysts; second, the text or a set of signifiers by
means of which the writer projects his world, the schematically presented or signified world; and third, there is
the concretized or imagined world, a synthesis of the
schematically signified world and the reader's creative
contribution. Linguistics, we understand, is dealing with
the string of words as an 'exchange of utterances', while
literary studies are concerned mainly with language as it
gives rise to the reader's construction of imaginary worlds
and their moral-philosophical stance. And closing the
inquiry, psychology and psychoanalysis have extended their
scope to include the study of the buried responses to
literary language in the reader's psyche and subconscious
mind. (19) But it is the relationship between the codified
and the concretized worlds on which we must focus here.
There is, of course, a considerable range of possible
conceptions of this relationship, a fact which is reflected,
for instance, in such disparate statements as George
Steiner's that 'criticism, analysis, "explication de texte",
commemoration ... are linguistic constructs scaffolded
about a previous linguistic construct' (20) and Roman

Ingarden's that the contests among literary critics are not about the words in the text, but about their opposing 'concretizations' of that text or, in the terminology used above, it is not the schematically signified but the concretized worlds which are in conflict. (21)

To return to Jakobson's suggestions about 'hierarchical' and 'multi-form whole-part relations', let us consider for a moment Stankiewicz's observation that 'since there is no clear demarcation-line between poetic and non-poetic language,' all we can say about poetic language is that it appears to be 'the message oriented towards itself' and that 'the message is an autonomous structure'. This Russian formalist insight is coupled with the Kantian position that 'poetic language is purposiveness in terms of the internal organization of the message, and purposelessness in terms of external reference'. Such interiorization, according to Stankiewicz, results in 'elements of the message entering into multiplex relations, analogous to those which obtain between the elements of the code'. I doubt whether the use of 'analogous' can be taken for granted; it seems an assumed conclusion. What I am primarily interested in, though, is his concept of 'multiplex relations' which transforms the 'linear sequence' of sign and signal into a poetic 'pluri-dimensional sequence', and his suggestion that 'the relations between units in the poetic message ... affect all levels of language, establish a tension between sound and meaning, grammar and vocabulary, phrases and higher construction.' (22) Probably, it is such 'higher constructions' which S.L. Bethell must have in mind when he states, somewhat categorically, that 'the most significant level, where the mind lingers, is not the verbal but the ideational – the final response is to events imaginatively recreated, not to word-meanings.' (23)

So far, two key aspects of works of literature have emerged which are difficult to reconcile: the 'linear speech product' or text as a sole objective basis of all investigations on the one hand and, on the other, that to which the elements of the text refer, their imaginative and ideational super-structure.

It may be helpful at this point to present, in outline, the suggestions for a delineation of interests which Roman Ingarden proposes in agreement with his studies since the 1930s. To see poetics as part of linguistics is the result of a narrow conception of works of literature: they are seen as verbal constructs, autonomous and largely self-

explanatory, like speech messages. But, in actual fact,
works of literature reveal themselves to be stratified
constructs with language as their indispensable skeleton.
If poetics were only a special field of linguistics, then no
problems ought to arise which cannot be solved by linguistic
means. However, the complex inter-relationship between
objects of the presented world and their schematic aspects
and, more seriously, all concretizations essential to
making sense of the presented world, and the 'multiplicity
in the concretization of artistic value' clearly do not pertain to the work's language itself. According to a strictly
linguistic view, then, these features ought to be banished
from literary criticism. Also, linguistics has not yet
successfully tackled such massive structures as are larger,
works of literature. The reason is that they are not
linear sequences, but constructs in which the meaning
units merely fixate 'that which has been imagined' and that
which is to be imagined. Without conceiving of works of
literature as multi-stratified constructs all this cannot be
appreciated. One should hold instead that the disciplines
of linguistics and poetics overlap, but that they have at the
same time large areas exclusive of one another. (24)

So far we have been dealing with literary language and
not specifically narrative language. This is partly because
the disagreements between linguistics and non-linguistic
poetics are of a general kind and include more specific
distinctions; partly, also, because the framework within
which I wish to study the nature of narrative can be applied
also to dramatic and lyrical modes of presentation.

Now let us look at two studies primarily concerned with
narrative and narrative language: David Lodge's 'Language
of Fiction' and 'The Novelist at the Crossroads'. Not
linguistic in any strict sense of the term, both works share
the central assumption that 'the fictional world of a novel
is a verbal world, determined at every point by the words
in which it is represented'. (25) What is problematical
here is this: either Lodge is giving us a tautology, equating
fictional and verbal world - a string of words - in which
case no doubt each part of the verbal world determines the
fictional world; or the fictional world is something different
from the verbal world but dependent on it; in this case, the
precise determination of the fictional world by its language
signals is a moot point. Lodge's position, as he himself
says, 'rests on the assumption that consciousness is
essentially conceptual, i.e. verbal'. He does admit that

there is 'non-verbal' experience, but rejects the notion that we can be 'conscious of that experience without verbal concepts'. (26)

Lodge's is a well-known position, and one which is not easily confuted. However, without complementing the verbal by a wider structural approach how can one explain such features as constellations of personae in a novel, juxtaposition of larger narrative sections, the fact that Ivan Ilich dies before he is born, patterns such as riddle structures in detective stories, our discoveries of a question-and-answer design, or the operational features and possible effects of narrative pace - all clearly aspects of fictional worlds? Granted, our discussion of these phenomena must be verbal. But we do not derive them immediately from the given string of words. And although we may verbalize our findings, we are rarely able to discover specific concrete evidence in the text for such large-scale inferences. And yet, we are not sliding down a rabbit hole, severing the threads which link us with reality, when we reconstruct the projected world by 'seeing' parallels, groups, blocks, correspondences, or chiasmic arrangements. Surely, such non-verbal phenomena as tripartition do matter in 'A Passage to India' or 'To the Lighthouse'.

Despite his invocation of a Muse as inspiring as Wittgenstein, Lodge's conception of the novel and its structure remains problematical, most obviously so when we read that 'meaning ... resides in the application of a concept to a thing in particular circumstances'. (27) For while this formulation proves perfectly useful when applied to individual words, phrases, sentences and, perhaps, even to groups of sentences, I cannot make out what, in this sense of the term, the meaning of a novel could be. At least, Lodge's view strikes me as a severe and unnecessary curtailment of both reading process and critical response.

In his attempt to refute Malcolm Bradbury's concept of structure, Lodge states that

what is achieved is certainly conditioned to some extent by what is prefigured, but in a more significant sense what is achieved, as it is achieved, displaces what has been prefigured, and alters the prefiguration of what is not yet achieved. (28)

This is quite true, and it is not clear why Bradbury has

given his argument a genetic bias. What Lodge's argument
fails to explain is the postfiguration that happens in the
reading process and which, I think, is ultimately responsible for the novel's meaning or, more exactly, its many
meanings.

It may be interesting, at this point, to return to Lodge's
seminal earlier work 'Language of Fiction' for his own
concept of structure. He clearly distinguishes two alternative critical procedures:

> (1) to isolate deliberately or at random one or more
> passages, and submit them to close and exhaustive
> analysis; or (2) to trace significant threads through the
> language of an entire novel. One might label these
> approaches 'textural' and 'structural' respectively. (29)

About the first course of action Lodge himself has mis-
givings, since 'any passage in a novel is largely determined
by its immediate and total contexts'. (30) Since to Lodge
the novel is merely a verbal construct, 'contexts' must
mean 'all the other words in the novel'. Instead, I would
argue the weakness of the first procedure on the grounds
that it disregards not only the total verbal context, but the
complex world which the reader constructs from the text
signs of the total work. Consequently, the ideational
superstructure which the reader hinges on each set of signs
is inferior to what it could be not merely on numerical
grounds. More often than not his interpretative abstractions are probably also wrong in the sense that the many
avenues which a reading of the total context would reveal to
be cul-de-sacs are open in the isolated passage, luring the
reader away from the novel's realm of adequate interpretations.

As to Lodge's alternative and his concept of 'structural',
it seems that textural and structural are in conflict for the
very reason that both refer to the same elements of the
novel, its linguistic meaning units. The only difference is
'exhaustive analysis' on the one hand and, on the other,
the search for 'significant threads'. Assuming Lodge's
textural analysis did cover the whole novel and his
structural approach did encompass as many threads as a
critic could possibly find, one could no longer distinguish
the two methods. It would, therefore, be more appropriate to term them 'selective close reading' and 'conceptual
textural approach' respectively.

Instead, I propose to reserve the term 'textural' for the discussion of the novel's visual and auditory elements, its stylistic aspects, its linguistic arrangement; in short, the surface text. Textural approach, then, is a special discipline within the wider structural investigation, focusing as it does on the work's surface text, while 'structural' is meant to comprise all aspects, textural and non-textural: the presentational process with its spatio-temporal narrative situation, acts of narrating, narrator personality, narrator-reader relationship, the novel's space-time world, its events and human acts, its personae and the inferences which all these suggest; in short, the total construct which the reader synthesizes with the indispensable help of extrinsic inter-textual and life experience on the basis of a given narrative text.

This is at the heart of our dilemma: the language of a literary construct is its basal property, and yet it is not enough. If it were, we should be able to identify a novel's language by comparing it with the language of everyday discourse. Since much of our workaday language and thought share the novel's mode of presentation, the procedure will not do. We cannot identify narrative language at its surface levels of sign and linguistic meaning, as Jan Mukarovsky, for example, has tried with poetic language. (31) Since narrative language contains all the 'objective' elements available to the reader, but since at the same time they are insufficient for the total construction of the narrative world, we must, if we wish to understand the nature of narrative, first investigate the role which narrative language plays in the erection of this 'total construction'.

NARRATIVE LANGUAGE AS A STRUCTURE OF SIGNS

Being dynamic, the process of reading cannot really be represented as an object of investigation. All we can do, in focusing on its essential features, is assume that we have retained in our consciousness a given narrative and that we are now studying, step by step, the referential implications of its text. For this purpose I have chosen the last section of Ernest Hemingway's story Indian Camp, indexing it to show how the text signs of a narrative may become activated in the reading consciousness (see Figure 3.1). (32) Such a discussion of the reading consciousness precludes, of course, speculation about possible subconscious responses, however significant.

Admittedly, this is a very incomplete catalogue of the signals and references which one could list.   All this schematic arrangement is trying to show is that in making statements about literary constructs, and in particular about narrative, we have to operate at different levels of abstraction in relation to the level of the text.   Second, and this I think is a crucial point, such statements are not all derived directly from the signals of the text: many are inferences about inferences.   In fact, to make plausible interpretative abstractions at a high level at all, 'thematic umbrella statements' (which few critics abstain from making), we do not use as our basis the string of words, but the concretized presentational process and the imagined world as well as the extrinsic material which the reader contributes from his total stock of knowledge.   It is this synthesis which places narrative in a metaphoric relation-ship with everyday life.   This does not mean that we should not link our abstractions back to individual words in the text; on the contrary, the degree to which we are able to 'verify' our concretized world and interpretative inferences may serve as a measure of the adequacy of our reading in terms of the text.

A further admission of incompleteness concerns the cumulative process in which each of the text signs is modified not only by the whole preceding text, but also by the reader's responses to it.   Some tentative suggestions must suffice here.   My third and final restriction is that we must neglect, for the time being, the discussion of the double nature of all aspects of the schematically signified and concretized process and world and the resulting distinction between what they allow the reader to do and how they constitute themselves in a specific act of reading.

Assuming that we have the whole story before us, the chosen passage strikes us first as a specific visual (or auditory) impression; we are aware of a fairly solid block of print and its sub-division as against the looser arrange-ment of print shapes, letters, and words in the preceding dialogue section.   In itself, this observation is of little value, but the reader involuntarily stores it to activate it later in the light of the total information.

To be able to determine the story's authorial narrative situation, we must first consider the spatial and temporal locus of the point of view from which the presented world is seen.   In Sentence I, the narrator or narrative voice is spatially somewhat removed so that the boat with father and

```
             va, st
        p,per      aex,t              s         p,per    s ⌐        ⌐        ⌐
                                                            psp
 I      They were seated in the boat, Nick in the           pt
                                                            per
            s      p      per   aex,t                       at
        stern, his father rowing.                       ⌐   ia

           s,p    e,t,pt              s              ⌐       psp
                                                            at
 II     The sun was coming over the hills.          ⌐       ia

           s,p    e    pt        e        s         ⌐       psp
                                                            at
 III    A bass jumped, making a circle in the water.⌐       ia

                                                            psp
          p,per aex      s         s            ⌐           pt       pp
                                                            per
 IV     Nick trailed his hand in the water.     ⌐           at
                                                            ia                wi

           s,p  ain                at,s             ⌐       psp
                                                            pt       pw
 V      It felt warm in the sharp chill                     per
                                                            at
              at,t                                          ia
        of the morning.                             ⌐

             t,at              s       aex    s     ⌐
                                                            nw
 VI     In the early morning on the lake sitting in         nr
                                                            nt
          s          s      p    per   aex                  psp
                                                            pt
        the stern of the boat with his father rowing,       per
                                                            nt
                  ain,sti                                   at
                                                            ia
        he felt quite sure that he would never die. ⌐       ⌐        ⌐
FIGURE 3.1
```

va	–	visual and auditory effects	surface
st	–	stylistic features	aspects

p	–	point of view	
psp	–	spatial locus of p.o.v.	
pt	–	temporal locus of p.o.v.	
ns	–	narrative situation including all aspects from p to nt	presentational process as
n	–	narrator or narrative voice	suggestive of
nw	–	narrator's relationship with presented world	concretized process (pp)
nr	–	narrator's relationship with reader	
nt	–	narrator's overall tone	

s	–	aspects of space	
t	–	aspects of time and tense	
e	–	events	presented world
aex	–	acts, physical	as suggestive of
ain	–	acts, mental	concretized
per	–	presented personae	world (pw)
sti	–	explicitly stated idea	
at	–	atmospheric qualities	

ia	–	interpretative abstractions	high-level
wi	–	work ideology	inferences

son is in focus; in II, the spatial locus of the point of observation appears to be moving close to Nick in order to describe the rising sun from his position; III suggests the same constellation, with the difference that the narrator is now focusing on the water nearby; in IV the narrator appears to be retracting to watch Nick trial his hand; in V he is moving into Nick's mind, registering the boy's sensation of warmth ('It felt,' not 'he' or 'Nick felt'), while in VI, finally, the narrator's spatial locus is moving away from the boat, the lake with its early-morning atmosphere, and the narrower focus on Nick, now in the form of thought report and omniscient observation.

It is less rewarding, but by no means easier, to define the narrator's temporal locus in this passage. Generally speaking, the temporal locus of the narrating voice appears to shift with what is being told, accompanying the action, as it were. This sense of an immediately presented world is, I believe, a result mainly of the subtle conflict in which the progressive verb forms with the epic preterite.

Our inferences about the narrator's tone must remain similarly tentative. In the story as a whole, as well as in its final passage, we notice a slight shift from distanced, 'objective' neutrality to a conspicuous technical nearness to the protagonist. It would seem that it is this physical proximity between narrator and central persona which, on the part of the reader, encourages the inference of a tone of controlled sympathy.

Objective as the narrator's position is throughout the greater part of the story, it is not surprising that there is no firmly established relationship between narrator and reader or any explicit references to the act of telling. As a result, the reader is made to shift with the narrator and to share his close contact with the boy's sensation of warmth and feeling of security at the end of the story.

As for the presented world and its filled analogue, the imagined world, there are first the personae, father and son, the one propelling, the other trailing; the one having made his son share in adult experience and now trying to take him back, the other, being taken along, exposed, and now on his way home; the one experienced in life, pain, and death, and the other, in the stern of the boat, recovering from too early, too acute an experience.

The two non-human occurrences in the passage, its events, stand in forceful contrast with the boy's central experience. Both sunrise and jumping bass are aspects of nature and life, a new day, of wholeness and ordered universe, of which Nick, in the end, feels himself an integral part. This makes sense also in terms of the atmospheric qualities which the reader may wish to attach to some features of the presented world. The chill of the morning can be seen as contrasted with the warmth of Nick's body, just as the chills of pain and death may appear as set against the warmth of sunlight and life.

Apart from the sense of stasis in motion which we derive mainly from the use of tense, there are other aspects of time worth considering. There is, for instance, the difference between the relative speed of the action at the beginning of the story, hastening, one feels, to fulfil and overthrow the father's expectations on the one hand and, on the other, the contemplative restfulness in the final section. This initial sense of coercion, the short time span of the action, and also the external aspect of brief reading time, in short, the general impression of brevity, add to the weight of Nick's experience a quality of painful poignancy. But then, again, we must not forget these other aspects of time in the presented action, such as the beginning of a new day and the implications of a temporal cycle suggestive of Nick's recovering vitality.

Perhaps the most clearly established aspects in Indian Camp are those of space. Accompanying Nick, the reader enters various spaces, crosses thresholds and moves closer and closer to the story's central space, a place of initiation and revelation; from the familiar shore, the stern of the boat and his father's arm around him, Nick crosses the lake, proceeds through the forest, enters village and shanty, and finds himself in front of a bunk; he returns through the forest, across the lake, alone in the stern of the boat, his father rowing. Somehow we feel compelled to link this circular journey to the circle made by the bass in the water, the circle of the sun and its orbit and, ultimately, the cycle of life. By this activity of linking and inferring, the reader, at the end of the story, sees Nick embedded in the widening horizons of water, hills, sun, and cosmic space.

When we are talking about stated ideas, we are dealing with the one area of a literary work in which the text functions as verbal construct in its own right. By stated ideas I mean directly presented statements (made by the narrator or presented as a persona's mental or speech act) apparently serving as interpretative guides. In picking up

stated ideas in a story, the reader is able to proceed
straight away to the pattern of interpretative abstractions –
which he is inferring at the same time by other means –
without first establishing an imagined world.   'He felt
quite sure that he would never die', refers, of course, to
a specific feeling experienced by a specific persona.
However, we notice at the same time its abstract quality
and interpretative weight, if we link this statement with the
concrete situation in the shanty and with the series of
abstract questions and answers in the dialogue preceding
our passage.   Considered in this manner, the story's final
statement is the solution which Nick gives himself as well
as the narrator's chief cue for our interpretation.

Those among us who take the intentional fallacy strictly
must skip the following and reject what could be said about
a story in terms of authorial register or those features
subtly indicative of the author's standpoint as implicit in
typographic layout, title, surrounding elements, etc.   In
our case the title's 'neutrality', in keeping with the general
presentational form, allows hardly any inferences at all.
One should, however, consider certain framing elements
which, although external to the story, nevertheless place
what is told in a larger context: the arrangement of
chapters (I to XV) and the italicized passages preceding the
stories from Indian Camp to The Undefeated. (33) Falla-
cious as such considerations may be to a literary theory
which treats the literary construct as an autotelic object,
not to take these features into account at all would be a
more serious misdemeanour.   When we read the volume, we
certainly do 'get an impression' of or draw conclusions,
however provisional, about the author's possible 'Weltanschauung'.   And we ask ourselves why he – and evidently
not the narrator – has placed the reminiscence of war,
'Everybody was drunk.   The whole battery ...' to 'I was
a kitchen corporal' in the vicinity of young Nick's
ordeal. (34)

If we were to draw inferences from all the details available in a narrative, i.e. the visual impression of the
printed text, text signals, presented world, the presentational process, and their concretized analogues, we would
obtain a large number of general statements many of which
would make sense in terms of the rest; some would be
difficult to link to others and some might be completely
isolated.   Such statements we are referring to as high-
level interpretative abstractions.   But except for a

research worker with a special aim, nobody reads stories in this manner. Instead, at a certain stage in the reading process and more or less consciously, we tend to take far-reaching interpretative decisions, we choose an interpretative standpoint towards which, more or less obstinately, all our further interpretative activity is oriented. Consequently, our interpretative abstractions will not only be reduced to those appropriate to our chosen interpretative stance, they will also appear as structured. This structured set of interpretative abstractions we should understand as a narrative's work ideology.

From what has been said it follows that work ideology is neither wholly objective, pertaining to the textual construct alone, nor purely subjective. Work ideology is rooted in the textual construct as far as it can be linked to aspects of the verbal and non-verbal elements of the text; it is rooted also in the reading consciousness in as far as the selected set of abstractions is a choice resulting from the reader's peculiar 'biographical situation', (35) his typified everyday experience and sense of inter-textuality, his total psychic and socio-cultural make-up at the moment of reading. The phrase 'in as far' is deliberate, since even in a very loose and seemingly incoherent narrative a great many interpretative abstractions appear as prestructured. As to the reader's biographical situation, it determines not only the direction of his interpretative orientation, but also the level of abstraction at which he places his work ideology. The distinction between interpretative abstractions and work ideology is useful because it allows for the reader who proceeds to draw interpretative inferences at a high level of abstraction without combining them into a set of summary statements about the narrative's moral-philosophical and ideological commitment.

As an illustration, let us draw such a structured set of interpretative inferences from what we have established about Hemingway's short story. In Indian Camp experience appears to be forced upon youth, unexpectedly and, paradoxically, also unintentionally. Through narrowing horizons a child's mind is made to enter a central space where it is to witness excruciating pain and suicide, the concentration into one moment of painful utterance and agonizing silence and the torturously powerful urge to enter as well as leave this world. But youth is released, not ready yet to link experience with existence. Ironically, it is the protective forces which serve as agents in this

process of initiation: their triumph of experience, mastery
and guidance is reversed to the shocked admission of
mightier forces being at work. The intellect asks questions
and receives answers repeating, at the ideational level, the
implications of the concrete situation. But there is resistance to such knowledge: the warmth of the body belies
death. Death is not a property of youth.

Obviously, the casual reader will skip the one or the
other rung of the interpretative ladder from visual-auditory
perception to high-level abstraction. But at the same time,
it is most unlikely that he can make valid interpretative
inferences without having first established from the concrete
datum of the narrative text the schematically signified
process of presentation and presented world and, in bringing to life these two with the help of his own stock of
literary and life experience, the concretized imagined
world.

Chapter 4

Narrative stratification and the dialectic of reading

In this chapter I wish to trace Roman Ingarden's conception of the literary work of art as summarized at the beginning of his 'The Cognition of the Literary Work of Art' and make suggestions, in addition to his observations, as to the way in which the structure of narrative differs from that of other literary modes. A critical summary of Ingarden's nine criteria will be the basis of the argument.
1 For Ingarden all works of literature are

multi-stratified constructs containing (a) the stratum of the sounds of the words and of linguistic units larger than words, (b) the stratum of linguistic meaning units such as sentences and sentence correlates, (c) the stratum of schematic aspects through which the various presented objects appear, and (d) the stratum of presented objects themselves.

In addition to what Ingarden includes in the first stratum I would also list typographic aspects of words and larger linguistic units, on the grounds that for the reader they are indispensable aspects and that they too have a potentially significant role to play in the total polyphony of aesthetic value qualities. Ingarden's second stratum (b) poses no problem; it is generally referred to as the surface text. But it is with strata (c) and (d) that this study must take issue. In accordance with our argument in chapter 1, that in narrative we are always dealing with two sets of signifieds (process and world) both of which have to be constructed by the reader, the stratum of schematic aspects as well as the stratum of objectivities must be further differentiated. Stratum (c1), or process as schema, and stratum (c2), the stratum of the schematically given world, are followed by strata (d1), or process as a set of objectivities, and (d2), the objectivities of the presented world. Depending on which of the two signifieds, process or world, is foregrounded in the stratum of the surface text, the reader will be able to concretize first (c1)–(d1) or (c2)–(d2).

In other words, the narrative text determines the sequence of concretization; the reader cannot concretize process and world simultaneously. In the statement 'She despised the miserable beggar' we first concretize the aspects of the presented world before we construct the narrator's physical and moral stance. By contrast, in beginnings such as 'Appelez-moi Thérèse' or 'Call me Ishmael' we first concretize aspects of the presentational process and also, as a secondary construction, tentative aspects of the presented world. In the course of reading, the latter are confirmed when we learn that Thérèse and Ishmael refer at the same time to personae of the presented world, to experiencing selves. As the beginning of 'The Great Gatsby' unfolds, the reader is guided to shift his sense of priority from the schematic presence of a narrator to the foregrounded presented world. The statement 'In my younger and more vulnerable days' starts with a reference to a speaking I, 'my', whereas 'younger ... days' makes us concretize, however tentatively, a lived past. Yet, the presentational process is still accessible as a secondary construction, at its centre a now older and, unless he is speaking ironically, also a less vulnerable person.

Although I do not accept the belief that 'there is nothing in discourse that is not matched in the sentence', I do think the reading act testifies that we are bound to synthesize abstract meaning at each point of the reading process as well as in retrospect. (1) Ingarden's exclusion of a set of abstract propositions as an umbrella interpretation from his schema of strata is carefully argued, but to my mind does not accurately reflect what in fact happens when we read literary works. Since we intend our world not merely in terms of objectivities but also ideologically, since we must interpret imaginary worlds as we do the social life-world by means of ideological structures, the reader's activities are not likely to stop after he has concretized a quasi-world. And if he cannot stop there (except by a deliberate act, e.g., by performing a phenomenological reduction) a philosophical-ideological stratum (e) must be stipulated in the literary work of art. However, the interpretative inferences drawn in this stratum are the result not only of a summary deep-structure transformation of the surface text, but are also abstracted from our concretizations, except where thematically significant abstract statements are directly provided in the surface text.

2 Ingarden's next step in the argument, that 'the material nature and form of individual strata are responsible for the special relationship among all strata and, at the same time, the formal unity of the work as a whole', perfectly meets the requirements of our enlarged stratified model.

3 The third point concerns the 'quasi-temporal extension' of the literary work, the 'ordered sequence of its parts such as sentences, sentence correlates, chapters,' or 'various kinds of dynamic development'. (2)   This forward dimension makes the reader respond step by step to all strata and their syntagmatic extension from beginning to end.   In terms of narrative structure this means, among other things, that the reader accumulates lacunae of indeterminacy and schematic aspects of both process and world, his step-by-step concretizations of these, as well as his interpretative inferences at each point of the reading process.   At the end of the reading act this noetic phase or gradual experiencing of the text changes to a retrospective noematic phase or the narrative as experienced.

4 'Contrary to the majority of sentences in scientific works, which are genuine propositions, the statements in literary works are quasi-propositions.' This is a fundamental observation which must be seen in relation to the phenomenological separation of artistic and aesthetic object as well as Husserl's notion of the reconstruction of meaning intention.   To simplify the matter somewhat let me add the following distinctions between (a) definitions (e.g., $a^2 + b^2 = c^2$), (b) pragmatic propositions, and (c) quasi-propositions.   Type (c) contains statements which may look like propositions of the kind defined as (a) and (b).   If the intended reader reception is not coded in the text itself, the system of frames within which we experience literary works, just as the social situations pertaining to pragmatic statements, supplies the cues for an aesthetic response. Nevertheless, we are always free to follow or disregard coded meaning intention, so that there are the appropriate and inappropriate modes of response, as shown in Figure 4.1.

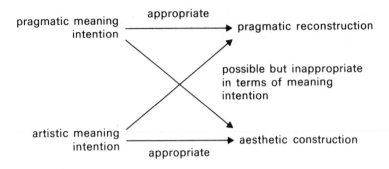

FIGURE 4.1

5 To be a valuable work of literature each of its strata
must contain valuable qualities of these two kinds:
artistically and aesthetically valuable qualities, the
latter of which are latent in works of literary art.
Their multiplicity effects a peculiar polyphony of
aesthetically valuable qualities which in turn determines
the quality of the value that constitutes itself in the work.
In a scientific work we may also find literary artistic
qualities which control certain aesthetically valuable
qualities.   In a scientific work, however, they are
merely a 'momentum ornans', linked to the work's essential function in a loose manner only or not at all.   Such
embellishment cannot transform a scientific work into a
work of literary art. (3)

Although it is, of course, possible to respond to artistic
objects in a pragmatic fashion or to pragmatic objects
aesthetically, it is the latent polyphony of aesthetic value
qualities which encourages the aesthetic construction of
meaning and undermines the pragmatic response.   As for
the narrative text, it is especially the interaction between
presentational process and presented world which contributes most to that polyphony.   Each stratum from print/
sound to work ideology, the relation of all strata to one
another, and the aspects of the forward reading dimension,
such as the rhythm of language, the temporal unfolding of
process and world in the reading consciousness, or the
gradual constitution of the overall aesthetic-philosophical
design and work ideology are all potential vehicles of
aesthetic value qualities.
   6 'The literary work of art – like any other work of

literature – must be distinguished from its concretizations
which arise during its reading (or in a stage performance
and its experience by an audience).' As it stands,
Ingarden's assertion is not easily reconciled with other
conceptions of literature, notably various linguistic
approaches. But if we take a work's concretization to mean
the reader's construction of an aesthetic object which is
constituted by a number of transformations of the surface
text, bridges can be built. As illustrated in chapter 1, we
should distinguish the following transformations: first, one
in which the narrative text is grasped as two sets of
schematic propositional meanings or the deep structures of
presentational process and presented world; the second, a
concretizing transformation in which process and world are
imaginatively objectified in terms of inter-textual and
everyday experience; and a third transformation by means
of which highly abstract interpretative inferences are drawn
and synthesized into work ideology.

> 7 Unlike its concretizations, the literary work is a
> schematic construct, i.e. some of its strata, especially
> the stratum of presented objects and that of its aspects,
> contain lacunae of indeterminacy, gaps which are
> partially replaced by concretizations. The overall
> concretization of a work of literature is still schematic,
> but to a lesser degree than the work itself.

In accordance with our enlarged scheme of stratification,
all we must add is that in narrative the reader's concretizing acts of consciousness are focused most strongly on the
creation of the double vision of presentational process and
presented world.

> 8 The lacunae of indeterminacy give way to specific
> concretizations in the sense that they are filled out, as it
> were, by more precise determinations of the presented
> object. The process of filling, however, is not itself
> sufficiently determined by the delimiting aspects of the
> presented object, so that it may vary in different
> concretizations.

In contradistinction to Ingarden, this study puts greater
emphasis on the variation between different individual
concretizations. Not merely may the imaginative constructions of process and world vary, they must be distinct in

separate readings of a narrative even by the same reader
because of his altered stock of typified experience (for
which the narrative itself is partly responsible), between
different readers because of their distinct 'biographical
situations,' (4) between epochs, regions, cultures or
classes, because their conceptions of world both as spatio-
temporal and ideological structure differ more or less
radically. Therefore, since there is no such thing as
identical concretization, and since the author can be
understood as the work's first reader, reading fictive narrative is always the aesthetic construction of a vision and
an implied authorial stance, and not a reconstruction of
meaning intention.

> 9 The literary work is a purely intentional construct with
> its ontological source in the creative acts of the author's
> consciousness and its physical foundation in the printed
> text or any other physical tool of reproduction (e.g.,
> tape). Owing to the stratification of its language, the
> literary work of art is inter-subjectively accessible as
> well as reproduceable; it is therefore an inter-subjec-
> tive, intentional object linked to a community of readers.
> As such, the literary work is nothing physical and trans-
> cends all acts of consciousness of author and reader
> alike. (5)

Ingarden's ninth point sums up a complex argument about the
ontological status of literary works of art, derived and
purely intentional objects, and inter-subjectivity, an
argument too involved to interpret in its entirety in this
study. All I wish to do is ask and propose a brief answer
to this question: if, as Ingarden says, the literary work of
art is nothing physical and transcends both authorial and
reading consciousness, how then can it be inter-subjectively accessible? One assumption must be that the
literary work is not given to the reader as an object,
except partly in as far as it is material shape. We must
further hold that it cannot be a purely subjective construct
either, since through its codification it acts as a schematic
guiding system for the reader's responses: there certainly
are wrong readings (though no single correct reading),
such as changes of or disregard for textual information.
The literary work is inter-subjectively accessible because
in its concretization there occurs an inter-relation of the
acts of consciousness of author and reader, and also, as a

secondary relationship between reader and reader; as we read the text, the schematic guiding system comes into existence, allowing and urging our concretizations to take shape. This schema is the result of, but not identical with, the author's meaning intention; at the same time it is the basis on which the reader constructs his meaning: verbal, imaginary and philosophical.

According to Husserl, such codified schemata permit the reconstruction of meaning intention. But identity of meaning intention and received meaning seems possible in two cases only: (a) in mathematical definitions and the statements of formal logic and (b) in codified empirical observation, where both referential meaning and modality can be and are checked against their source items in the world-out-there. In the literary work, however, we are dealing with an altogether different situation: (c) fictional statements or quasi-propositions of which the reader's aesthetic construction of meaning can only be said to be an approximation of the artistic meaning intention. Further, in narrative, it is above all else the construction with the help of our stockpiled inter-textual and everyday typifications of both process and world which guarantees the possibility of that approximation, but at the same time makes highly unlikely the identical reconstruction of the artistic intention.

A helpful case in the discussion is the novelistic documentary which partakes of (b) coded empirical observation as well as (c) realistic statement. A strictly documentary reading would have to reconstruct meaning exclusively in the sense of rule (b), while a realistic reading must construct meaning in terms of rule (c). Both possibilities are allowed for by the codified schemata of the novelistic documentaries that I know. In all other literary works, especially narrative works from realistic fiction to fantasy, the reader's stock of inter-textual and everyday experience necessary to make sense of the text renders impossible the objective reconstruction of meaning intention. Not unlike the social interaction of human consciousness, the reading of works of literary art is an approximating interpretation, an inter-subjectively guided aesthetic construction.

Let us now test our assertions about narrative stratification and forward reading dimension by looking more closely at selected fictional statements and then at a short story as an example of a total narrative structure. Near the beginning of Bernard Malamud's 'A New Life' we read, 'bearded, fatigued, lonely, Levin set down a valise and suitcase and looked around in a strange land for welcome.' Apart from its immediate visual and auditory qualities, the surface text provides us with a set of aspects of space, time, acts and persona, evoking in the reading consciousness a scene as if performed on a stage and also a host of expectations, very tentative no doubt, waiting to be rejected, modified, or fulfilled. This activity of mentally staging that which is presented is construing or concretizing our imagined world. This world is still small, mostly on the forestage, but nevertheless established.

But this is only one side of the phenomena of the print shapes, language signs, and their linguistic grouping, the one which our more immediate responses are inclined to reveal. The other comes to light when we apply a radically different attitude of consciousness, one of focusing not on the concretized world itself but on the process of its presentation. Although we are still dealing with the same linguistic unit, we are now fabricating something which is essentially different from our staged world. Viewed in this manner every word and, I am inclined to argue, even the punctuation may disclose something about the spatial and temporal position from which the presented world is being observed, the relationship which exists between speaker and world, between speaker and reader, the intended personality of the speaker, or his ideological stance.

At the end of 'A New Life' our answers to these problems, though by no means easier to find, will be considerably more comprehensive. But even this one sentence is a rich resource. First we are given a view of Levin's face, then an interpretation of his physical and mental states; then we move away from him to watch his movements as well as the objects he is handling; we witness his looking around, but at the same time we slip into his mind to interpret his environment as strange and his glance as expressing expectation. This shifting position of the locus of observation is the first aspect of the presentational process which can be established with considerable accuracy. Our other inferences, as for example a certain sympathy toward Levin on the part of the speaker, or the observer's relatively close temporal locus, require much more information and are constituted only gradually in reading further.

One aspect, vital to our grasp of the kind of presenta-

tional process employed, concerns the speaker's very
activity of speaking: whether he is mainly discussing,
debating, confessing, adoring, imploring, praying,
attacking or narrating. Any of these activities may of
course be modified by any one or more of the others; which
of these is predominant and structure-carrying, though,
can be secured only in retrospect, i.e. with the whole text
at our disposal. From this vantage point, then, we can
say that the sentence in question is a typical sample, so
that 'Levin set down a valise' and 'looked around' are
characteristic aspects of an act of telling which, experienced as juxtaposed to its referential meaning, support our
understanding of presentational process and presented
world as narrative structure.

On the one hand, then, there is the identity of the
linguistic units as vehicles of presented world and presentational process and, on the other, the clear distinction
between the different ways they are constituted in the
reading consciousness. This paradox of being embedded
in the one surface text, indeed in one and the same word,
and requiring for its construction two distinct manners of
reading, may serve as the basis for a definition of works of
narrative literature.

Narrative could be defined as a reader's realization of a
language construct in which linguistic features are predominant, the meaning units of which contain at the same
time aspects of the presentational process and the presented
world requiring for its aesthetic construction distinct acts
of consciousness. In the performance of these acts the
presented world gradually emerges as a complex cluster of
aspects of time, space, events and human acts, narrated
personae, atmospheric qualities, and a set of ideological
positions, while the presentational process unfolds itself
step by step as a presenting persona's shifting spatial and
temporal locus, his acts of viewing the world and rendering
it to the reader, a narrator personality and his moral
stance which the reader synthesizes as his ideological
attitude. (6) Since in every fictional narrative there are
two fundamentally different modalities, that of the presentational process and that of the author as sender of the
total message, the conclusions drawn about the presentational process cannot be equated with the implied authorial
stance. Only the careful, separate construction of
presented world and presentational process and their
interpreted interaction allows the inference of an overall
authorial position or work ideology.

We must now consider language structures which play an important role in narratives but do not seem to fulfil the requirement of interaction of process and world, because either the aspects of the presentational process or those of the presented world are absent. I am thinking in particular of such devices as dialogue without 'verba dicendi', free indirect style as dominant in 'figural narrative situation', (7) authorial commentary, authorial first-person reader advice, first-person narrator interjection, or two kinds of interior monologue.

> 'What is your owner's name?' 'He is old Yang From Wanshien.' 'I'll remember not to ship on his boat – I mean the new one he'll have to get after his Noise Suppressor wrecks this one.' (John Hersey, 'A Single Pebble')

The linguistic units here foreground one aspect of our definition of narrative, namely the presented world in the form of speech acts and their fictive referents. By implication, we also learn something about the speakers, but now the speakers are personae of the presented world and no longer an aspect of the presentational process. This example, therefore, fails to fulfil one condition of the definition, a condition which, however, is provided by the narrative context. Drama, a close relation of dialogue, supports this view in that its overall presentational process is not revealed through the spoken language but through its physical performance: it is its staging which provides the concretized unity promised by the text.

In Ernest Hemingway's Hills Like White Elephants, a story often cited for its dramatic character, the ratio between narrative and scenic elements is roughly five to seven. The story's 67 cases of dialogue without 'verba dicendi' are balanced by 33 instances of dialogue with narrator comment and ten passages of pure narration. Furthermore, the introductory narrative-descriptive passage of nine and a half lines establishes firmly the overall authorial narrative situation, while the concluding section of seven lines of straight narration and two lines of dialogue with narrator comment release the reader with a definite sense of having read a story rather than having enacted a piece of drama.

The strange pain of his heart that was broken seemed to

consume him. That he should love her? That this was
love! That he should be ripped open in this way! Him a
doctor! How they would all jeer if they knew! It was
agony to him to think that they might know. (D.H.
Lawrence, The Horse Dealer's Daughter)

In the first sentence the relationship between acting and
narrating personae is intact. The surface text is the
vehicle of both narrated world and its process of presentation. But with 'That he should love her?' the narrative
situation becomes ambiguous. Either the narrator is
asking a rhetorical question or the narrated persona's
stream of thought is given in the form of free indirect
speech. In the first case, the narrator would be commenting directly on the doctor's attitude to Mabel Pervin, the
emphasis being strongly on the narrator's reflections about
his narrated world and a certain distance between narrator
and narrated persona. In the second case, we are adopt-
ing a very different attitude of consciousness in facing a
figural situation. Now, the first and last sentences
operate as guides, escorting us from the story's overall
authorial narrative situation into a figural situation and
back again. There is a sudden shift of focus which the
reader must make in order to switch from the doctor's
omnisciently presented feelings to his immediately
expressed thoughts. Instead of listening to the narrator's
interpretation, he is now eavesdropping on Doctor
Fergusson's panic-stricken thoughts from 'That he should
love her?' to 'How they would all jeer if they knew!' But
this stream of though contains aspects of the presented
world only – a persona's acts of consciousness – while the
narrator appears strangely suspended from the story's
medium, waiting for his turn. In strictly figural presentation, then, the linguistic units of the surface text function
exclusively as vehicles of aspects of the presented world,
a reversal of the situation in narrative self-reflection and
commentary. That we nevertheless tend to respond to
figural situations as if we were facing ordinary narration
is probably the result of their enveloping narrative elements
which the reader accepts as the guiding framework.
    The following three examples from 'Joseph Andrews' may
serve to illustrate the relationship between narrative as
defined above and such devices as a narrator's statement of
a 'universal truth', independent of the presented world, a
narrator's statement of a general idea as linked with the
presented world, and reader advice.

It is a trite but true observation, that examples work more forcibly on the mind than precepts: and if this be just in what is odious and blameable, it is more strongly so in what is amiable and praiseworthy. (Book I, ch. i)

Another philosopher, whose name also at present escapes my memory, hath somewhere said, that resolutions taken in the absence of the beloved object are very apt to vanish in its presence; on both which wise sayings the following chapter may serve as a comment. (Book I, ch. vii)

And now, reader, taking these hints along with you, you may, if you please, proceed to the sequel of this our true history. (Book III, ch. i)

The first example is a general observation, explicitly stated by the narrator, which is not by itself connected with the presented action but likely to be linked with it by the reader. Seen from our specific angle, the linguistic units carry information about the narrator only; all that we are given is the narrator's speech act which, strictly speaking, allows no specific inferences about the narrated world. The second case is a variation of the first in that the speech act is again predominant, while the world hinted at by the narrator is not the narrated world but a secondary one serving the story world as illustration and not vice versa, as the narrator is trying to have us believe. The third instance is related to both these cases in that it does not contain data about the presented world. It differs from them, however, in the sense that it imparts information not so much about the narrator's philosophical outlook as about his relationship with the reader, a relationship perhaps best described as jovial, ironical and mocking.
The inexhaustible 'Tristram Shandy' provides the follow-ing illustrations of the kind of first-person narration in the world of which the narrator takes an active part. 'On the fifth day of November, 1718 ... was I Tristram Shandy, Gentleman, brought forth into this scurvy and disastrous world of ours' (Book I, ch. v). This sentence contains both narrated world and narrative process and, specifically, the narrating and experiencing selves. The 'I' is under-stood as the vehicle of two related personae, belonging to two distinct realms of experience and separated by a con-siderable span of time. But even such a minor feature as

the date, while evidently disclosing a temporal aspect of the narrated world, carries and conveys some tentative information about the narrator's personality: his scurrilous accuracy and ribald irreverence. 'Scurvy and disastrous', likewise, are qualifiers not so much of the presented fictional universe as a hint at the narrator's own sarcastic conception of the world at large and the 'Leibnizians' in particular. It would appear, then, that in first-person narration there is always a latent tendency of shifting the focus increasingly to the presentational process until all that is given is the very activity of narrating, in which case the narrating and experiencing selves have fused into one. In such coalescence, first-person narration approaches lyrical modes of presentation: we are dealing with a fusion of presented world and presentational process. (8)

But what is happening when the narrator interrupts his activity of telling by an interjection such as 'Shut the door' (Book I, ch. i), something which is a part neither of the presented world nor of his self-reflection? Expletives of this kind apparently belong to an implied second world, the world of which the narrator's act of composing his story is an element, while at the same time communicating something about the narrator's state of mind. And even in 'O there is a sweet era in the life of man, when ... a story read of two lovers, separated from each other by cruel parents ...' (Book VII, ch. xxxi), the double aspect of presentational process and presented world is retained. Although the episode is carried through by means of breathtaking participial constructions until it resolves itself, relieved it seems, in the clauses 'they fly into each others arms, and both drop down dead with joy', a story is being told and a narrator's presence felt. And, as is true of 'Tristram Shandy' in general, the latter aspect is predominant, with its joy of narrative tomfoolery sparked off by an exuberant apostrophe.

In such cases, however, as 'I wish I had been born on the Moon or any other planet' and 'To such, however, as do not choose to go so far back into these things, I can give no better advice, than that they skip over the remaining part of this chapter' (Book I, ch. iv), the presented world in the above sense has ceased to exist. In the first instance, this is because the narration is oriented back toward its source – the narrating self – and in the second, because reader advice in establishing immediate communication between speaker and listener reduces the triangual relationship of narrative between narrator, presented world and reader to a linear connection between narrator and reader. But reader advice is interesting also for a different reason: while the temporal relationship between narrator and presented world is ultimately one between narrative present and narrated past – even if the presentational process appears to accompany the action – in the case of reader address the narrator establishes a tentative link between the narrative present and the future event of any possible reading situation.

Interior monologue is commonly discussed as one of these modes of presentation: direct speech, indirect speech, 'style indirect libre', and interior monologue. Or, according to Derek Bickerton's classification, 'soliloquy is inner speech rendered in direct speech, ... omniscient description is inner speech rendered in indirect speech, ... indirect interior monologue is inner speech rendered in free indirect speech', the speech form of Stanzel's figural narrative situation, and 'direct interior monologue is inner speech rendered in free direct speech.' (9) Indispensable as these distinctions are, they do not tell us anything about the varying relationships in each category between presented world and presentational process, changes which may be highly significant for the interpretation of narrative constructs. The distinction which I wish to draw is between interior monologue as embedded in other narrative situations and interior monologue as a structure–carrying feature.

In the first case, the double aspect of narrated world and narrative process operates not unlike that in a figural situation: speech act and narrated world are both experienced by the reader as presented world, a world which is determined by an overall narrative situation other than 'direct interior monologue'. 'Mr Bloom, about to speak, closed his lips again. Martin Cunningham's large eyes. Looking away now. Sympathetic human man he is. Intelligent. Like Shakespeare's face. Always a good word to say.... He looked at me.... He knows' ('Ulysses', New York: Random House, 1946, p. 95). The first sentence serves both as a foothold in the overall narrative situation of am omniscient observer reporting the protagonist's response to Martin Cunningham's modest views, and as a guide assisting the reader to bridge the gap between the external, physical world of Leopold Bloom's closed lips to the mental world of his thoughts about Cunningham.

Molly Bloom's long, silent, unpunctuated pillow talk is quite different: '... when I put the rose in my hair like the Andalusian girls used or shall I wear a red yes and how he kissed me under the Moorish wall ...' occurs toward the end of some 45 pages of uninterrupted interior monologue. The authorial guidance characteristic of much of Leopold's thoughts has handed over its narrative responsibility to a persona of the presented world. As a result, its one part, young Molly putting a rose in her hair, is now the total presented world, while its second part, Molly in bed reminiscing, assumes the role of the overall narrative situation. And it is indeed with a strong sense of Molly as a narrator that we close the book.

With these variations in mind, we may return to the question of narrative stratification. Having adopted, in principle, Ingarden's conception of literary language as stratified, and having defined narrative in terms of its homogeneous surface text capable of carrying, simultaneously, two heterogeneous kinds of aspect, those of the narrated world and those pertaining to its presentational process, we can now proceed to outline the manner in which narrative constructs constitute themselves in the reading consciousness.

As has been shown, the activation of presented world and presentational process requires first that the reader attend to two distinctive objects, demanding in turn the application of two radically different attitudes of consciousness. In terms of stratification this means, second, that the reader in doing so moves within two distinct strata; and third, that there is always an ontological priority either of world over process, where the presented world allows the construction of process, or of process over world, when the presentational process is foregrounded but allows world to be construed. (10) The essence of the lyrical mode could be defined analogously by the flowing into one stratum of the strata of presented world and presentational process, while in the language of staged drama the stratum of presentational process is altogether buried.

When we read a work of narrative literature, then, we are confronted first with (a) the stratum of print shapes and their visual and auditory effects and, having performed the activities of perception and apperception, we proceed to (b) the stratum of the surface text and its linguistic meaning units. These units carry in their one homogeneous structure two heterogeneous sets of aspects, aspects which

pertain to the narrated world and its presentational
process, respectively, and which are activated by the
reader separately and consecutively in strata (c) and (d),
or vice versa, where the characteristic features of narrative manifest themselves. The stratum of the narrated and
imagined world (c) is seen here as consisting of two sub-
strata, (c1) the presented world in its schematic givenness
in the text and (c2) its concretized form, the imagined world
itself. In the ordinary narrative statement foregrounding
the presented world the reader having constituted stratum
(c2), is in a position to proceed to (d) the stratum of the
presentational process. Like stratum (c), this fourth
stratum must be understood as encompassing both the
schematic aspects of presentational process (d1) and its
concretized analogue (d2). But in spite of the fact that in
the ordinary case mentioned we can construct the presentational process only after we have established the imagined
world, the two strata are none the less closely related:
since in many ways they are both mental analogues of our
actual reality, they are constructed by the reader in a
similar manner.

(c1) and (c2)	(d1) and (d2)
presented (schematic) and	presentational process
imagined (concretized) world	(schematic and concretized)
spatial aspects	spatial locus of narrator
temporal aspects	temporal locus of narrator
narrated events and acts	acts of narrating
stated ideas	stated ideas
atmospheric qualities	atmospheric qualities
narrated personae	narrating persona/ae

In stratum (e) high-level interpretative abstractions are
made: a set of inferences about the narrative as a whole
which we draw with the help of (a), (b), (c) and (d) and such
extrinsic information as prefaces or larger frameworks
within which narratives may be placed; and second, work
ideology or interpretation at a high level of abstraction as
relevant to the reader's own moral, intellectual, socio-
cultural, and biographical position.
    Counting (c1), (c2), (d1) and (d2) as separate strata and
including the ideational level of narrative constructs as the
concluding stratum means setting seven strata against
Ingarden's four. This, I think, is a necessary modification
for the reasons that the activities of the reader in

establishing the two pairs of strata are different in essence and status and, also, that the activity of drawing high-level abstractions appears to be one further necessary rung on the same interpretative ladder. In accordance with our conception of the typifying activity of consciousness we cannot as readers but perform interpretative deep structure operations: in our retrospective attempt to intend and grasp the story's meaning we always form highly abstract summary propositions.

'All human beings,' Malcolm Bradbury observes, 'are narrators, seeking to reconcile what they see and what they say, seeking to make whole and credible the world they speak into existence.' (11)   One feels inclined to complement this view by suggesting that all human beings are readers, seeking to reconcile what they read with what they see, seeking to make sense of a whole in terms of the world in which they exist.   Indeed, the former requires the latter if we wish to understand the nature of narrative, since, as I believe, it is through the activities of a reading consciousness that texts come to life. (12)

Applied to narrative, coming to life means that the acts of telling and the presented world which are buried in the signs of the text are activated step by step in the process of reading until the whole dynamic quasi-world and mediation of a story are established.   Further, any narrative in the process of being concretized strikes the reader as a world in motion.   'The wholeness of telling seems driven by experience, human understanding, compassion,' (13) says Bradbury with a story's author in mind, and, what is more important for the reader, presentational process and presented world have retained and reflect this dynamic quality in their step-by-step unfolding and quasi-temporal dimension.

One could argue that drama deserves the epithet of 'a world in motion' even more legitimately than narrative.   But let us keep the following essential distinctions in mind. First, the setting in motion of the dramatic world hidden in the test has already been achieved by a producer and his actors, so that the audience is faced with a largely concretized world.   Second, and this is another significant difference between dramatic and narrative art, the spatial aspects of the stage, such as decor, costumes, and props have a stability not unlike those of the physical objects of the actual world.   By contrast, the spatial locus of a narrator and, more obviously, the spatial aspects of the

narrated world are dynamic; they change, chameleon-
fashion, according to both context and reading situation.

The lyrical poem, although strictly speaking also a
process, appears to be present in the reading consciousness
as one entity owing to its size and the intensity of the fusion
of presentational process and presented world. It can be
experienced in a monothetic act of consciousness.

For these reasons the lyrical poem has lent itself to
criticism characterized by a terminology of closed shape
(cf. monuments, urns, icons, etc.) and has supported the
prejudice against the temporal qualities of works of literature in favour of their architectonic features. (14)   The
juxtaposition of architectural to temporal aspects, however,
is not only artificial but also misleading since, as is driven
home by the reading of narratives of some size, it is the
latter which furnish the former with their dynamic qualities.

To be able to talk about both presentational process and
presented world at any given moment in the reading process
and, at the same time, about their cumulative unfolding
along the temporal extension of reading, various strategies
have been proposed.   In the linguistic camp, Manfred
Bierwisch makes the distinction between 'textual microstructure' referring to the 'area of the short-term memory
and that which can be constructed ... during the process of
understanding' and 'macrostructure' or the 'construction of
fables, the interlacing of episodes.' He sees 'an essential
mediation between the macrostructure and microstructure
which results in the total effect' and demands that 'a rational
literary theory must encompass both realms.' That the two
structures are clearly distinct is demonstrated, Bierwisch
says, by the fact that in translation the microstructures
have to be replaced by new microstructures, while the
macrostructures are 'effortlessly carried from one language
to another.'   I doubt whether such transactions are effort-
less, but the distinction no doubt is valid.   Unfortunately,
Bierwisch has to admit, as do the majority of linguists,
that 'our present knowledge does not enable us to say anything meaningful about the type of relationship.' (15)

Thus deserted, we return to Roman Ingarden and one of
his more recent followers, Wolfgang Iser.   In close
alliance with the Polish philosopher, Iser disclosed his own
phenomenological outlook with the claim that 'reading causes
the literary work to unfold its inherently dynamic character'
and that 'the convergence of text and reader brings the
literary work into existence, and this convergence can

never be precisely pinpointed, but must always remain
virtual, as it is not to be identified either with the reality
of the text or with the individual disposition of the reader.'
But Iser goes beyond Ingarden in understanding the
'dynamic process of recreation' by the reader as 'steered
by two main structural components within the text: first,
the repertoire of familiar literary patterns and recurrent
themes, together with allusions to familiar social and
historical contexts; second, techniques or strategies used
to set the familiar against the unfamiliar.' The oscillation
between the alien and familiar in the text brings about the
fundamental 'dialectic of the structure of reading' which
finds a synthesis in the reader's 'chance to formulate the
unformulated.' (16) Let me contribute a few points to
Roman Ingarden's position and Wolfgang Iser's findings by
discussing the dynamics of narrative experience as it is
likely to manifest itself during a reading of Alex la Guma's
short story, Blankets. (17)

Choker, a thug, has been stabbed. While he is lying in
a lean-to waiting for the ambulance, his mind wanders, and
fragments of his past mingle with his perception of his
surroundings. On the stretcher in the speeding ambulance
Choker, astonished, feels the clean bedding and warm
blankets, which cover him for the first time in his life, a
life of squalor, violence and hopelessness.

The dynamics of reading strikes us first as an accumulation of printshapes, linguistic relationships and linguistic
meaning units. 'Choker ... on the floor ... assorted ...
junk ... an old blanket ... stabbed three times ... blankets
... filthy and smelly ...' are experienced at a visual-
auditory level, but also as features triggering off an
activity commonly referred to as imaginative reader response. Although a full description of the operational
features of this intricate activity may never be possible, a
few observations can be made. As we are beginning to
imagine Choker's narrow world, we note that we are
performing leaps in trying to conjure up a meaningful
continuum of mental images.

There are gaps which we have to bridge, Roman
Ingarden's lacunae of indeterminacy, areas which are
responsible for the schematic nature of the presented world
as well as the presentational process. In the same way in
which we accumulate the text's verbal features we store
these unfilled lacunae, filling them tentatively as we read
on and revising our interpretative decisions in the light of

new textual information. This process of concretization
and its results, the concretized work of literature, are, as
Ingarden has taken pains to demonstrate, an ontologically
necessary response on the part of the reader to the problem
set for him by the author.

In order to specify one area of concretization, let me
draw a distinction between primary and secondary concretization. If primary concretization refers to the filling of
the immediately given schematic world, secondary concretization could be said to occur whenever the reader places
the thus constructed world in its wider enveloping physical
and social context. Our activity of primary concretization
is called upon, for instance, when we read that Choker is
haunted by images of his past and the memory that 'the
agonized sounds of the bedspring woke the baby in the bath-
tub on the floor, and it began to cry, its toothless voice
rising in a high-pitched wail that grew louder and louder.'
The ensuing passage, 'Choker opened his eyes as the wail
grew to a crescendo,' again belongs clearly to the narrated
present. But the text supports the illusion of the identity
of the two presented worlds of past and present. 'Wail' is
a part in both sections, and the definite article in the second
establishes an even closer link with the first. Understanding here, then, means first to construct both past and
present as separate worlds; second, to see the one concrete
reality of Choker lying on the floor, experiencing past and
present as one; and, third, to link, by interpretative
inference, the concrete past and present worlds in terms of
their common outcry of pain and helplessness. Secondary
concretization, on the other hand, could be said to take
place, for example, when we people the enveloping District
Six with those bystanders in 'tattered trousers' and
'laddered stockings' and add their likely attitudes and
values, their fears and hopes, as far as our extrinsic
knowledge allows, and in so doing give not only life but also
socio-political significance to a very brief text.

Contrary to hard-headed approaches through language and
in accordance with what has been said so far, we accumulate, besides verbal units and lacunae of indeterminacy,
also our concretizations. So that we retain not only the
clause, 'he was used to blankets like this,' but also the
world of poverty and social frustration to which it alludes.

At the same time, we project, at any given moment in the
reading process and again more or less tentatively,
possible future courses which the action could take as well

as their possible implications. Such protentions accompany
our reading, waiting to be rejected, modified, or fulfilled.

'"Ja. But look what he done to others"' inculcates on the
reading consciousness a first notion of Choker's own violent
life and guilt and, also, expectations of further clarification
of the protagonist's character. But throughout the story
his guilt is contrasted with the evocation of the hostile
social conditions under which he must survive. And when
at the end we read that 'his murderous fingers touched the
folded edge of the bedding', the relationship between thug
and victim is brought home with a vengeance. Our protentions are both qualified and fulfilled.

There is also the question and the speculations which it
sparks off as to Choker's rescue or death. Naive as they
may seem, such protentions are pertinent to at least part of
the story's effect, especially since the narrator ends without betraying the injured man's fate. However, our retrospective view of the story causes us to drop protentions of
this kind as futile speculation. At the end of the story we
know that Choker's death or rescue is immaterial if compared with his whole past life, a life we feel compelled to
equate with that threadbare blanket in the fold of which
'vermin waited like irregular troops in ambush'.

This step-by-step process of stock-piling words and
lacunae, retentions and protentions, and their fulfilment or
modification is complicated by a process of quite a different
nature: that of constituting in the reading consciousness
sets into which the various items of narrative process and
narrated world group themselves. In this way we store
each element not only as it appears in its quasi-temporal
linguistic arrangement, but also selectively in terms of the
features of space and time, action and personae, so that at
the end of our reading we are in a position to retrieve
information pertaining to the dynamics of both the gradual
process of the unfolding narrative as well as its interacting structural sets. Blankets, for example, is quite
conspicuously dominated by spatial features which, almost
automatically, appear to form a meaningful pattern in the
reader's mind: the 'jigsaw puzzle' of wet, sweaty bodies,
the 'crumpled, grey-white pillow', the 'half-healed wound'
or the 'rubbed smear of lipstick', the 'faded curtain',
'bedsprings', 'sagging bedstead', 'thin cotton blanket',
'cardboard-patched window', or the 'squeezed-out wash-
rag' of Choker's face make sense not merely as a catalogue
of individual images, but as a design. And even the

prominence of spatial detail on its own is a significant fact
of the story's work intention: the tangible creation of the
material reality of specific social conditions.

But in concretizing we shift not only between the immediately given and its implied enveloping horizons, or
between aspects in a linguistic sequence and as grouped in
sets, but also between different levels of tangibility.   If
we focus for a moemnt on a level of pure inference, the
stratum of high-level interpretative abstraction, we notice
that almost at any given moment in the reading process
fragmentary and provisional inferences are being drawn.
And like all other aspects accumulated in the reading
consciousness, these noetic abstractions, too, are subject
to possible rejection, modification, or fulfilment.

Now the question must be raised and answered how the
reader is able to move so effortlessly – or so it seems –
from the print shape on the page to such interpretative
comments as, for instance, that Choker's present condition
of having been stabbed is simply the concrete expression of
his existence as well as that of a whole suppressed class.

To the devout disciple of verbal analysis, reading stories
can appear problematic only in the sense that the reader
may have difficulties in coping with the author's diction and
style.   But I think that apart from its linguistic obstacles
reading is always problematic in terms of the text's unfolding situations to which the reader is juxtaposed as he
constructs them.   And there is more than mere confrontation.   Reading, not unlike living, is coming to terms with
such situations.   To attempt an answer to our question,
then, let me enlist the assistance of Alfred Schutz and his
conception of the social life-world, a more or less
problematic world which we interpret with the help of our
'typified knowledge at hand'.   According to Schutz, when
man is faced with something unfamiliar 'in the midst of the
unstructured field of unproblematic familiarity', the
situation has 'topical relevance', it merely 'appeals to his
curiosity' and 'attracts his attention'.   'Interpretative
relevance' refers to our task to interpret what has fallen
into our horizon of perception; we must 'subsume' this new
situation, 'as to its typicality, under the various typical
prior experiences which constitute ... [our] actual stock of
knowledge at hand.'   For something to have 'motivational
relevance' it must be related to our 'future behaviour'.
Two basic kinds of motivational relevance are possible:
the one which is expressed by 'in-order-to motives', the

other by 'because motives', the former suggesting an a
priori, the latter an a posteriori position. Or, in
Schutz's formulation, 'whereas the in-order-to relevances
motivationally emanate from the already established paramount project, the because relevances deal with the
motivation for the establishment of the paramount project
itself.' (18)

In the reading process these three types of relevance
play two different roles. They occur first in the reader's
progression from the perception of the printed sign to the
construction of the imagined world and inference of high-
level abstractions: what we read may arouse our curiosity
and hold our attention, prove problematic in a linguistic-
semantic sense, or challenge us to read on because we feel
that there must be a solution to the problem which the
language of the passage poses. Title and opening sentence
in our story set in motion an operation in the reading
consciousness which, in spite of its textual indeterminacy,
is steered loosely by the directional nature of the expectations which they arouse. At a verbal level, whatever can
be linked with blankets will be tested as to its relevatory
potential and, at the level of the narrated world, whatever
promises to shed light on Choker's physical condition as
well as its causes will be activated as interpretative aids.

Second, Schutz's types of relevance play a role within
the strata of the presentational process and the presented
and imagined worlds in that the quasi-reality in our consciousness, analogue that it is of our actual world, is
always experienced as more or less problematic. The
'high-pitched wail' of the baby's 'toothless voice' and the
'crescendo' of the siren's wail strike us as an unfamiliar
combination of familiar phenomena; we may hesitate for a
moment, but will quickly understand and read on: the
situation could be said to have topical relevance. But the
distinctions here are as sliding as those drawn in Schutz's
life-world, and what may be merely topically relevant to
one reader may cause considerable interpretative difficulties to another. In fact, one could argue that almost the
whole enterprise of reading, the total process of linking
elements within the text and oscillating between the bodies
of knowledge about actual and narrated world is at the heart
of Schutz's type of interpretative relevance.

Turning to motivational relevance, we must remember
that the term refers to man as an actor in the social life-
world; although the reader is actively engaged in the two

senses of being spoken to and of constructing a fuller world
out of its schematic presentation, he can only fill, not alter
the given. It is for this reason that there are only because-
motives and no in-order-to motives in the reading of texts.
Because we have construed Choker and his hostile environment in a particular way, we understand the 'murderous
fingers' which touch the thick, new, warm blanket at the
end of the story as essentially innocent.

We must now ask what kinds of typified knowledge we
employ whenever the reading consciousness is confronted
with a story text. As an answer, I should like to modify
Alfred Schutz's concepts by distinguishing between typified
knowledge of the everyday world and specifically literary
knowledge or inter-textual experience. Further, in reading Blankets, for instance, we are tapping specific areas of
such typifications. As to everyday knowledge, we have at
our disposal what we know about slum conditions in general,
the South African social scene, and District Six in Cape
Town, the storehouse of Alex la Gama's material.

Quite different in kind are our inter-textual typifications
of our literary knowledge. The experienced reader is
alerted, for instance, to the mechanics and possible
thematic functions of flash-back technique; he can
distinguish easily between the stages of the tripartite
montage, with the protagonist's mind retreating further and
further into the past and then again approaching the narrated present. But not only can he solve with relative ease
the story's technical difficulties, he is also prepared for
their role in terms of the story's ideational core: the
montage of fragments of Choker's past into his present
situation makes available relevant aspects of the thug's
whole life and puts his present predicament in a socially
significant perspective.

It would be gratifying to find out how much of such knowledge is tapped at each sentence and at each stratum of the
emerging construct of our imagined world. An answer
here is, of course, heavily dependent on the differences not
only between specific narratives but also between individual
readers. One small general observation, however, may be
worth making. There seems to exist a peculiar relationship between the stratification of narratives and the
reader's stock of typified knowledge: the progression at
any given moment in the reading process from visual-
auditory sign to interpretative abstraction at a high level,
a movement which has been shown to be bound up with the

essential nature of works of literature, appears to be paralleled by an increasing complexity in the typified extrinsic knowledge of which the reader must avail himself. The imagining of the narrator's spatial locus and the spatial aspects of the narrated world in Blankets, for example, requires considerably less extrinsic knowledge than, for instance, our construction of the narrating and acting personae or the formulation of a work ideology. Regrettably, I do not have the equipment to follow up the implications which this curious parallel may have for our conception of the actual world, but I suspect that Roman Ingarden, in his Polish works, has more to say on the matter.

Earlier I called the cumulative process of any first reading 'noetic'. In Edmund Husserl's terminology, 'noetic' refers to the act of experiencing, 'noematic' to that which has been experienced. (19) Obviously, at each step of the reading process we pass through noetic as well as noematic phases, since each step, as it is taken, recedes into the past as something which has been accomplished. In this chapter the term noetic is used to stress the incompleteness and preliminary nature of each phenomenon of the reading process if compared with the whole. Only when we have completed our first reading of a story do the phenomena of the concretized imagined world and the inferences which we draw take on the relative momentary stability of an overall 'noema'.

The difference between reading in progress and retrospective view can be described only as radical. In the former, everything is in the making, 'in statu nascendi'; in the latter the concretized work appears as shaped. This second possibility I should like to term the 'noematic' phase of reading. Some of the disagreements between story readers and claims for an erotics of art on the one hand and, on the other, story critics and hermeneutics are brought into sharp focus if one keeps this distinction in mind. Readers are interested above all in the story's dynamic qualities, its 'noesis', whereas critics attempt operative explanations of the whole, an exercise for which they require an overall 'noema'. Ironically though, there is, strictly speaking, no such thing as a story's noema; there are only noematic aspects which, for fleeting moments, conjure up the illusion that we have grasped the whole. It is with these qualifications in mind that I wish to make a few brief comments on the retrospective view which the reader may entertain of a story like Blankets.

With the reader's response to the last word of the text, the reading process and, consequently, also the story undergo a decisive change. The reader's forward orientation, his accumulation of protentions and his openness to the gradual modification of his concretizations are suddenly replaced by an attitude of preparedness for the experience of a meaningful total configuration. The immediate concrete situation of the injured man waiting for the ambulance is now before us, and we feel urged to make sense of its full range of implications. In the light of the whole story we understand, for instance, the necessity of violence; we accept that the protagonist's awareness is bound to be restricted to the ugly strategies of survival; we know that there cannot be room for social consciousness where morality has been reduced to the thug's code of honour and where man views his world not as particularly hostile, as does the reader, but with the unquestioning acceptance of someone born into it. Like Ezekiel Mphahlele in the story In Corner B, or Alan Paton in The Waste Land, Alex la Guma has created a powerful indirect indictment of racial discrimination and suppression by presenting a non-white-only action and confining the white man's role to the performance of a charitable act.

But to avoid the impression of a fully stable overall noema which the reader could grasp once and for all, I wish to resume briefly my earlier notion of a story as a world in motion. There are the forward motions of reading, the depth motion of the concretization of the presentational process and the imagined world at any given moment of reading, the dynamics of narrative process and imagined world themselves, and the motion of their continuous interpretations by the changing individual reading consciousness, different readers, social groups, nations and epochs.

At the same time it is important to remember (and our brief discussion of Blankets supports this) that the dynamics of a story do not simply spring from the intrinsic qualities of certain narrative elements. Rather, they are the result of an interplay of intrinsic and extrinsic phenomena, a dialectic which underlies all reading. Indeed, narrative comes into being only when this dialectic operates. To sum up, its essential features are these: first, the interaction at any given moment in the reading process of the textual information and the typifications of everyday as well as inter-textual knowledge, resulting in partial concretizations of narrative process and imagined world; second, the

oscillation between these accumulated concretizations and
the total textual information with a momentary overall
concretization as synthesis; third, the interplay of the full
range of interpretative abstractions drawn from narrative
process and imagined world on the one hand and, on the
other, the reader's system of values or moral-philosophical
position, forming what I have termed the narrative's work
ideology; and, four, the synthesis by which, paradoxically
perhaps, the reader is changed by a work which he has
partly constructed himself. (20)

Chapter 5

Ladders of fictionality

The distinctions which I shall draw in this chapter are the result of a narrow focus on the essential features of modes of narrating and their corresponding modes of reading, in terms of their graded relationship with actual reality or, in Edmund Husserl's words, the 'world-out-there'. Further, the modes of projecting (author), presenting (text), and appresenting or concretizing (the filling in by the reader to make coherent the schematically given world) must not be equated with literary compositions, but merely manifest themselves in various combinations and to differing degrees in the reading of specific works.

Let us begin again with our working definition of narrative as a literary form in which a narrative attitude is structure-carrying, the other two major attitudes being an existential attitude, or the expression of an immediate state of being, (1) and a gestural attitude, which constitutes itself by staged or stageable language. (2) The three attitudes can be best demarcated with the help of a schema of stratification. If works of literature unfold in the reading consciousness in a series of strata and if these strata are (a) the stratum of print or sound, (b) the stratum of linguistic meaning units, (c1) the stratum of the schematically signified or presented world, (c2) its appresented or concretized equivalent, (d1) the stratum of the schematically given presentational process, (d2) its appresented or concretized equivalent, and (e) the ideational stratum of interpretative abstraction, then we may define as follows. (3) While narrative language allows the clear differentiation between presented world and presentational process, or strata (c1/c2) and (d1/d2), the existential attitude and its language defy such separation; here presentational process and presented world have merged. The essential property of gestural language is the very absence of the presentational process, or strata (d1) and (d2).

To ask now whether a story is fiction, partly fiction, or non-fiction is to presuppose a graded scale by which one can measure a text, while the scale in turn reflects one of the various notions of fiction, such as something made or a construct, a system of lies or something invented. The concept of narrative as something made applies equally to non-fiction and cannot therefore serve as a distinctive characteristic. The issue of fictional truth cannot be discussed in this study. There remains, then, the distinction between invented and non-invented narrative or, rather, a ladder of varying degrees of fabrication.

With the exception of the reproduction of spoken or printed language itself, all texts are, of course, invented. Furthermore, all invented texts are the results of authors' prepredicative as well as predicative experiences of the world; and so, when we say that a story is fiction, we are referring as much to the author's projection (or his imagined world) as to his correlative system of verbal clues and what it presents and also, but in a different sense, to the imagined world which the reader assembles from the linguistic construct as his basis. A careful look at the different ways in which the world-out-there appears to be related to a variety of modes of narrative projection, presentation, and appresentation or concretization may yield a few useful delineations; of these the following ladders give a schematic view.

Ladder I

1 the world-out-there (non-linguistic and linguistic)
2 1 as apperceived by the author ⎱ preceding, accompanying,
3 2 as apprehended by the author⎰ and determining 4 and 5
4 projected world: the prepredicative and partly predicative features of the author's imagined world
5 purely predicative or formulated version of 4
6 text: physical manifestation of 5; printed, spoken, on tape, record, etc.
7 6 as apperceived by the reader
8 7 as understood as a construct of linguistic meaning units
9 8 understood as presenting a schematic world

10 reader's appresented world: filled version of 9,
    accomplished with the help of 14 and 15
11 8 understood as providing a schematic presentational
    process
12 reader's appresented version of 11, accomplished by
    means of 14 and 15
13 reader's interpretational abstractions as drawn from 10
    and 12
14 1 as apperceived by the reader ⎫ preceding, accompanying,
15 14 as apprehended by the reader⎭ and determining 7 to 13

Ladder II

3 the world–out–there as apprehended by the author
4 projected world
      4.1 documentary projection: selection of specific
          features of recollection of and traceable
          relationship with 3
or 4.2 realistic projection: eidetic features of objects
          and their bonds of 3
or 4.3 mythic projection: patterning of aspects of 3 in
          addition to their typical bonds
or 4.4 allegorical projection: fusion of objects and
          ideas of 3
or 4.5 fantasy projection: distortion of eidetic
          features of 3
or 4.6 any combination of 4.1 to 4.5
5 predicative version of 4
6 text
      6.1 to 6.6, as text analogues to 4.1 to 4.6

Ladder III

6 text
7 6 as apperceived by the reader
8 7 as understood as a construct of linguistic meaning
    units
9 reader's experience of schematic consturct
10 reader's appresented or concretized world
      10.1 documentary appresentation: restricted to
          filling in of specific extrinsic factual evidence
          and to 'pairing' (or that part of appresentation
          absolutely necessary for the reader to make
          sense of the schematically given world)

or 10.2   realistic appresentation: filling by means of typified everyday knowledge at hand or 14 and 15

or 10.3   mythic appresentation: inferential patterning of appresented world

or 10.4   allegorical appresentation: prescribed and mandatory patterning of guided and restricted appresentation

or 10.5   fantasy appresentation: filling in by means of free combination of typified knowledge and reader's dream and fantasy worlds as well as strong urge to discover meaning-giving patterns in order to be able to link fantasy world back to 14 and 15

or 10.6   any combination of 10.1 to 10.5

Our ladders suggest that the modes of authorial projection, on the one hand, and the reader's modes of appresentation, on the other, can be delimited by the relationship between the worlds they intend and the world-out-there. Further, since each of these intended worlds is the result of specific directional activities on the part of the author and, reciprocally, on the part of the reader, one can juxtapose to the projected world as the outcome of 'authorial reduction' the readers' appresentations as effected by 'aesthetic reconstruction'. (4)   Indeeed, the former requires the latter if the story is to exist as story and not simply remain text.

In the case of documentary narrative we tend to assume that the projected world in the writer's consciousness is identical with the world-out-there.   But even in this mode there is the personally coloured reflection of apperceptions of external reality and the admixtures of selection, omission, and even interpolation.   On the other hand, though documentary projection cannot be said to be factual in any strict sense of the term, there is a sense in which the distinction between non-fiction and fiction holds.   Only in non-fictional projection can each spatial and temporal detail, or aspects of events and human acts be argued to have a traceable source object in the actual world.   Or, viewed from the position of the writer, only in non-fictional projection does the author attend consistently to individual objects in the world-out-there.   Or, in terms of ontological status, while (with the exception of reproduced language) there is no immediate verbal reflection of fact, only the linguistic encoding of apperceived and apprehended fact, there is indeed immediate verbal rendering of fiction since fiction only exists as an act of consciousness.

I am restricting the discussion of non-fictional (or minimally fictional) narrative to documentation. I am nevertheless aware of such imaginative components in historiography as selection, omission, interpolation (or the filling in by the historian's 'a priori imagination' of that which is not available as fact but necessary for our understanding), construction, and critical interpretation. (5) As far as this 'a priori imagination' is operative in the projection of a coherent world, history and non-fiction story are closely related. The dissimilarities are not in the presented worlds themselves, but in their presentational processes which, in documentary literature, are largely borrowed from the manifold techniques of fictional narrative.

To proceed, then, from a documentary mode of projection to a documentary text, a system of adequate linguistic formulae is required which points to a set of facts embedded in the continuum of the world-out-there. By contrast, an author moves from a realistic mode or projection to a realistic text if he employs concepts which do not refer to what Husserl calls 'this-theres' in the world-out-there, but have their source objects solely in the sedimented eidetic features of the world-as-it-appears-to-him or, to use Alfred Schutz's terminology, in his 'stock-piled typifications' of the everyday world. This differentia is noteworthy since documentation and realism cannot be distinguished at the level of linguistic structure. A mythic projection is characterized by the fact that through its surface world inter-related areas of meaning appear which are suggestive of a set of ideas; accordingly, mythic texts are linguistic structures in which are contained clues as to both that coherent world and this pattern of meaning. Proceeding from an allegorical projection to an allegorical text means transforming the projected fusion of aspects of objects and ideas into linguistic formulae of the nature of 'highway Salvation'. Lastly, essential to fantasy projection and its text is the replacement of the bonds between the eidetic features of our knowledge of the everyday world by unfamiliar links.

Conversely, if he is to read adequately (i.e. if his reading does not contradict the potential of the text) the reader will respond to these modes of projection buried in

the text by reciprocal modes of appresentation. For the
literary critic this is an intriguing field, since the distinctions between modes of appresentation allow him to describe
works of literature in terms of reader response. But first
I wish to confute the widespread belief that we react to
documentation and realism as to the specific, whereas we
read a mythic or allegorical text as something more general.
To do this, let me apply Husserl's distinctions between
formalization versus deformalization and generalization
vis-a-vis specialization.

Husserl separates lucidly 'generalization and specialization' from 'the reduction of what has material content to a
formal generality of a purely logical kind, or conversely the
process of filling in with content what is logically formal.'
Formalization, so understood, is the transformation of
material content into a purely logical form, the process
from authorial projection to text; while deformalization is
the filling with content of an 'empty logico-mathematical
form', the process of building a skeletal world out of the
text. By contrast, specialization is directed towards
'eidetic singularities', for example, the numbers two,
three, four, or five, whereas generalization points towards
a 'highest genus', for instance, 'numerical quantity in
general'. (6) Applied to reading, this means that deformalization refers to acts which give mental-material content
to linguistic formulae or to moving from the stratum of
linguistic meaning units to that of the schematic world,
appresentation to the filling of the undetermined areas
within this skeletal construct. (7)

Since a documentary text is intended by its author as a
system of linguistic meaning units with traceable source
objects in the world-out-there, adequate, i.e. documentary,
reading must tend towards the mental reconstruction of these
very same objects. Accordingly, the reader's provision of
mental-material content for the linguistic formulae should
always be directed toward the recognition of a 'this-there'
in the world-out-there. If lack of evidence impedes these
acts of detailed reconstruction, the reader must be content
with a world which remains in large parts schematic. To
describe this narrower activity of filling, we could adopt
the term 'pairing'. (8)

There is nothing to prevent us from reading a documentary
text as if it were realistic, even mythical. However, in
the light of the acts of consciousness manifest in the text
such reading must be considered as inappropriate. The

reader would have to disregard, for instance, the authorial discouragement of private appresentation which is so marked a feature in 'In Cold Blood'. For Truman Capote has left no doubt that the presented world can be checked, and ought to be if further information is required, in 'the village of Holcomb', Kansas, and its police records, aspects which are not part of the reader's general knowledge of the world. Also, as a consequence of such authorial limitation of subjective appresentation, the construction in the reading consciousness of the ideational stratum is deeply affected: the reader feels reluctant to allow his interpretative inferences to play freely; instead, we tend to restrict them to such ideas as we would hold if faced with the actual documented case itself.

While in documentation the text relates to a specific entity in the world-out-there, something very different takes place in the realistic mode. Since there is no traceable object of which the language is a sign and since language in itself is merely a system of eidetic features of our visions of the world, the 'realistic world' is made up in the reading consciousness alone by the interplay of the text and the typifications of the reader's stock-piled knowledge of actual reality. Consequently, reading at a realistic level can be defined as consisting of eidetic recognition and deformalization plus appresentation in terms of our typified knowledge of the everyday world. What we appresent from a realistic text, therefore, belongs to a very different sphere of being if compared with the reader's grasp of a documentary text. And even if a realistic novel employs isolated features which do signify a 'this-there', their irrealization through their fictional surroundings is fundamental and irreversible. Consider, for instance, the following examples.

In this angle stood Greshambury House, and the gardens and grounds around it filled up the space so made. There was an entrance with large gates at each end of the village, and each gate was guarded by the effigies of two huge pagans with clubs, such being the crest borne by the family; from each entrance a broad road, quite straight, running through to a majestic avenue of limes, led up to the house. This was built in the richest, perhaps we should rather say in the purest, style of Tudor architecture. (Anthony Trollope, 'Doctor Thorne', ch. 1)

Mr Thorne's house was called Ullathorne Court, and was

properly so called; for the house itself formed two sides
of a quadrangle, which was completed on the other two
sides by a wall about twenty feet high.... From the
gateway two paths led obliquely across the court....
Ullathorne is a high building for a country house, for it
possesses three storeys; and in each storey the windows
are of the same sort as that described, though varying in
size. (Anthony Trollope, 'Barchester Towers', ch. XXII)

Although both houses can be tracked down to Montacute
House in Somerset, their presentation in the novels lacks
all specificity; and not even a more detailed combination of
essential features than Trollope supplies could achieve a
sense of a unique 'this-there'. (9) Instead, our typifications of Tudor architecture, gates, effigies, club-bearing
figures, terraces, country houses, or windows are called
upon to fabricate first a skeletal and then a filled world, so
that we ourselves create what the text does not provide.
In 'Life on the Mississippi' (1883) Samuel Langhorne
Clemens records that:

Every town and village along that vast stretch of double
river frontage had a best dwelling, finest dwelling,
mansion – the home of the wealthiest and most conspicuous
citizen. It is easy to describe it: large grassy yard,
with ... ('Life on the Mississippi')

What follows is a catalogue of the essential features of the
'big, square, two-storey "frame" house', with its portico,
columns, iron knocker, 'a parlour, fifteen feet by fifteen',
or 'mahogany centre-table'. It is fascinating to see how
the eidetic generalities of this inventory are transformed
into the eidetic singularities of Huck's admiring description
of the Grangerford House in chapter XVII of 'Huckleberry
Finn' (1885); or, in other words, how the historical and
typifying account of a number of houses of that area and era
is fictionalized by the subordination of their essential
features to the idiosyncrasies of the fictive narrator's
response to one imaginative house.

It was a mighty nice family, and a mighty nice house, too.
I hadn't seen no house out in the country before that was
so nice and had so much style.... There warn't no bed
in the parlour, not a sign of a bed. ('Adventures of
Huckleberry Finn', ch. XVII).

Yet, however personal Huck's narration may seem compared with the typifying account of 'Life on the Mississippi', we are furnished merely with the schematic aspects of the presentational process (Huck as narrator, his spatial and temporal locus in relation to what he tells, his activities of telling, and his attitude to the reader and the presented world) and those of the presented world (with its spatial and temporal features, action, and personae) which we must deformalize and appresent. Indeed, both Trollope and Mark Twain keep the aspects of the world-out-there 'at arm's length', as Joseph Conrad, in the Preface to 'The Secret Agent', says he did during the composition of that novel, 'lest they should rush in and overwhelm each page of the story.'

The pith of the mythic mode of appresentation is the reader's guided discovery of a pattern of meaning bestowing sense on the fictional world beyond its verisimilitude. Two activities of consciousness must concur to make this possible: the patterning activity of authorial projection buried in the text and the reader's readiness to let things fall into shape beyond the appearance of the appresented surface. Since mythic narrative is not simply a linguistically filtered vision of the eidetic features of the world-out-there, as is its realist relation, but an interpretation of an eidetic view of the world-as-it-appears-to-the-author, its guiding principles are powerfully present, readily recognizable, and will therefore affect our reading accordingly.

There is much more of the mythic (and even fantastic) in the realistic novel than is commonly acknowledged. The time-honoured distinction between novel and romance, for instance, is an awkward attempt to solve this problem. But what to do with works like Kafka's 'The Trial'? It is certainly not a realistic novel, but even less a romance. It would be much more practical to employ the term novel in a more general sense and make the distinction by means of such adjectives as realistic, mythic, allegorical, fantastic, or a combination of these, to indicate the structure-carrying mode or modes. Also, this method would allow for the fact that these distinctions are merely different degrees of fictionality if measured by the world-out-there and not, as the 'natural novel theory' (10) claims, a measure of how much actual 'life' and 'fact' is subsumed in a narrative.

To return to the mythic modes of projection, presentation, and appresentation, they are not restricted to realis-

tic surfaces; they can operate also in slightly disrupted as
well as highly fantastic fictional worlds. This does not
affect their essential nature, only their function: failure
to recognize mythic patterning in a realistic narrative does
not in any way interfere with the reader's grasp of the
action's basal meaning, while in a fantasy world this very
patterning may be his sole interpretative footing. But
before I attempt an illustration of how a mythic mode of
appresentation can affect our comprehension of a novel, let
me briefly speculate on the possible span of such interpretations of our view of reality. Keeping in mind that author
and reader are consciousnesses facing the world-out-there
and bringing their responses to bear on language, we can
say that their visions may range from a world in which man
is threatened and annihilated to one of which he is a wholly
integrated part, from a state of absolute rejection to a state
of grace; or, psychoanalytically speaking, from paranoia
to primary narcissism. George Bendemann, K., or Gregor
Samsa are personae caught in patterns of the first kind,
while the protagonist in the concluding situations of the
vast majority of European 'Märchen', for instance, approach
the opposite pole. A synoptic discussion of Joseph Conrad's
'Nostromo' will show what kind of mythic design may be
apprehended somewhere between these extremes.

When we read 'Nostromo' as a realistic novel about
Costaguana, 'an imaginary republic on one or other side of
the Isthmus of Panama but so imagined as to be unidentifi-
able', (11) we cannot help but arrange, in addition to our
mode of realistic appresentation, the spatial aspects of
Costaguana into a peculiarly consistent 'moulage': Sulaco
appears as shut off and protected from the rest of the world
by such natural barriers as mountains and sea. Further,
it seems to order itself in concentric circles with the Casa
Gould at the centre, the circles themselves being connoted
by such object symbols as the Goulds' garden wall, the wall
of Sulaco, the flat expanse of the plateau, the steep coast,
and the rock face of the Cordillera. At the same time the
novel's spatial features appear to group themselves at
different levels of altitude: there is the lowest plane of the
Golfo Placido and the Isabels, followed by the harbour and
campo, Sulaco itself, the mine and, lastly, the majestic
heights of Higuerota.

This manner of reading is the first step in a mythical mode
of appresentation; the next step is to conceive of the spatial
middle as a thematic centre. The Casa Gould, at the heart

of concentrically arranged lines of force delineating
specific and graded areas of meaning, is both cradle and
life-centre, 'the inner Cabinet', of the new community.
Likewise, Sulaco as a whole is grasped as a configuration
of the struggling and constantly threatened human community.
Remoteness and isolation, internal organization and, above
all, the mythic religious quality of the 'sanctuary of peace'
in this 'enormous semi-circular temple', are redolent of
Ernst Cassirer's insights that 'hallowing begins when a
specific zone is detached from space as a whole' and that
'this concept of a religious hallowing manifested concur-
rently as a spatial delimitation has found its linguistic
deposit in the world "templum"', which 'signifies that which
is cut out, delimited'. (12)

Against this background of the human community as the
superimposition of an area of meaning on inimically indifferent nature, man on his own is viewed as physically and
morally weak. He may refuse to entrust himself to the
community and die outside its sanctuary, 'just outside the
cloud veil', as does Decoud; betray its trust and thus
remove himself from its centre, as does Nostromo; or
sacrifice a personal relationship within the community for
financial power, as does Harry Gould. On the other hand,
man is presented also as capable of committing himself to
playing a responsible part in the commonwealth. Emilia
Gould, Nostromo before the theft, or Dr Monygham, who
rehabilitates himself through sacrifice, testify to man's
defiance of those 'dark powers' and accomplishment of the
'commonest decencies of organized society'. The
community, however, remains threatened, and at the end of
'Nostromo' its fate is left precariously balanced.

In a mythic mode of appresentation, then, the surface
world pales before its ideas, so that the ideational elements
merely implied in the presented world become the guiding
principles with which this very surface is reappraised.
By contrast, reading allegorically is determined by the
overt presence of inter-related ideational features in the
preceding strata. At the visual level of print this
'intrusion' can often be recognized by capitalization, in the
stratum of linguistic meaning units by naming. But, most
important, in the stratum of the schematically given world
these ideational features are fused with the schematized
objects into one concrete-abstract scheme, so that the
objects attain an abstract quality, while conversely the
ideas are objectified. The reader - if he is to read

appropriately – must respect this fusion by performing four distinct activities.

First, there is the eidetic recognition of the schematized objects and personae on the one hand and, on the other, the understanding of their abstract qualities.   In this way village, highway, town, hill, valley, country, mountain, man, woman, child, lord, or parson are experienced as separate from their attributes morality, salvation, carnal policy, difficulty, humiliation, coveting, caution, obstinacy, discretion, patience, desire of vainglory, or two-tongues respectively.   Second, in a synthesizing act the reader attaches these abstract qualities to the objects and personae and so is able to grasp the essential features of the 'village Morality', 'highway Salvation', the 'town Carnal Policy', a man called 'Obstinate', the woman 'Discretion', the 'Lord Desire of Vain Glory', or 'Parson Two-Tongues'.

Third, eidetic recognition and synthesis of concrete and abstract aspects are succeeded by a process of guided deformalization and appresentation in which the reader fills in the merely schematically given world by means of his typifications of everyday and inter-textual knowledge and, more decisively, the conceptual range laid down by the general qualities attributed to the concrete aspects of this world.   As in documentary reading, then, allegorical appresentation is rigorously curtailed; not, however, by an obligation to the world-out-there, but rather owing to the fusion of the stratum of the presented world with that of interpretative abstraction.   Lastly, having given mental-material content to the schematic construct, the reader now performs an act of formalization by inferring from the appresented allegorical world an interpretative design similar in some points to that discovered in mythic reading. But, unlike the procedure adopted in a mythical mode, he now formalizes in accordance with the rigid rules which inform the presented world in allegorical narrative.   As a result, such guided systematization tends to produce in the reading consciousness a relatively stable ideational pattern, such as a theology, political theory, or, more generally, an ideology. (13)

Of narratives in which fantasy projection is the structure-carrying mode we say that the surface world is ruptured. But what is actually happening when we read such passages as the following?

    ... a forest with sparks of purple and ... golden fire

gemming the foliage; a region, not of trees and shadow, but of ... altar and temple, of pyramid, obelisk, and sphinx. (Charlotte Bronte, 'Villette', ch. XXXVIII)

I kicked at the dilapidated door of the ... pigsty ... two horses, enormous creatures with powerful flanks tucked close to their bodies ... by sheer strength of buttocking squeezed out of that door hole. (Franz Kafka, A Country Doctor)

She's swelling up, swells till her back's splitting out of the white uniform and she's let her arms section out long enough to wrap around the three of them five, six times. She looks around her with a swivel of her huge head. (Ken Kesey, 'One Flew Over the Cuckoo's Nest')

Head with legs sings merrily in the streets, led along by a beggar. The head is an egg. A stupid old woman prises open the egg-head. Foetus. Its singing is its cries of unspeakable agony. The old woman sets fire to the foetus. (R.D. Laing, The Bird of Paradise)

We certainly grasp the various linguistic structures, we recognize the syntactic arrangements; at the same time we also understand words and phrases as isolated meaning units. 'Sparks', 'foliage', 'altar', 'dilapidated door', 'powerful flanks', 'white uniform', 'she looks around', 'stupid old woman', or 'foetus' can all be comprehended separately as in a realistic mode of reading. However, as long as we attend to these items realistically, they do not fit together. It is the connections within the schematic spatio-temporal matrix, between acts and events and personae which differ radically from those available in our typified knowledge of the everyday world. Therefore, we must allow the bonds between the essences sedimented in our consciousness to be replaced by the new links offered in the text. This peculiar manner of reading is probably facilitated by our typified memories of dream fantasies and inter-textual experience, especially of fantasy literature. No reading of Kafka or any Kafkaesque story will ever again produce that fascinated astonishment with which we first witnessed Gregor Samsa and his pathetic attempts at being accepted by his embarrassed family. At one blow, as it were, a whole new set of interpretative tools was then supplied and has since been at hand.

Further, since the thus appresented or concretized world still remains inexplicable and strange in terms of our everyday experience, we respond to a forceful impulse to search for an ideational superstructure comparable to those metaphysical schemata which we continuously superimpose on our apperception of the world-out-there. In this manner, we associate Kafka's 'gigantic insect' with a human community which rids itself of its parasitic member, the penal settlement with legal conceptions of the Old and New Testaments, or those underlying Germanic 'Spiegelstrafen' as against modern punitive practices, or Richard Eastman's phantom ship with a world foundering in mismanagement and man no longer able to cling to a faith for which there is neither evidence nor hope.

We have so far been concerned only with the schematically presented world and its effect on modes of reading. A glance at the presentational process will provide further distinctions. For the documentary mode of projection alone can we stipulate fairly strict rules governing the presentational processes employed. Here the range of narrators available to the author is severely restricted: the narrative situation must meet the demands of objectivity, neutrality; in short, of factuality. This precludes, for instance, the author's choice of whether the narrator should be outside or inside the action; it precludes also omniscience and, generally, the manipulation of mind action unless revealed and identified as such by the personae themselves. The 'true account' of 'In Cold Blood', a genuine documentation in most other respects, is in part fictionalized when the author transforms a posteriori information about the personae's thoughts into free indirect speech projected onto the temporal plane of the murder. On the other hand, manipulation here is based on fact: the personae's thoughts are not the result of authorial surmise but of the novelistic treatment of documentation. (14) In all other modes, the restrictions on presentational procedure can be lifted at will. Even in realistic or naturalistic narrative such unrealistic devices as omniscience, free indirect speech, or the rendering of the imbecile mind, as for example in Benjy's section in 'The Sound and the Fury', demonstrate that our labels of 'illusion of reality' or 'verisimilitude' want qualifying.

Consideration, then, of both the schematically given world and its presentational process produces evidence for the view that with the exception of documentation in the

sense defined above, all modes of projection, presentation,
and appresentation from realism to fantasy are but rungs on
a ladder of irrealization. Only documentary narrative
could therefore be called non-symbolic, since it is rooted
in a set of linguistic analogues of the apperceived external
world. All other modes are symbolic in the sense that even
the most vivid realism is an analogue of an analogue of the
apperceived world-out-there or, in Alfred Schutz's words,
a 'sign of a sign'.

Up to this point our discussion has centred on the relationship between artistic construction and aesthetic
reconstruction. But the modes of projection, presentation
and appresentation can be seen also as the results of
various forms of authorial or 'artistic' reduction, requiring
in turn reciprocal forms of aesthetic reduction; they are
the results of 'acts of segregation and placement'. (15)
Concomitant with such reductions go horizonal qualities of
which the essential features vary in each of the modes
under consideration. Maurice Natanson, in his discussion
of the horizonal character of novels, lists the following
aspects as necessary conditions for the grasp of a literary
microcosm in the reading consciousness:

> First, a temporal-spatial matrix of some order is
> necessary for the characters and action. Second, the
> story presenting the action presupposes that this matrix
> has functional limits which set off what occurred prior
> to the story told as well as what might occur after the
> story ends. Third, the action involved is action for
> characters. Their world is interpreted by them. Its
> meanings are disclosed originally through their action.
> Fourth, that there is and that there continues to be a
> coherent reality for the characters throughout the narra-
> tive, a reality that is inter-subjective, that embraces
> their lives, is a necessary condition for the possibility
> of their world. And fifth, underlying every possible
> element of the literary work is the horizon which defines
> and limits the world created. (16)

All these are necessary yet still not sufficient conditions
for our cognition of narrative; they must be complemented,
in agreement with our initial working definition, by the
features of the presentational process with its aspects of
the spatial and temporal locus of point of view, the activities
of telling, the persona of the narrator (however tentatively

suggested) and the relationship between narrator, presented world, and reader. Both presented world and presentational process are horizonal and differently so in the five modes defined above.

The horizonal quality of documentation does not go beyond 'segregation and placement', because it refers to an action which meshes into an actual past and an actual future, its outer horizon being a threshold to an enveloping wider action rather than a conclusive border. By contrast, in the realistic mode the hedging around is complete and final. There is no immediate passage between the realistically appresented and the apperceived-apprehended worlds; they remain apart, similar though they may look. Moving from documentation and realism to mythic telling, we discover an increase in horizonal quality. For in the mythic mode the reader is bound to respect not only the rigorous bracketing of the world-out-there, but also the internal organization into areas of greater and lesser significance, each of which is marked off by its own border. Such intrinsic horizonal arrangement is present also in the allegorical mode, with the difference that now the hemmed-in areas of meaning are not forcefully suggested but prescribed and mandatory.

The most striking sense, though, of a horizon which hedges a world of its own issues from fantasy narrative. In addition to imparted internal horizons, it is its external border which powerfully shuts off the fictional world from other spheres. In fact, the reader must cross several thresholds before he can enter the realm of fantasy or he falls into it, as it were, when the writer has deliberately refused to point out the steps. The very shock which the reader of a fantasy story may experience is the result of a fall or leap or, in Alfred Schutz's formulation, a 'radical modification in the tension of our consciousness'. (17) As an illustration of a fantasy world into which the reader is gently introduced and from which he is even more gently released, let me outline the horizonal features of the beginning and ending of 'Alice's Adventures in Wonderland'.

Alice is 'sitting by her sister on the bank', peeping into her book and drowsily thinking of what she could do, 'when suddenly a White Rabbit with pink eyes ran close by her.' Alice's drowsiness and the sudden appearance of the bunny prepare us ever so smoothly for our entry into the 'Märchen' world in which we hear the rabbit speak. At the same time, the narrator anticipates our recrossing the horizon of this dream world at the end with his aside '(when she thought it

over afterwards ...)'. Toward the close of the narrative
the reader's passage from the Queen's Court to his everyday sphere is as easy, albeit a good deal more elaborate.
Having herself crossed the threshold from dream to waking
in her sister's lap, Alice is reported to narrate the
'Adventures' of her curious dream.

And after Alice has become part again of the farmyard
reality, the older girl herself begins to daydream of Alice
and her wonder world. Unlike Alice, however, she can
only 'half believe' her dream and is bound to understand its
details in terms of her actual surroundings. The Rabbit is
explained to be the rustling grass, the splashing mouse the
ripples on the pool; rattling teacups become tinkling sheep-
bells, the Queen's agitated cries the shepherd's call, and
all the other images 'change to the confused clamour of the
busy farmyard'. In a very special sense, then, internal
horizons have been created as part of a sense-making
mechanism which Alice's dreaming consciousness has
superimposed on a confused and accidental reality. The
reader, having experienced both, is gently returned to the
sphere of the realistic story and can now undertake the last
crossing on his own, the passage from realism to reality.

In 'Alice's Adventures in Wonderland' the various
horizons pertain to the presented world only, and our
entries and exist are guided by the same narrative voice
with more or less the same spatial and temporal locus in
relation to what it tells and more or less the same tonal
quality. But what about the presentational process? Does
it not also have a bearing on a narrative's horizonal
qualities? Indeed it has. Whenever a narrator hands over
his authority of telling to one or more other narrators or
any other source of information, the perceptive reader will
sense that he has entered a sphere different from the one in
which he has accommodated himself. This holds true even
in the case in which a number of narrators focus on the
same region of the fictional world.

There are the cyclical framework narratives such as
'1001 Nights', 'Decameron', or 'The Canterbury Tales' in
which the reader's many transits from one enveloping
narrative situation to the presentational processes pertaining to each single story play a prominent aesthetic
role. There are also narratives like 'Rashomon' in
which various narrators present their views of what we
tend to call one and the same objective set of facts. But
although the horizons here are anything but conspicuous,

we nevertheless feel transported by each narrator to a
different realm of experience, so that we wonder whether
it is sensible to speak of one objective reality at all. A
more complex case is 'As I Lay Dying' with its fifteen
different narrators and their fragmentary visions of one
total fictional mosaic. But again, although we are furnished
with the central data of coffin and journey by all of them,
each experience is as locked up in itself and as jealously
guarded as is the corpse of Addie Bundren. In addition,
there are significant differences between the outside views,
the conflicting attitudes inside the family, the psychic and
mad response and, in central position, the consciousness of
the dead. Since here the presentational process tends to
subsume the presented world, we can no longer talk about
the reflections of one and the same reality in a number of
consciousnesses, but rather state that it is only to such
reflections that we can attach any meaning. (18)

An early example of the main narrator handing over to a
secondary one is cited by Erich Auerbach in 'Mimesis'.
Encolpius, Petronius's narrator in 'Trimalchio's Banquet',
gives us another guest's description of the host's wife and
his milieu, so that we are informed by one who tells from
the vantage point of admiration and intimate knowledge:
'the viewpoint is transferred to a point within the picture'
and 'the picture thus gains depth'. Petronius, Auerbach
explains, accomplishes two things with this device: 'on the
one hand the most intense subjectivity, which is even
heightened by individuality of language, and, on the other
hand, an objective intent – for the aim is an objective
description of the company at table, including the speaker,
through a subjective procedure.' (19) Paradoxically, by
entering the sphere of the secondary narrator we have
moved a step further away from our own everyday experience
and now find ourselves in a realm more intensely fictional
than Encolpius's, while at the same time we receive a more
credible, and indeed more realistic, account than the
primary narrator would be able to provide.

Strictly speaking, we step inside such narrower horizons
whenever a persona other than the primary narrator speaks
or thinks: in direct speech; in letters as those in
'Wuthering Heights' or 'Lord Jim'; in free indirect speech,
as for instance towards the end of James Joyce's story A
Painful Case, or The Dead, and D.H. Lawrence's The Odour
of Chrysanthemums or The Horse Dealer's Daughter; in
interior monologue, as for example in Molly Bloom's silent

soliloquy in 'Ulysses'; or in diary entries as those in 'A Portrait of the Artist as a Young Man'. Here, in giving way towards the end to dialogue and first-person account, the authorial-figural guidance of the major part of the novel has handed over narrative responsibility to the now self-responsible, though by no means mature, artist. In fact, the emphatic horizonal quality of the concluding section drives home Joyce's ironic detachment from Stephen's intellectual pretentions as forcefully as it does the protagonist's relative independence.

To sum up the argument of this chapter, there are not simply literary objects identifiable as documentary, realistic, mythic, allegorical, and fantasy stories, but rather attitudes of consciousness on the part of the authors which have entered, more or less successfully, the stories' material foundations, their texts, and corresponding attitudes of consciousness on the part of the reader, if adequate reading is to be accomplished. Further, the attitude of story reading has as its essence the distinction between the stratum of the presented world and that of its presentational process, each of which is made up of features of space, time, acts and events, personae, atmospheric qualities, stated ideas, and an abstractable work ideology. Within this general attitude specific distinctions between non-fictional and various fictional modes can be drawn according to (a) the inter-relationship between their seven strata, (b) various modes of deformalization and appresentation, (c) the horizonal qualities of presented world and presentational process, and (d) the graded relationship between the deformalized and appresented fictional worlds, on the one hand, and the world-out-there, on the other.

Chapter 6

Bracketed world and reader construction in the modern short story

At a very general level, brevity in literary forms could be described as a drastic curtailment of linguistic material or reduction of the total language material defined by the horizon of a writer's linguistic competence. Given this obvious linguistic diminution, however, brevity in the many short literary forms appears structured in vastly different ways. Though ultimately always a question of authorial choice, 'brevitas' in the various types of short narrative displays distinct structures which we can describe, just as extended forms are large as the result of specific techniques of 'amplificatio'. Amplifying devices requiring considerable amounts of linguistic material to be aesthetically satisfying are, for example, the presentation of the matrices of cities and societies, physical or psychological development and decay, generation patterns, adventure chains, historical periods, or the use of multiple presentational or presented narrative strands. Such centrifugal macrostructural concerns contrast with the centripetal structures which the reader must activate in short fiction.

Centripetal structures are arrangements at the semantic level which do not immediately cause linguistic reduction and thus overall brevity. Just as the numerical restriction of signifiers does not automatically mean a compression at the level of the signified world (a brief anecdote is capable of vast leaps in presented time and space), so too can the relations between centripetal semantic structures and overall linguistic brevity merely be called a loose interdependence, a tendency.

The range of explanations as to why the short story is short has been vast. There are, for example, Bret Harte's loosely sociological comment that 'perhaps the proverbial

haste of American life was some inducement to its brevity',
the suggestion by Frederick B. Perkins that 'It compares
with other prose compositions as the lyric does with the
epic ... [or] as a melody with an opera or a sonata', Danforth Ross's discovery of a tight pattern of recognition and
irony in Aristotle's sense, Robert W. Neal's stress on
signified personae 'in conclusive action, each according to
his own character, in a time of crisis', or the more probing
considerations by Norman Friedman, who explores possible
combinations of short and long actions with 'static' and
'dynamic structures'. (1)

   To Frank O'Connor the modern short story is the literary
form in which a tradition of formal brevity meets with the
theme of the 'Little Man' or 'submerged population'; to
Bonaro Overstreet it is defined by its absorption of the
psychological standpoint. The more recent inquiry by
Theodor Wolpers attempts to isolate typical attitudes of
telling underlying brief narrative forms. Fascinating and
helpful as some of these propositions are, they cannot, as
does Vladimir Propp's morphology, yield a grammar of
'functions' typical of the modern short story. It is simply
too heterogeneous a genre, embracing too many narrative
types, to lend itself to rigorous structural description.
Literary scholarship may have to remain content with as
inclusive a view as H.S. Canby's, that the modern short
story 'reveals itself as merely a special case and particular
development of the endless succession of distinctly short
narratives'. (2)

   A somewhat less ambitious undertaking would be to
isolate a specific type within this elusive genre by describing its structure from the viewpoint of its emergence in the
act of reading: the structure of the boundary situation
story. A brief look at what reduction means in some other
types of short narrative will furnish a set of contrasting
patterns.

   Compared with its relatively open presented world, J.P.
Hebel's anecdote Unexpected Reunion (1811) displays
drastic linguistic compression. Shortly before his wedding
in a Swedish town a young miner is killed below ground.
Fifty years later his body, preserved by iron vitriol, is
found in the mine. The miner's fiancée, now an old bent
spinster, recognizes her beloved and attends his funeral in
her Sunday dress. Brevity here means an almost complete
suppression of the paradigmatic plane (an extreme case of
Roman Jakobson's definition of prose) and the compression

to a bare minimum of logical and chronological items of the
syntagmatic sequence. This contrasts with a temporally
and spatially extended signified world filling the gap of fifty
years between the miner's accident and his burial: the
destruction of Lisbon by an earthquake, the Seven Years'
War, the abolition of the Jesuit Order, the Liberation of
America, the Conquest of Prussia by Napoleon. These
temporal and spatial determinations are, however, merely
named as in a catalogue, so that they remain restricted to
their role of indicating the passage of time. Unlike the
structure of the novella in which the presentation of the
extraordinary event is given elaborate syntagmatic development and even some paradigmatic expansion, Hebel's anecdote is an illustration of extreme linguistic compression
around an extraordinary event. For these reasons Unexpected Reunion is not a close relation of the modern short
story, despite its influence on later writers of short fiction,
especially on Franz Kafka. (3)

Neither the horror story of the last century, from Poe's
The Fall of the House of Usher (1839) to the Gothic stories
of Ambrose Bierce, Robert Louis Stevenson, or James's
The Turn of the Screw (1898), nor Hawthorne's brief moral
tale are easily recognizable in the types of the twentieth-
century short story. With its stress on the atmospheric
qualities of the threateningly numinous, the former dates
itself as part of the Gothic tradition, while the latter's
pointed ideological concern appears now to be somewhat at
odds with its illustrative devices. On the one hand, there
is the centripetal moral point, especially the sin of scientific purism, as in The Birthmark (1843) or in Rappaccini's
Daughter (1844), towards which the tales are designed; on
the other, there are such centrifugal aspects as the foregrounded didactic implied author and unequivocal interpretative guidance combined with elements of the marvellous
and romance. Thus the two types of story are clearly set
apart from the multiple reductions operative in both the
presentational process and the presented world of the
modern short story.

Poe's theory and practice have probably had their most
far-reaching effects on twentieth-century narrative through
the action and plot story from such thrillers as The Tell-
Tale Heart (1843) to O. Henry's mass production of tightly
woven external action and surprise endings. In this type
of story the presentational process is strictly bridled
towards its functions of guaranteeing causal nexus as well

as the concealment and disclosure of information, while the
personae, acts and events of the signified world must allow
for two coherent structures of reading: a foregrounded and
misleading one and another which, sparked off by a surprising solution, in the end supersedes the former. In
this, a story such as O. Henry's The Gift of the Magi
(1905) is related to the structure of riddles, except that its
reader is not trying to solve an enigma; he does not doubt
his grasp of the fictive world he has constructed until he is
told that he has been tricked. There is also a structural
affinity with the joke, except that the story's twist is a
causal continuation of disguised information and not an
absurdity requiring for its cognition a bisociative act of
consciousness. (4) Though extensively used by O. Henry
and his emulators up to the present, this structural pattern
has its own history from Washington Irving's The Little Man
in Black (1807), or Hawthorne's Mrs. Bullfrog (1837) to
Fitz-James O'Brien's A Terrible Night (1856), Thomas B.
Aldrich's The Lady with the Balmoral, Miss Hepzibah's
Lover (both 1859) or Marjorie Daw (1873), Ambrose Bierce's
An Occurrence at Owl Creek Bridge and The Boarded
Window (1891), or Kate Chopin's Desiree's Baby (1894).

Naturally, the action and plot story lives on side by side
with more ambitiously innovative forms and indeed also
inside other types as a submerged structure. Its evident
relations are the popular thriller, the Western, the
character-formula, love stories, or science fiction narratives with their more or less radically altered socio-
technical matrices of the presented world. (5) The last
type in particular has recently entered the mainstream of
narrative experimentation by a liaison with the devices of
metafiction. (6)

The traditional evaluative distinctions between the
'formula-story' and 'the genuinely artistic short story'; or
between 'popular fiction's technicoloured myths' and the
'literary short story' are none of this chapter's business. (7) But let me briefly note that the rejection or
disregard of popular narrative common until recently at
most teaching institutions and still flourishing in less well-
informed literature departments is the result of an uncriti-
cally applied interpretative process developed for the discussion of paradigmatically or metaphoridally complex
structures. (8) A study of the reception of popular narrative both in its ontological and historical aspects would
yield a very different and certainly more fruitfully descrip-

tive grasp of that vast and influential branch of literary production.

The formal consciousness and practical accomplishment of the short story towards the end of the last century was not only an awareness of a structure of words and taut macrostructural arrangements, but also of the structures of corresponding acts of reading.   In Poe's theory the 'unique or single effect', the controlling influence of the denouement on the composition, or the rigorous functionality of each word in the entire story go with such notions of reception as the significance of brief reading time, the completion of the act of reading at 'one sitting', that the reader's focused excitement cannot be long sustained, or that only in a very brief narrative a writer can maintain full control over the reading consciousness. (9)   Like Poe, Chekhov balances his compositional observations with statements about the reading performance.   Dense brevity or 'the compactness that makes short things alive' are best achieved, he says, by a deliberate curtailment of authorial intrusion, especially of the moralizing kind, a 'sloughing off at one stroke [of] – all that is useless', brief and relevant description of 'Nature', characterization which is limited to psychological detail, a rigorous reduction of the signified personae, and an emphasis on the self–presentation of the particular.   Correspondingly, 'when you shut your eyes you get a picture', psychology becomes 'clear from the hero's actions', and the reader can 'add for himself the subjective elements that are lacking in the story.' (10)   Henry James too, whose fascination with the explosive power of psychological detail prevented him from writing more than a mere twelve stories of approximately and under 7000 words, saw this double aspect of 'innumerably repeated chemical reductions' and the 'compactness into which the imagination may cut thick, as into the rich density of wedding–cake'. (11)

Thus practically and theoretically equipped, the short story, towards the end of the last century, began to explore also a work ideology more probing than anything attempted since Hawthorne's moral tale.   The result was to become the dominant type of the modern short story over about half a century.   But before we turn to the boundary situation story itself, two further decisive influences need to be summarized: a number of nouvelles treating pointed existential situations, and a core of theoretical statements by European existential thinkers.

From roughly the middle of the nineteenth to the first
decade of the twentieth century a handful of nouvelles by
writers in Europe and the USA exhibit structures organized
towards pointed situations in which a presented persona, a
narrator, or the implied reader in a flash of insight become
aware of meaningful as against meaningless existence.
There is the revolt against man's walled-in existence,
partly realized by the narrator in Melville's story Bartleby:
Scribener (1856), the religious fulfilment granted to
Félicité in the concluding revelation of Flaubert's A Simple
Heart (1877), or Ivan's religious-existential experience in
Tolstoy's The Death of Ivan Ilych (1886). Familiar, too,
are the moral shock suffered by Marlow in Heart of Darkness (1902) as a result of his meeting Kurtz, or Aschen-
bach's protracted and final acceptance of his decay and
death in Thomas Mann's Death in Venice (1912).

In these stories the principles of 'amplification' and
'brevitas' are combined to form what Henry James called
the 'shapely nouvelle'. (12) Amplification is constituted
by cumulative encounters and gradual withdrawal in
Bartleby, the banal chain of events in a life of service and
catalogue of personal disappointments in A Simple Heart,
the summary overview of Ivan Ilych's shallow life and
increasingly detailed presentation of his disease in
Tolstoy's tale, Marlow's ominously gradual physical and
mental approach towards darkness, or the elaborate post-
ponement of death in Mann's 'Erzählung'. By contrast, the
centripetal structural features are defined by each story's
core situation of gravitational existential significance
towards which the narrative material is organized: final
vision or revelation, rejection of false moral premises, and
the gain of a state of authenticity.

We are able to make the previous observations precisely
because our reading performance appears split into two
contrasting phases: a dynamic phase of accumulation and
storing and an almost static one in which we are guided to
construct empathetically a boundary situation. Once we
have concretized the focal situation, the accumulated
material of the first phase is experienced as background
for a highlighted vision. In the reading consciousness,
subordinated accumulated information and foregrounded
reduced world are thus constructed and abstracted to shape
a complex aesthetic-ideological experience.

To be sure, such pointed existential situations have not
been the prerogative of literature alone. Rather, we are

dealing here with a case of inter-textuality beyond the
strictly literary.   In 'Being and Time' Martin Heidegger,
for example, pays tribute to the insight he obtained from
Tolstoy's The Death of Ivan Ilych, while conversely a
good deal of modern literature reflects the speculation of
existential philosophy. (13)   Indeed, both literature and
existential thought have crystallized those narrowly horizonal experiences which Karl Jaspers terms 'boundary
situations'. (14)   They are situations of sudden grief,
pain, loss, guilt, disappointment, betrayal, disillusionment,
or, above all, confrontation with death, in which man feels
called upon to come to grips with himself and to make fundamental decisions concerning the meaning of his existence
not normally made under the conditions of daily routine.
Although existentialist thinkers differ in their interpretation of boundary situations and especially of death, they
all, from Kierkegaard to Camus, share the concept of
pointed situations of heightened awareness in which we
wrest from life an authentic existence or stare absurdity
in the face.
    Around the end of the last century the structural accom-
plishment of the short story merged with the formal-
ideological concern of the boundary situation, central to a
number of nouvelles as well as to the analytical writing of
some existentialist philosophers, to mould a distinct
narrative type: the boundary situation story.   In it the
linguistic material is no longer harnessed to serve primarily
an extraordinary event, external action, gripping atmosphere, or a tightly structured causality.   Compression of
the linguistic surface is now combined with the reduced
spatio-temporal matrix of the presented world, the subordination of the presentational process to this constricted
fictional frame, and a narrowing down of the ideological
field to private existential issues.   Thus, the boundary
situation story is the story of the bracketed world.
    In this type of story the exclusion of total enveloping
experience in favour of a few isolated items of consciousness is strikingly apparent in the spatial reductions which
both author and reader perform.   Poignant insights are
suffered and gained in a stable in Chekhov's story Lament
(1886), in front of an open grave in Stephen Crane's The
Upturned Face (1900), in a bazaar in Joyce's Araby (1914),
in an office room in Katherine Mansfield's The Fly (1922),
on a small island in Hemingway's The End of Something
(1925), in a shanty in Indian Camp (1925), or at the table

at a railway station in Hills Like White Elephants (1927), on
a deathbed in Katherine Ann Porter's The Jilting of Granny
Weatherall (1930), in a railway carriage in Pirandello's War
(1930), on a cot in Hemingway's The Snows of Kilimanjaro
(1936), in a prison cell in Sartre's The Wall (1939), in a
make-shift hospital in Heinrich Böll's Traveller if You
Come to Spa ... (1950), on a hospital bed in Ilse
Aichinger's Story in Reverse (1952), in a pot-hole in Gerd
Gaiser's Why Don't You Let Yourself up for a Change?
(1955), under the discarded body of a bus in a scrapyard in
Alan Paton's The Waste Land (1961), or in an airport toilet
in Nadine Gordimer's No Place Like (1971). In accordance
with spatial reduction the stories' presented time too tends
to be deliberately curtailed to the span it takes to dig and
fill a grave under enemy fire, the moments of a brief conversation, of a death agony, or the minutes in which a vital
decision is shunned or an ultimate choice made.

As the protagonist of The Waste Land gets off the bus, the
week's pay in his pocket, he is confronted by thugs. He
runs for his life, hurling himself into the barbed-wire
desert of a junk yard, desperately wielding his stick at his
closest pursuer. He manages to hide beneath the wreck of
a bus, where he realizes that the young man he hit was his
own son: he is dead. In the reduced space of his filthy
hideout the man understands his personal tragedy as the
tragedy of his people.

Unlike the foregrounding of the presentational process in
Hawthorne's illustrated moral or in the stories of metafiction, process in the boundary situation story is strictly
subservient to the governing spatio-temporal and ideological
focus on a pointed experience. In authorial narration this
is evident in the almost complete absence of explanation or
interpretation. The 'author's hands and feet' are concealed, as Chekhov demanded for the sake of objectivity and
brevity, (15) and frequent use is made of scenic presentation (extremely so by Hemingway in Hills Like White
Elephants and The Killers) and free indirect style (e.g.,
in Life of Ma Parker, The Man I Killed, or No Place Like).
In first-person narration, on the other hand, a very
different device of reduction is often employed: the
narrator with limited powers of interpretation. There are
the insensitive narrator (as for instance in A Rose from
Emily or My Pale Brother) as well as the sensitive but
inexperienced narrator (as in The Sisters, That Evening
Sun, I Want to Know Why, or My Old Man), leaving it again

fully to the reader to construct for himself the impact of
the existential point.

The boundary situation story forces us to hone away our
stock of ideological typifications until it is narrowed down
to the thematic core of a poignant personal problem.   This
is illustrated by our experience of James Duffy, who in
James Joyce's A Painful Case (1914), asks himself why he
has sentenced to death the woman he ought to have loved and
receives as an answer a shattering sense of loneliness;
Elizabeth's grasp of the unbridgeable separateness between
her husband and herself and admission of guilt in D.H.
Lawrence's Odour of Chrysanthemums (1911); a man's
shock realization of the full meaning for him of the loss of
his son in War (1930); a girl's saddening but controlled
insight that the father of the child she is expecting does not
really love her in Hills Like White Elephants (1927); or a
woman's abrupt decision rather to face uncertainty than to
return to an unjust society in No Place Like (1971).
Dialectically interacting as are the structures of narrative
text and reading act, identification with the implied reader
of the boundary situation story means a radical bracketing
of the actual reader's consciousness of a permanently
present and all-embracing social reality.   For he must
first construct (a construction only possible paradoxically
on the grounds of his total experience) in sharp relief the
narrowly defined existential situation before he can fully
place it in the wider structure of his own ideological stance.

Having stated and briefly illustrated the fact of reduction
in the boundary situation story, we must now show how this
narrowing down is accomplished in terms of macrostructural
narrative strategy.   There are three dominant structures:
a linear one, inherited from the nouvelle, in which the
existential situation is the climax of a chronological development; second, a circular structure with the presented
situation acting as temporal horizon into which the expository material is projected; and, third, a focal structure
consisting of nothing but the boundary situation itself.

In the first structure the gradual change from a series of
impressions of a wider experience to a particular and
decisive one acts as a kind of funnel.   We recognize this
funnelling effect in Stephen Crane's The Open Boat (1889);
or Thomas Mann's Tobias Mindernickel (1898), in which the
protagonist's lonely life begins to look more promising when
he obtains a little dog as a companion, but which culminates
in Tobias's attempt at securing his pet's permanent depen-

dence on him by injuring it with a bread knife. Kafka's
The Judgment (1913), Joyce's Araby, A Painful Case, or
The Dead (all 1914), D.H. Lawrence's The Horse Dealer's
Daughter (1922), Somerset Maugham's The Outstation
(1924), Hemingway's The Short Happy Life of Francis
Macomber (1936), in which climactic preparation is
developed almost to the extent of that operative in the
nouvelle, Steinbeck's Flight (1938), Sartre's The Wall
(1939), or Doris Lessing's A Sunrise on the Veld (1951):
all illustrate the linear structure in which a final boundary
situation forms the climax to an expository narrative phase.

Linear structure in Joyce's A Painful Case, for instance,
is constituted by a sequence of chronologically arranged
narrative units: an authorial characterization of James
Duffy mainly through spatial detail (a shallow river, a room
without carpets or pictures, an iron bedstead, a single
blanket, etc.) as an ascetic, pedantic person without
friends; the introduction of Mrs Sinico as foil; their brief
relationship; his rejection of her love and Mrs Sinico's
apparent psychological deterioration and suicide. This
expository structure is followed by the rapid sequence of
Duffy's responses leading up to the concluding existential
situation: his sense of disgust at learning of Mrs Sinico's
death, embarrassment, uneasiness, feeling of loss,
sympathy and pity, self-accusation, acknowledgment of
guilt and crushing insight that 'he was alone'.

While the linear arrangement of narrative phases must be
able to sustain in the reading consciousness an arc of
tension from beginning to boundary situation, the second
kind of design can accomplish a compelling sense of imme-
diacy by projecting the past and its expository information
into the horizon of the narrated present. In this manner
past and present are fused in Ambrose Bierce's An Occurrence at Owl Creek Bridge (1891), a story still closer to
the action and plot narrative than to its later relations,
Katherine Mansfield's Life of Ma Parker and The Fly (1922),
Edith Wharton's Roman Fever (1934), Hemingway's The
Snows of Kilimanjaro (1936), Wolfgang Borchert's My Pale
Brother (1847), Aichinger's Story in Reverse (1952), or
Gerd Gaiser's The Man I Killed (1956), a story with
multiple temporal horizons.

In The Snows of Kilimanjaro, for example, the cogent
horizon of the narrated present is Harry's approaching
death as he is lying on a cot in the African bush. Into this
frame is projected, in the form of the protagonist's delirious

reminiscences, an essential part of his existence which he
had consistently pushed aside. Instead, he had lived off
his own physical vitality, women and money, scavenging
like the vultures and hyena which are now anticipating his
death. In concise units a sequence of striking memories
crystallize in his mind: his experiences as a soldier in
Thrace, images from the Alps or a trout stream in the Black
Forest, memories from Constantinople, or his reminiscence
of Williamson, the dying bombing officer. As Harry
approaches his death, he knows that he should have given
artistic shape to those experiences; and in a sense he does
so now, even if only in his feverish consciousness. With
his realization of the image of snow-covered Kilimanjaro he
has not only reached his death, but also accomplished a
moral-artistic comeback. In this final image the framing
boundary situation and the thematized past are both fused
and transcended.

But the most radical bracketing of general experience is
achieved in those stories in which the boundary situation
constitutes the sole and total compass of the presented
world. This arrangement is structure-carrying, for
instance, in The Upturned Face, The Sisters, The End of
Something, The Killers, Hills Like White Elephants, War,
Supper, or Traveller if You Come to Spa ... .

In Luigi Pirandello's story War this focal structure
cogently guides the act of reading. Seven people in a
stuffy carriage at a provincial station near Rome talk about
the loss of sons in the war. Two personae are foregrounded: a 'fat woman' whose son has just left for the front and
an old man who has actually lost his son but represses his
grief by speculating about sacrifice and national duty.
When the woman asks the seemingly silly question, '"Then
... is your son really dead?"' the man breaks 'into harrow-
ing, heartrending, uncontrollable sobs'. The brief time-
span of the conversation and the compelling spatial
constriction of the carriage do not permit any digression to
disturb the boundary situation, so that its focused power
exposes the man's attitude as false ideology and grants him
the authentic experience of bereavement.

Just as the artistic object only comes to life in its
aesthetic reconstruction, so too do the three described
forms of bracketing depend on three distinct structures of
reading response, three different kinds of reader 'epoche'.
The reader's construction of the first or linear kind can
best be called guided bracketing; his experience is at the

same time an accumulation – though vastly reduced if compared with the acts of storing required in the nouvelle – and a being led towards a climax, followed by a concentrated realization of the story's structural core, the boundary situation.

The second kind of response, corresponding to circular structures, is a horizonally determined act of reading: the reader is guided to establish a temporal frame in terms of which he must activate all past information as a homogeneous Now. By temporal thematization, especially by means of structured memory, his acts of construction are funnelled towards his realization of the situational frame, the boundary situation.

Lastly, in the 'pure' boundary situation, the reader's acts of bracketing are no longer guided or funnelled. Confronted with the bare existential situation, which is neither introduced nor expanded by the filling material of a thematized past, the reader must radically and at one stroke set aside his stock of general typifications. In so doing, he himself transforms the presented crisis into the existential experience of the reading act. As his hermeneutic identification with the implied reader compels him thus to perform the boundary situation, he experiences his reading as both reduced construction and abandonment.

About half a century of exploration appears to have exhausted the structural potential of the boundary situation story. As new types of story are given the spotlight on the stage of narrative experimentation, its formal-ideological stance begins to look strangely old fashioned. Foremost among these new types is the metastory, the short form of metafiction, its structure constituting a total revolt against the reductions of the older type. From Jorge Luis Borge's early narratives in the 1930s and 1940s to the recent publications of John Barth, Robert Coover, or William H. Gass, the metastory explodes the frame of its predecessor's restricted world, harnessed presentational process, and narrowly philosophical work ideology. (16) It focuses anew on narrative as unrestricted 'ludus', on telling as conversational free play, and on the multiple, heterogeneous artistic-aesthetic concerns of literariness itself as its loose ideological commitment. (17) No matter what shortcomings its critics have already discovered and however quickly it may have to give way to new types of story telling, its very prominence now suggests that both as a structure and a reading performance the metastory has freed aspects of narrative art long tied up by its powerful predecessor.

Chapter 7

Narrative strands: presented and presentational

The multiple choice of routes between the Clashing or Wandering Rocks instead of the single course between Charybdis and Scylla only partly illustrates the distinction between multi-strand and single-strand narration, just as the 'meanwhile back at the ranch' formula merely indicates one special case of stranded narrative. They both signal to the reader that the separate parts of the presented world must be constructed as spliced entities first before they can be related to one another. Again, the ardent attention structuralists have given to action sequences tends to support this limited, indeed one-sided view of narrative structure.

In contradistinction, it seems to me that multi-strand structure is one of those central narrative possibilities which highlights the usefulness of our definition of presentational process and presented world as the two sets of signifieds of the surface text by allowing the discovery of two kinds of strands: presented strands (spliced or multi-strand world) and presentational strands (spliced or multi-strand process). (1) Conversely, the possible schematic presence in the surface text and the reader's construction of presented and presentational strands shows lucidly not only the ontological separateness as sets of signifieds of world and process but also their potential structural inter-action.

In reading narrative texts, the reader must be prepared to design not only the double vision of a single or homogeneous process and a single or homogeneous world, but also their double-strand or multi-strand equivalents. More technically speaking, an important part of inter-textuality is the reader's expectation of noetic as well as noematic strands, or strands dealing with the experiencing of an imagined world and strands pertaining to that world as experienced. In single-strand narrative the reader constructs the linear continua of aspects of space, time (chronological as well as non-chronological), and personae of both process and world. In multi-strand narrative, the reader may encounter the following structural possibilities: presentational strands and homogeneous world, presentational strands and heterogeneous world, presentational strands and heterogeneous worlds, whereby process and world become homogeneous; single-strand process and heterogeneous world, and single-strand process and heterogeneous world, whereby the presented world becomes homogeneous in the end. A further complication is the possible subordination of presented and presentational strands to overarching structural principles, as for example in the Chinese box arrangement of worlds within a presented world or various levels of presentational process in frame tales and other narratives.

The distinctions between single and multi-strand narrative can be schematically illustrated with the help of the model of a maze which we may try to grasp by (a) describing from the viewpoint of one consciousness the linear sequence of a route from beginning to end, (b) describing in a scanning fashion, e.g., up and down on a scale from left to right, (c) having a number of consciousness describe the linear sequence of a course from beginning to end, or (d) having a number of consciousnesses scan in the manner of (b).

What in his imaginative realization of world and process are the guiding cues allowing the reader to identify narrative strands? In both presented and presentational strands it is above all structural leaps as to personae and spatial aspects which indicate a change from one strand to another, while the temporal aspects may or may not differ from those of other strands. As a result of his sense of continuity and discontinuity, the reader will construct separate macro-structural units over and above the microstructural text schema, which he stores and brings into play as subsequent textual information requires.

Textual coding as well as imaginative objectification of presented and presentational strands can be expressed also in terms of syntagmatic and paradigmatic relationships. But while in the sentence the relations of contiguity and association are of microstructural nature, applied to narra-tive strands, they must be understood as high-order relationships or macrostructural links at the level of large-scale narrative patterns. Syntagmatic coding of the presented world allows the reader to realize a construct in which the contiguity of spatial and temporal aspects, aspects of personae as well as ideological structures, plays a dominant role. Likewise, the syntagmatic coding of the presentational process is experienced by the reader as a continuum of narrating authority, of a recognizable identical narrating persona or voice. This does not deny the possibility of quasi-physical or ideological development as to world or process. What it means is that both are constructed by the reader as single-strand as long as they do not change radically; i.e. as long as the narrating persona is not replaced by another narrator and as long as there is no radical change of presented personae or groups of personae.

By contrast, multi-strand arrangement in both process and world may be understood as macrostructural paradigmatic structures. Instead of one continuum of the presented world an author may choose a number of alternative worlds, or a heterogeneous world and, by the same token, instead of one continuous coherent presentational process he may decide on alternative processes with different narrating personae. But the matter becomes somewhat more complicated when, as pointed out above, a writer subordinates narrative strands to units of a higher structural order or, in linguistic terms, when he uses at the same time both syntagmatic and paradigmatic macrostructural coding of presented world and presentational process. In the first case, the reader is required to construct Chinese box effects of worlds within the presented world; in the latter he must realize individual consciousnesses or speakers assuming for a while the role of narrator under the umbrella of the governing presentational process. Both cases can be found in 'Ulysses' and 'Light in August', discussed below.

In practice, of course, our logical distinctions hardly ever appear in a 'pure' form; this, however, does not diminish their epistemological value: once we have understood the principle and not merely a special case of multi-strand narrative, our reading will be richer in the full structural sense. The examples to follow are thus meant to illustrate a theory of narrative strands which in turn may widen our horizon of structural expectations.

1 MULTI-STRAND OR HETEROGENEOUS PROCESS

Presentational strands and homogeneous world: This case is problematic in that the object of observation is the very result of the observing and rendering acts of different narrators or presenting consciousnesses. The following examples must therefore be understood 'cum grano salis'. In 'Rashomon', as in 'As I Lay Dying' or 'The Sound and the Fury', a number of narrators/consciousnesses provide a cumulative list of aspects of the presented world which allow the reader to design the adumbrational appearance of central events, acts, and personae embedded in the same spatio-temporal matrix. On the one hand, it is precisely the discrepancy between the seemingly identical core to which the different consciousnesses attend and the actual view held by each which is at the structural and philosophical centre of these works. On the other hand, the fact that such an identical core world does not exist does not detract from its structural function; it exists as an unstated assumption on the part of the reader, an assumption to be destroyed by the narratives: world is intended by individual consciousnesses, and inter-subjective agreement is the thin layer of ice on which social interaction precariously unfolds.

Presentational strands and heterogeneous world: In this the reader experiences both process and world as stranded. Well-studied examples are 'Wuthering Heights' or 'Lord Jim', in which a number of presentational sources, narrators and letters, are employed to allow the reader to assemble heterogeneous portions of the presented worlds: the contrasting everyday and not so natural elements in 'Wuthering Heights' and the opposing worlds of Jim as a member of Western and Eastern communities in Conrad's novel.

Heterogeneous process and world changing to homogeneous process and world: To a certain extent at least this is explored in Faulkner's 'The Sound and the Fury', where the presentational personae of Benjy, Quentin, and Jason and their separate worlds give way in the concluding section to authorial narration with its more balanced grasp of the Compson family. The observation that the authorial view coincides to a very high degree with Dilsey's does not at all diminish the value of the novel as an example; no matter with which presented persona a narrating persona sympathizes, the authorial view is constructed as the reliable centre of orientation which, in giving position and function to the idiosyncratic preceding strands, balances the narrative as a whole.

2 SINGLE-STRAND OR HOMOGENEOUS PROCESS

Single-strand process and homogeneous world: A vast number of narratives, especially first-person narratives, exemplify the homogeneity of both presentational process and presented world: the coherent process with its central narrating persona is set against the continuum of a presented world.   In Salinger's 'The Catcher in the Rye' the narrating speech act of Holden Caulfield is as homogeneous as the world which the speaking persona projects for the reader.   It does not matter whether there are spatial or temporal leaps in either process or world, as long as in both sets of signified aspects of recurring personae and recognizably interlinked patterns of human acts guarantee the reader's sense of coherence.

Single-strand process and heterogeneous world: In this case the continuity of the presentational process is set against a number of contradictory as well as complementary fragments of the presented world.   In Robert Coover's The Magic Poker, for example, the mischievous and frivolously irreverent first-person narrator lends a modicum of coherence to a multiply fragmented world.

Single-strand process and heterogeneous world becoming a homogeneous world: Here again, stranded narrative means that we are dealing with one coherent set of signifieds, the presentational process, with the second, the presented world, split up into sections with differing aspects of presented space and personae.   However, the crucial point is that toward the end of the narrative all or some of the sections are fused into a single presented world.   A lucid example is Stephen Crane's The Bride Comes to Yellow Sky, which may also be seen as a structural stepping stone to the more complex patterns of narrative strands discussed below.

The continuum of an authorial and omniscient narrator is juxtaposed to three clearly marked strands of the presented world, with a concluding section in which strands 1 and 3 are combined.   Strand 1 gives the reader the newly-weds, Sheriff Potter and his young wife, on the train from San Antonio to Yellow Sky.   The train approaches the Rio

Grande 'at an angle, and the apex was Yellow Sky'.
Potter is uneasy, not only because of his new condition,
but above all because he feels he has betrayed the citizens
of Yellow Sky by concealing from them his intended
marriage.   Contrary to the spatio-temporal dynamics of the
first strand, strand 2 provides the spatially and temporally
restricted action of a small group of men in the Weary
Gentleman Saloon of Yellow Sky.   The main function of
this strand is the complication of strand 1 by establishing
two opposing forces, Scratchy Wilson and Sheriff Jack
Potter: '"Jack Potter's in San Anton ...   He's the town
marshal ...   He goes out and fights Scratchy when he gets
on one of those tears."'   The conclusion, '"Here he
comes," they said', allows the reader to concretize
Scratchy outside the saloon and at the same time link strand
2 with strand 3, which opens with, 'A man in a maroon-
coloured flannel shirt ...'.   This strand is concerned with
drunken Scratchy's challenge to the people of Yellow Sky
and especially to Jack Potter.   Two issues need to be
resolved in the last section: the Sheriff's sense of guilt
and Scratchy's aggression.   A major point of the story,
though, is the change of the expected violent collision into
harmony.   It is the very offence of Potter's secret wedding
which turns out to be the positive agent in the confrontation
with Scratchy: a sheriff without a gun is no opponent even
for an inebriated Scratchy Wilson, so that Scratchy and
Jack part on a friendly note.   Both the macrostructural
fusion of the presented strands and the microstructural
items of the surface text interlink to produce a parodic
reversal of the show-down situation of the Western.

Apart from its structural function as one complex cluster
of aspects of Joyce's Dublin in the total design of
'Ulysses', the episode of The Wandering Rocks is an
exercise in and virtuoso display of the two fundamental
techniques of story telling discussed in this chapter: multi-
strand and single-strand narrative.   To the multi-strand
scanning of the city labyrinth in sections 1 to 18 is juxtaposed the single-strand rendering of the Viceregal proces-
sion.

As indicated in Joyce's schema, the multi-strand presentation of a city can be signified in a variety of ways.   If we
focus on the dominant spatial aspects of the presented
world, the streets (squares, lanes, shops, or restaurants)
best characterize the author's method.   If we try to grasp
Dublin with the help of the body metaphor, the narrative can

be compared to an incision made into an organ, laying bare
the sections of a large number of severed blood vessels.
This metaphor of the sections of a fragmented city expressed
in terms of multiply cross-sectioned life is consolidated by
Leopold Bloom's image of 'infants cuddled in a ball in blood-
red wombs like livers of slaughtered cows. <u>Lots</u> <u>of</u> <u>them</u>
<u>like</u> <u>that</u> <u>at</u> <u>this</u> <u>moment</u> <u>all</u> <u>over</u> <u>the</u> <u>world</u>.' (2) This, in
principle, is precisely what James Joyce has accomplished
in The Wandering Rocks. He has to present a large number
of citizens - Joyce's symbol for chapter 10 - roughly at the
same time all over the central part of Dublin.

If we look at the episode in terms of art, the catchword
is mechanics or, more accurately, mechanics of narrative
arrangement. While section 19 could be regarded as
ordinary or simple narration operating like a series a+b+c+d
... + n or single-strand action sequence, sections 1 to 18
could be characterized by a series a1+k3+d2+a3+f4+ ... +n
or multi-strand sequence. Or, in the terminology of the
Russian Formalists, sections 1 to 18 illustrate the mechanics of changing 'fable' into 'sujet'. As far as the presentational process is concerned, we must distinguish between
the primary authorial narrative situation characteristic of
both sections 1 to 18 and the concluding section on the one
hand, and, on the other, a number of subordinated narrative situations in which presented personae assume narrative authority either as consciousnesses or speakers for
short time-spans. But while authorial guidance remains
the governing presentational principle throughout The
Wandering Rocks, the treatment of the spatial locus of
telling is distinct. In sections 1 to 18 the authorial
narrator's 'post of observation' leaps rapidly from one part
of central Dublin to another, whereas in section 19 it
follows the steady progress of the Viceroy's carriage along
its route.

In the concluding section the relative temporal stasis
(between 3 and 4 p.m.), spatial dynamics, and rapidly
changing presented personae of the preceding sections are
replaced by chronological progression (from 3 to 4 p.m.),
linearity of spatial aspects (a continuum of streets, bridges,
squares, or quays), and a group of central personae,
William Humble, Earl of Dudley, Lady Dudley, and their
party. Despite these differences, both the heterogeneous
world of sections 1 to 18 and the homogeneous world of the
last section grant the reader an experience of coherence.
But the methods by which this is codified are very different:

in the first instance coherence is signalled by the presence
in the various sections of aspects of space and personae
from other fragments; in the second case, coherence is
not constructed from fragmentation but more immediately
given in the identity of a central persona and a continuum of
spatial and temporal aspects.

For the reader the two views of Dublin illustrated by the
two antithetic narrative techniques do not simply stand
opposed to one another, a heterogeneous, chaotic and
complex society as against a linear, homogeneous and
purposefully directed one. Through synthesizing acts of
consciousness the reader experiences the two aspect
clusters as one complex 'noema', Joyce's Dublin,
schematically given by means of two kinds of 'noesis', two
distinct ways of experiencing: heterogeneous and
homogeneous.

In many respects Faulkner's 'Light in August' appears
conventional if compared with 'The Sound and the Fury';
however, as far as a writer's exploration of multi-strand
narrative is concerned, 'Light in August' is as innovative
and structurally complex as the earlier novel. Indeed,
Faulkner has accomplished an intricate multi-strand
narrative on a large scale. As in The Bride Comes to
Yellow Sky and The Wandering Rocks episode of 'Ulysses',
multi-strand structure here means multi-strand world
presented from an overall authorial narrative situation.
And yet, 'Light in August' also approaches the technique of
stranded process by granting a number of subordinate
narrating personae considerable autonomy.

To glance at as complex a tale as 'Light in August' from
the singular viewpoint of multi-strand narrative means to
neglect structural aspects which would have to play a
prominent role in a holistic reading. No attention can
here be paid to the multiple flashbacks transforming the
past into the present, the rhythm resulting from the changes
between panoramic view and close-up description, summary
and detailed report, the allocation of different tenses to
presented personae, the arcs of tension and phases of the
presented world in which the narrative unfolds in recognizable units along the temporal extension of the reading
process, or a set of adequately abstracted interpretative
inferences. All we can do is list the narrative strands,
sketch their inter-relationships, and make suggestions as
to their functions in the act of reading.

For clarity's sake, I wish to catalogue the strands of the

presented world as major and minor strands according to
their length.   In the order in which the reader constructs
them, there are the large strands of Lena (S1), Byron (S2),
Joe (S3), Hightower (S4), and the Hineses (S5), related
to a group of smaller strands comprising those of Armstid
and his wife(s1), the people of Jefferson (s2), the Sheriff
and his Deputy (s3/s4; their strands are experienced as
spliced later in the novel), the Negro messenger (s5),
Brown (s6), Gavin Stevens (s7), Percy Grimm (s8), and the
furniture dealer and his wife (s9).

Clearly, the study of narrative strategy demonstrates the
artificiality of the distinction between the technical and
thematic function of strands.   Whenever we construct
strands as related to other strands, their relational side
is always at the same time a semantic aspect; indeed, we
experience strands as interlinked because the link means
something.   Or, in Saussure's terminology, any structural
relationship is itself a sign, a signifier and a signified.
Thus it is only partly true that 'Light in August' is a
'character-dominated' novel in which 'each character
carries his own structure'. (3)   Each of the major strands
certainly presents a personal history, but that history is
what it is because of its network of links or absence of
relations with other strands.   Lena's and Joe's strands (S1
and S3), for example, never meet; the continuum of enduring
affection, procreation, and calm confidence, on the one
hand, and, on the other, the gradual destruction of a
personality and the social outrage which that personality
consequently effects are experienced by the reader as
separate, opposed, and irreconcilable.

There is also Hightower's initial refusal of his life
history (S4) to be fused with and thus complicated by other
personal histories.   When in the second part of chapter 13
Byron Bunch tries to involve Hightower in the turmoil of the
present, he resists desperately: '"I wont! I wont! I have
bought immunity."'   In the end, though, his strand is
linked with both Lena's (S1 and Joe's (S3), suggesting at
least the possibility of the old man's social reintegration.
Unlike the strands which are not directly linked, and unlike
the Hightower strand which for a while resists linkage with
other strands, the strand at the centre of which stands
Byron is the central integrating force of the novel.   It is
to him, a man of shy integrity, that the major strands of the
narrative are drawn and it is he who establishes communication and thus community.

Another way in which the structural relationships of strands act as signs is the manner in which the reader is allowed to construct certain strands only at advanced stages in the reading process. In particular, the highly significant strands of the Hineses and Percy Grimm are introduced relatively late. The first answers burning questions about the social and psychological beginnings of Joe Christmas, the second provides his execution and castration; the former illustrates Faulkner's special kind of suspense through withholding vital psychological information, while the latter displays his taut control and economy in introducing and dismissing an agent of a strictly limited though central task. Other late introduced strands provide the additional agents of the community, the Sheriff and his Deputy, Brown as foil to Byron Bunch, but also witnesses and their commentary, such as the Negro and his report of Joe's frenzy in the black church, Gavin Stevens and his intellectual interpretation and, finally, the furniture dealer's concluding story.

It is this last strand which deserves special attention as far as the novel's narrative strategy is concerned. Not only does it contain Lena's final words as reported by the furniture dealer, '"Ain't nobody never said for you [Byron] to quit,"' and his interpretation, 'I reckon she knew that when she settled down this time, it would likely be for the rest of her life,' but it also serves as frame together with the Armstid strand at the beginning of the novel. And again, frame does not mean something merely technical; the kind of frame which we must construct, the two small strands of two ordinary men and their wives, supplies the enveloping everyday sphere within which the strands of social outrage and tragedy are embedded.

Apart from being elements of a semantically organized narrative strategy, the various strands function also as strings of aspect clusters of the presented world, aspects of personal tragedies (Joe, Joanna, the Hineses, Hightower, or even Brown), the community of Jefferson (a number of unidentified personae, the Sheriff, his Deputy, the Negro messenger, Gavin Stevens, Percy Grimm, as well as the outsiders Hightower, Joanna, Joe, Brown, or Byron), and the continuity of ordinary social life (Lena, Byron; Armstid, the furniture dealer and their wives). Summarily commenting on the destinies of the presented personae in 'Light in August', one critic sees 'individual freedom or compulsion ... primarily determined by a character's success or failure

in dealing with his past'. (4)   This certainly applies to the
major strands and perhaps also to the Grimm strand (s8),
except that the catalogue of aspects of Joe Christmas's life
history which the reader is invited to accumulate leaves
little doubt that Joe's is not the kind of past with which one
can deal successfully at all.   But the presented strands not
only allow us to design personal histories; they also make
us imagine a community through the way they are intertwined in the centre of the novel.   To enable 'the individual
and the community' to be 'obverse reflections of each
other', (5) Faulkner invites the reader to construe the
continua of strands as well as their interaction; as in our
experience of actual social life, our constructions are thus
the solutions of a partly determined jigsaw puzzle.   But
neither personal tragedy nor shocked community should form
the sole focus of the reader's imaginative objectification of
the narrative.   Just as over-emphasis on the hero of
Shakespearean tragedy undermines the concern of the
Renaissance audience with the restored order of the
community, so would a reading stressing the novel's tragic
elements at the expense of their enveloping workaday society
result in a badly distorted construction; both must be
experienced as defining each other.

Some strands in 'Light in August' function as subordinated
presentational process and in so doing relate our reading
experience to that of 'As I Lay Dying' or 'The Sound and the
Fury'.   Not every speech act or string of thoughts, though,
is discerned by the reader as subordinated process; they
are simply part of the physical and mental acts of the
presented world.   What clearly codes them as presentational
process is the introduction and/or conclusion by the
governing process of a continuum of speech and thought
without interruption by a controlling narrative authority.

In the minor strands, agents and narrators are clearly
coded as distinct.   Gavin Stevens is not merely the passive
intellectual as against the perverted activist Percy Grimm:
their introduction sketches their roles as presenting and
presented personae, respectively.   The Grimm strand (s8)
is introduced and continued authorially from 'In the town on
that day lived a young man named Percy Grimm' to the
prophetic authorial generalization, 'They are not to lose it,
in whatever peaceful valleys, beside whatever placid and
reassuring streams of old age', while the authorial,
ironical introduction of Gavin Stevens merely identifies him
as intellectual commentator and then hands the presentational

process fully over to him: 'Gavin Stevens though had a different theory.   He is the District Attorney, a Harvard graduate, a Phi Beta Kappa.'   Similar presentational functions are attached to the strands of Armstid, the Negro messenger, Mrs Hines, and the furniture dealer, whose introduction in the present tense, 'There lives in the eastern part of the state a furniture repairer and dealer', makes possible the reader's temporal integration of the fiction into the living society of the day.

Like tripartite arrangements of parts (as, e.g., in 'To the Lighthouse' or 'A Passage to India'), question-and-answer patterns (as, e.g., in Camus's 'L'Etranger'), or riddle structures (as, e.g., in the myth of Oedipus and the Sphinx or modern detective narrative), presentational and presented strands are structural matrices of a higher order superimposed on the microstructural schema of the narrative surface text.   Their logico-imaginative realization on the part of the reader requires the mental acts of splicing and synthesizing: splicing, when process and/or world are integrally coded; and synthesizing, when process and/or world are spliced in the text into separate strands.   In performing these acts the reader brings to light further aspects of the potential polyphony of aesthetic value qualities of narrative art.

Chapter 8

Acts of narrating: transformations of presentational control

Narrative structure has room for a large variety of acts of narrating apart from reporting, describing, or remembering. We find acts of teaching, reprimanding, exhorting, ridiculing, explaining, projecting, comparing, prophesying, or abstracting. At the same time, such acts are always the codified expression of specific directional activities of consciousness; they are not merely acts of explaining or abstracting, but always acts of explaining something, prophesying something, or ridiculing something. (1) Further, in the majority of linguistic constructs and certainly in all narrative structures the directional activity of consciousness or intentionality is not restricted to the relationship between a subject (speaking, thinking) and his intentional object (the signified world). Intentionality in narrative always also includes an implied (and/or stated) reader who is constructed in the reading process by the actual reader in combination with his grasp of presentational process and presented world. (2) And even though the implied reader, as every other objectivity in the literary construct, is not fully defined, his concretization by the reader is schematically guided in all types of narrative. In any specific reading situation the actual reader's construction of the implied reader is central to the establishment of narrative meaning. (3)

The available typologies of point of view, narrative situation, or narrative transmission (Friedemann, Friedman, Booth, Stanzel, Bickerton, Hamburger, or Chatman) are based on quantity of knowledge, distinctions by pronoun, the physical relationship between narrator and presented world, or the discrepancy between or congruity of the information supplied by the narrator and the information

gathered by the reader. (4)   At its simplest, critical
terminology speaks of omniscience, limited omniscience,
objective narration; first-person authorial, peripheral and
central; third-person authorial and figural; I-origo;
reliable, unreliable, insensitive or naive narration; or
stresses an inside and outside perspective (Uspensky). (5)
Such distinctions have proved useful when they have been
drawn in conjunction with questions of signification.   As
merely technical operations, leaving the construction of
meaning to other studies, they leave us empty-handed if not
empty-headed.   There is, however, another kind of
structural question which automatically raises semantic
issues.   In fact, it cannot be answered without pointing at
the same time to ideologically charged relationships.   The
question is: in what way are presentational process,
presented world, and implied reader functions of one
another?

In a sense the question is as much the result of an
investigation as its starting point.   It assumes, for
example, that when we consider a number of narratives we
will indeed discover such a functional relationship, a
recognizable pattern underlying the general structure of
narrative.   Its answer presupposes further that we have
asked and satisfied a number of subordinate queries, such
as whether we can discover a graded series of separate
relations between process and world, world and implied
reader, or process and implied reader.   And if so, we must
also have found out whether these relationships are structures of diminishing or increasing control and, conversely,
increasing or diminishing dependency.   And if we remind
ourselves that intrinsic functions, through their concretization by the actual reader, also acquire an extrinsic role, we
must also raise the larger question of how the relations
between process, world, and implied reader operate in
terms of the all-embracing authorial stance which the actual
reader always ultimately construes.

As to the last item, there is first a negative answer; a
positive one will emerge in the course of this chapter.
Neither our construction of implied reader, nor that of the
presented world, and certainly not our grasp of the presentational process can be equated with the authorial stance;
especially not when there does not seem to be any obvious
difference between the presentational speaker (as against
presented speakers) and what the author might have wished
to say.   This is forcefully illustrated, I believe, by the

presentational structure of Genesis with its authorial narrator.   For the author(s) who designed the tale in its different forms must have had far-reaching politico-religious aims in employing the kind of process and narrator they did.   By contrast, the narrator's attitude is narrowly and pointedly defined. (6)

Ordinarily, our combined construction of process, implied reader and presented world provides sufficient clues for us to infer a likely authorial commitment.   There are, however, examples where the authorial stance is <u>not</u> coded in the text.   In these cases neither process nor implied reader or world can be used as interpretative guides; we are then bound to rely also on extraneous information.   An instance of this will be discussed below.

As far as the other questions go, our subordinate responses suggest as a comprehensive answer a dynamic pattern of structural interdependencies.   When we argued in the first chapter that one can discover a scale from authoritarian telling in creation myths to a more 'democratic' form of narrating in metafiction, we covered only part of the issue.   That is, as far as the suppression or foregrounding of the presentational process is concerned, they are indeed the extreme poles on a scale.   The present problem, how-ever, requires a substantial schematic extension as well as stratification of that scale.   It appears that the relation between presentational process or, for the focus of this chapter, especially the narrator, the presented world and the implied reader can undergo the transformations shown in Table 8.1

TABLE 8.1

N / \\ W — R	Narrator	authority	partner	minor
	World	defined by Narrator defining reader	negotiable	defining Narrator judged by reader
	Reader	minor	partner	authority

The schema presents a chiastic relationship, whereby the

narrator scale proceeds from a maximum of overt control
over presented world and implied reader to a minimum of
authority, the implied reader scale from a minimum of
independence to a maximum of authority. Somewhere in
between, narrator and reader are partners dealing with a
negotiable presented world. This, of course, is a
structural overstatement of actual relations in narrative
art. But the point is that we can indeed discover a kind of
formula according to which the relations between presentational process and the implied reader are transformed or,
more accurately, gradually reversed around the axis of the
presented world.

In its multiple dynamic appearance in narrative art, the
inter-relationship between process, world and reader as
forms of diminishing and increasing control constitute a
true structure in Jean Piaget's sense. In any narrative
they are construed as a tightly interdependent and coherent
whole whose parts do not operate in isolation; their
construction in different narratives displays a transformational dynamic; and together they are experienced by the
reader as a self-sufficient, self-regulating system. (7)

Let us now test the validity and usefulness of our schema
by differentiating its simple tripartite arrangement with the
help of different types of narrative and selected examples.
The following argument and concluding chart (Table 8.2) are
the extended and reduced answers, respectively, to our
initial question.

Our statements in chapter 1 about the presentational
process of Genesis are valid also in our present discussion.
The acts of narrating are treated as if they did not constitute
a fictive speech act but the factual statements of a witness
and authority, thus negating query or doubt on the part of
the reader/listener. Consequently, the implied reader is
indirectly defined as obedient, believing and child-like, a
minor who must accept as fact and law a presented world
which already includes him as a dependent creature, in fact,
as victim. Such control over world and reader by the
presentational process, though in a less apparently
authoritarian manner, is present also in a number of other
types of narrative.

In the parables of the New Testament, for example, a
lucid structure of wrong and right, of punishment and reward
is established in the guise of a straightforward and familiar
fictive world by a divine speaker to an audience incapable
of grasping the more complex message of the 'mysteries of

the kingdom of heaven'. (8)   Proceeding by analogy, the
speaker leaves no doubt as to the correct application of the
tale.   Speaker, world, and implied reader/listener are
thus tied together in a relationship of intellectual, psychological and spiritual interdependence, defining the speaker
as controlling his message, his pedagogic means, especially
the presented world as teaching aid, and the minds of his
audience as a community of believers with limited intellectual
faculties.

   Though completely different in other respects, the
European 'Märchen' displays a similarly wide discrepancy
between its stipulated naive audience and knowing speaker.
The narrator's superiority, however, is not so much
intellectual as artistic-aesthetic and psychological, the
presentational process being concentrated on the deferred
fulfilment of the wishful expectations aroused in the reader/
listener at the beginning of the narrative. (9)   This central
aspect of the 'naive moral' in combination with features of
the marvellous subsumed under one arc of tension characterizes the control which the narrator exerts over his world
and audience as significantly reduced if compared with the
preceding types of story.   But even if it is merely aesthetic, control can still be powerful.   When in the reading
situation of the bed-time story we tie our children to the
world we speak into existence, they are spellbound.

   Unlike the artistic-aesthetically organized 'Märchen',
the European Saint's legend has a clear ideological focus.
It is addressed to a theologically structured community of
believers, thus re-enforcing an actually existing relationship of dependence between an actual controlling authority
and a controlled audience.   In reflecting the process of
canonization – in which the potential saint posthumously
undergoes two trials at the hands of the 'congregatio
rituum', proceeding from the status of 'servus dei' to that
of 'beatus', until he is finally declared 'sanctus' by the
Pope – the presented world of the Saint's legend provides
a miniature image of the hierarchy of ecclesiastical power in
actual life, thus acting as tool of control in the everyday
life of medieval Europe. (10)   But even outside its historical context of reception, the distribution of roles among our
three components, narrator, world, and implied reader is
still clear: the narrator is grasped as an informed and
loyal member of an established power structure, the presented world as an aspect of a complex theology and its
administration, and the implied reader as a faithful member
of an all-embracing and meaning-giving organization.

A special case of narrative is prophecy. In it a speaker projects as fact a disastrous future world to a historically contemporaneous audience of believers who have gone astray. The biblical prophecies of Isaiah, Jeremiah, Ezekiel, Jonah, Haggai, or Zechariah employ multiple frames of presentational speakers before the actual prophecy is given as the prophet's vision. In addition, they contain signals roughly indicating the time when the prophecy was supposed to have been made. (11) In terms of our scale, the important observation to make is that while in Genesis the attitude of the implied audience is compellingly defined as reverence, the addressee of the prophecies of the Old Testament is granted the relative autonomy of revolt. Yet it is also quite apparent that deviation from the prescribed path will not be tolerated in the long run and authority will be re-established by drastic means. Like all fictive narrative, prophecy has a factual politico-ideological and a symbolic aspect, both directed towards the same goal of theocratic control: historical occurrence and usage on the one hand and, on the other, the fictive schema of a dystopia.

In strictly allegorical narrative as understood in chapter 5 the relation between narrator and implied reader is that between an ideologist offering his message in the guise of a semi-concrete vision and a disciple not quite capable of handling pure theory. The double aspect central to allegoric texts of quasi-physical elements, especially personae and spatial detail, combined with abstractions which the reader is unequivocally guided to assemble into a coherent theological or political matrix, defines the narrator as a controlling ideological visionary and the implied reader as a naive disciple. In the case of extended narrative allegory though, control tends to be less forceful than in some previous types of story, for the simple reason that the manifold of narrated details and above all the unfolding sequence of acts and events are experienced by the reader as acquiring at least a modicum of autonomy: to a certain degree they obtain in the reading consciousness the status of being accumulated for their own sake. Especially in 'The Pilgrim's Progress', where the reader is constantly reminded of the narrator's ideological goal, the very quantity of adventures and the resulting sense of overflowing narrative energy, in warring against the narrative's religious core, grants the reader a certain degree of independence.

A somewhat more mature reader is stipulated in the

narrative of ideas with its prominence of abstract discourse
in both the presentational process and the presented world.
Control manifests itself in the direct and indirect ways in
which the reader is urged to appreciate and ultimately share
the ideological stance which he must construct from the
interplay of stated abstractions. In the extreme case of
the narrative of ideas the relation between narrator, world,
and implied reader is thus one between an ideologist, his
ideology, and a disciple. Exaggerated though this may
sound, despite Aldous Huxley's attempts, for example, at
embedding his philosophy in a concrete world of peace, the
reader of his 'Island' is very much defined in this way.
And even a novel of ideas as concretely located as Saul
Bellow's 'Mr Sammler's Planet' drew the reproach of
being concealed fascist ideology. The point is not whether
the attack is fair or unfair, though I do believe it to be
mistaken, but rather that it illustrates the actual reader's
realization and resentment of being controlled. 'Herzog',
in spite of its presentation of at least as much abstract discourse, is experienced as a far less threatening novel.
Since its stated ideas are aspects above all of Herzog's
frustration, symptoms of his disease, and since the presentational process does not coerce us to assemble them into a
coherent ideology, in other words, since a fictive concrete
world rather than its ideological interpretation is what the
reader is primarily persuaded to construct, we do not feel
alerted to the threat of direct ideological control.

What is commonly known about the various forms of omniscient narrative allows us to allocate them to a relatively
broad band in our scale, covering a range of relations of
control. From the viewpoint of this chapter little can be
added to the widely accepted definition of omniscience,
except that between the complex semantic unit of an all-
knowing narrator who moves effortlessly between the
spheres of mental and physical acts and events, the spatio-
temporally unrestricted world and mental processes of its
personae, and a reader who is permitted to share that
knowledge there also exists a recognizable structure of
interdependence. By means of suspended information,
linkages, explanation, and interpretation of the presented
world the clairvoyant speaker of the narrative guides the
reader's construction to approximate to his own and in so
doing defines him as someone who is being introduced to
some knowledge beyond his ken: an initiate. In the actual
reading experience of omniscient novels this sense of

dependence is usually concealed. Instead, we are led to develop a sense more of being the narrator's partner, if not his chum. This illusion is the result of the narrator's confiding voice and his appeals to the reader's intelligence, education, and sensitivity. An implied reader is thus established with whom the actual reader, a victim of flattery, is only too pleased to identify. This merely disguises the dominant structure of control; our illusion of partnership spares our feelings and indeed makes us desire the yoke of dependence to which we are put.

Two kinds of reduction of omniscience are frequently found: the narrator's retreat to the confines of his own consciousness and mental processes, on the one hand, and his restriction of his knowledge to the reflection of the phenomenal external world, on the other. The first kind of reduction is central to confessional narrative, the second characterizes so-called objective presentation. What happens to our system of relations of dependence in each of these? Since in the first type of story the narrator focuses on the activities of his own consciousness, especially on acts of remembering, the reader is made a confidant, as much imposed upon as permitted to share the narrator's largely private affairs. (12) Objective narration, in contrast, is the attempt to present nothing but aspects of the phenomenal world-out-there. Consequently, the narrator is shrunk to a non-interpreting neutral bystander merely recording the messages of his sense organs. A number of attempts of this kind have been made, but perhaps the most rigorous curtailment of process and world can be found in some of Alain Robbe-Grillet's work. In his story La Plage in 'Instantanés', for example, the reader is guided to assemble mainly optical and some aural impressions. And were it not for the odd 'sans doute' we could indeed believe that camera and tape recorder were reflecting the pretty scene selected by the author. (13)

But how does this deliberate and radical reduction affect the structure of dependencies between process, world, and implied reader? Is the reader fettered or liberated to the degree to which process and world are reduced? Perhaps the definition of the three elements as acts of observation, evidence, and witness best characterizes the new distribution of control. But at the same time, the very restriction of the implied reader to a mere witness of schematically sketched physical details tends to grant the actual reader a new freedom. Although the narrator is still in total control of the presented phenomena, their severe reduction allows if not invites the reader to concretize with his own stock-piled experience a merely skeletal world. The assumption here is that reduction to objectivity is a highly artificial restriction of consciousness. And unless the reader deliberately plays Robbe-Grillet's game by imposing similar restrictions on his reading consciousness, his stock of inter-textual and everyday typifications will grant him a more complex vision than is coded in the text. What is significant here in terms of control is the relative freedom of the actual reader to assume the stance of the nouveau narrator by performing corresponding reductions of his stock-of-knowledge-at-hand or to transcend the reduced schema coded in the text by appresentational concretization.

The riddle constitutes a turning point in our scale. Unlike its pragmatic relations in some Old Germanic juris-diction where solution or failure to solve the riddle signified life or death, or the examination of today which still retains traces of the threat of its historical forebears, the fictive riddle as structure-carrying, as for instance in the detective story, grants the reader the fundamental security of the reading situation. Nevertheless, its implied reader must decode the enigma of the presented world which may be fragmentarily revealed or further disguised by the narrator. His control over the reader is defined by the discrepancy between his knowledge of the solution and the reader's ignorance. On the other hand, every riddle embodies its solution, so that the decoder is always potentially in a psoition of being able to match the narrator's superior knowledge. (14) The reader's discovery of the solution annuls the narrator's advantage: both narrator and reader now control the enigma.

In the way in which the reader constructs the relations of control in narrative communication, the various forms of unreliable narration are closely related to the riddle. Indeed, it makes sense to regard narrative unreliability as a special case of riddle structure. There is, for example, the extreme case in which the narrator turns out to be a liar who all along has presented a false world, as in James's story The Liar (1888) (15) and in Camus's 'The Fall', or the more frequent case of narrative with an insensitive narrator providing a misinterpreted world. In the first instance, the reader's design of meaning requires the unmasking of the narrator and replacement of his false world by a more appropriate substitute; in the second case,

the reader must assess the narrator's mental shortcomings
and shift the misinterpreted world so that it coincides with
what he infers to be the implied authorial stance. In the
first case, the reader thus acts as rebel, in the second as
perceptive moderator. As to the dynamics of control, the
reader's adequate construction of both types of story results
in a double reversal: of the narrator's position of authority
to that of victim, and the implied reader's role from that of
victim to one of authority. If, on the other hand, the actual
reader fails to recognize the narrator's unreliability, i.e.
if he construes a trusting instead of a suspicious implied
reader, he defines himself as the victim of the presentational
process.

The structural opposition of the implied reader who in the
course of the story acquires or surpasses the narrator's
insights and the actual reader who may or may not be able
to follow suit can be recognized also in jokes and satires.
In the joke, a speaker offers a world developing towards a
logical climax which, however, is never reached but
suddenly debunked by the unexpected substitution of an alien
and incompatible realm of thought. What is crucial about
the structure of jokes is that it is not the speaker who
identifies that substituted sphere as incompatible, but the
reader who, by an act of bisociation, as Arthur Koestler
puts it, realizes the clash.

Yet it is not so much the inherent structure of the joke
which 'decapitates the logical development of the situation',
for the joke's structure is merely the matrix on which the
bisociation can occur. (16) It is the actual reader/listener
who must decapitate and bisociate, so that the explosion of
laughter may take place. If the reader grasps the given
linguistic sequence as an ordinary string of words (or sees
the incompatibility but not the point of convergence between
the two discourses) and thus fails to bisociate its alien
elements, the joke falls flat: the actual reader has failed to
identify with the stipulated reader and cannot share the
narrator's wit. The relations of control manifest themselves in the situation of a narrator who by presenting two
incompatible universes of discourse as one coherent
linguistic sequence challenges the reader's capacity for bisociation. By missing the point, the reader defines himself as fool; through the explosion of laughter, he becomes
the jester's partner, now himself in a position of assuming
the role of narrator.

In satire a similar situation of textual steering and

reader construction prevails, only on a considerably
extended scale. While the joke comes into existence in the
realization of its point, satire requires the cumulative bisociation by the actual reader of the given artistic distortion and the merely implied plane of familiar social
reality. (17) Satiric distortion can take very different
tacks. There are the temporal distortions of historical
defamiliarization as in Thomas Mann's novella The Law or
the dystopic projections of Huxley's 'Brave New World' or
Orwell's '1984'. Spatial and fantasy displacement are
characteristic of 'Gulliver's Travels'; the distortion of
social morality establishes the satiric gap in 'A Modest
Proposal', while an anthropomorphized animal world
gurantees the sense of 'Entfremdung' in 'Animal Farm'.
Also, the reader's tasks of bisociation differ markedly not
only as to the kind of displacement he must realize, but also
to the degree of distortion. Hardly any reader will fail to
discover parallels between Orwell's animal society and
recent historical political structures; Thomas Mann's The
Law, on the other hand, makes substantial demands on the
reader's abilities of bisociative linkage.

The implied reader of satire, then, performs the double
function of grasping the codified distortions as a coherent
presented world and, at the same time, of construing the
parallel ridiculed actual world by reading against the grain
of the text. Consequently, the actual reader is again given
the chance of identifying with the implied reader and
becoming a co-satirist; or he may fail to bisociate and so
declare himself to be a part of the ridiculed world. As co-
satirist, the reader has acquired the position of judge,
though his judgment tends to be bound to that of the narrator
or, in the case of a naive narrator, to that of the implied
author.

Our comments on metafiction can be restricted to the
observation that its narrator acts as a player in the game
of story telling, inviting the reader to join him as partner.
In the short pieces of John Barth's 'Lost in the Fun House',
Robert Coover's 'Descants and Pricksongs', Jorge Luis
Borges's 'Labyrinths', or William H. Gass's 'Willie
Master's Lonesome Wife', as well as in such long works as
Vladimir Nabokov's 'Pale Fire', Barth's 'The Sotweed
Factor', or Thomas Pynchon's 'Gravity's Rainbow' the
relationship between narrator, presented world, and
implied reader as player, game, and playmate is one of
reduced dependency and control. Unlike some previously

discussed narrative forms in which the implied reader is
taught truth and told to act accordingly, or the types in
which the narrator controls a secret which the reader must
discover by intellectual effort or else remain victim, metafiction does not disguise its presentational process and
relationship with the reader. Even where the reader is
attacked, satirized, or fooled, this very presentational
activity is disclosed as such. Hence he feels on a par
with the narrator and experiences his own acts of concretizing as simply having fun.

A further step on our ladder of narrative types leads us
to structures in which the implied reader must be constructed as being superior to the narrator at the end of the tale
as far as knowledge and understanding are concerned.
Compared with the first few types on our scale, this
constitutes a reversal of the relations of control between
narrator, presented world, and reader. Narrators who
lack control over the world they speak of and the reader are
the narrator as child, the handicapped speaker, the perse-
cuted narrator and the narrator who has lost the insight of
his being victimized, the dehumanized narrator. In this
order the implied reader is to be realized as adult, nurse,
rescuer or psychiatrist, and self-reliant moral judge.

Apart from the phrases in which the implied mature narrator's interpretations are superimposed on the child's
thoughts, James Joyce's short story The Sisters is a young
boy's response to the death of an old man, his friend
Father Flynn. There is the central concrete situation of
death, on the one hand, and, on the other, the child's
bewildered view as presentational process. The presented
world which emerges from it includes the external aspects
of a public view, especially that of the unsympathetic
Cotter, and the private view of Nannie and Eliza, the
sisters of the dead, who are apparently covering up some
unpleasant details in Father Flynn's life, and such internal
aspects as the boy's memories, doubts, fears, and struggle
to understand. Indeed, fear and curiosity are the
conflicting poles of his consciousness: the former characterizing him as a child, the latter announcing his will to
grow up. His old friend's death pointedly confirms this
opposition. The narrator experiences it as both the loss
of a guardian and the liberation from an impediment to self-
realization. As he is filled with fear at the word
'paralysis' and yet wishes 'to be nearer to it and to look
upon its deadly work', the narrator is made to describe his

own initiation into the disillusioning complexity of adult life. At the same time, the reader is guided to concretize a fictive explanation, as part of the larger ones of 'Dubliners' as a whole and 'Ulysses', of Joyce's own repulsion by and fascination with the city of his youth. However handicapped by the fragmentary information the narrator is permitted to supply, the reader is never in the position of the bewildered boy. He is an initiated adult able and obliged to understand the narrator's insecurity; he assumes the attitude of a guardian who sympathizes with a child growing up, while the narrator appears ruled to a large extent by the world he himself presents.

Handicapped narrators appear as physically or mentally retarded: as dwarf in 'The Tin Drum' or as idiot in 'The Sound and the Fury'. But while the narrator in Grass's novel uses his apparent handicap to picaresque advantage, Benjy in Faulkner's narrative is truly the victim of the world which he stammers. Here, the implied reader is a nurse assembling as best he can the patient's incoherent linguistic scraps into a provisional pattern, until subsequent information by other narrators allows him to make full sense of Benjy's tale. We may be annoyed with the author for making us struggle more than ordinary reading demands, but we must sympathize with the narrator; that is, if we accept the attitude of the stipulated reader. If we do, the degree to which the narrator is deprived of control is matched by the degree to which the reader's responsibility and authority rise.

Another form of handicap is decrepitude. In the Chilean José Donoso's 'The Obscene Bird of Night' (El Obsceno Pajaro de la Noche', 1970) the old narrator is the victim for a while of a group of six senile women in the convent house where he spends his last days. By debasing himself he is accepted as the seventh witch. But the relationship between victim narrator, victimizing world, and protective reader is by no means stable. Its changes produce a rhythm and sphere of meaning of its own as the narrator defines himself as 'Mudito; Don Jerónimo's secretary; Iris's dog; Humberto Penaloza, the sensitive prose writer who offers us, in these simple pages, such a deeply felt and artistic vision of the vanished world of yesterday, when the springtime of innocence blossomed in the wisteria gardens; the seventh witch,' until at the end of the novel he literally fades away as an intangible shadow, handing over his narrative authority to the detached voice of the implied author. (18)

The final position on our scale is reserved for the narrator who is not only the victim of the presented world, but deprived also of the moral faculties to judge it. By contrast, the reader who experiences the portrayed objectivities as brutal is given the responsibility of an independent moral judge. This, in essence, is how the relations of control between narrator, world, and reader is handled by Tadeus Borovsky in his short story Supper. (19) The emotionally detached, mechanical, but technically precise first-person narrator sketches an evening in a concentration camp. In front of the prisoners a group of Russians is executed by an SS firing squad. Brutalized by the common sight of destruction of life, a Jewish inmate insists that the human brain can be eaten raw.

The narrator's reduction to a robot witness has a profound work-ideological effect. No clues whatsoever are found in the text as to the interpretative stance which the reader may be meant to assume. As in Robbe-Grillet's story, the reader has a choice. In fact, a cynical reader would be technically justified in taking the narrator's speech acts literally; i.e. accept them as satisfactory. For the outcry of which the narrator is no longer capable is not signalled to be performed by the reader. And yet we react with a sense of moral loathing. Not because we are told to do so even indirectly by the text, but because we are guided by the interaction in the reading consciousness of our imaginative construction of the text on the one hand, and, on the other, by the context of historical events and the moral consensus of the human community outside Borovsky's fiction.

It is self-evident that few actual narratives illustrate only one position on our scale and no other. While some stories certainly do, the vast majority of narrative partakes of a range of such typified allocations. Especially the novel which, as Baxtin observed, is capable of subsuming a variety of discourse, tends to cover a number of types in our graded series of control relationships. (20) Most picaresque tales, for example, begin with a victimized narrator who, in the course of the story, attains relative independence from the world he depicts; i.e. the narrative moves from right to left in our schema. A variation of this structure is found in the story of Lucius in Apuleius's 'The Golden Ass', who, over eleven books, narrates his metamorphosis from a youth enjoying life and love to a donkey threatened with castration and seduced by a noble lady –

'Lector intende: laetaberis' - until he is finally retrans-
formed by Isis. (21)   Apuleius's adventure and fantasy
novel displays a pattern of changing relations of control
from somewhere in the middle of our scale to the right and
back again to its starting point.   Or, finally, there is the
structure of deliberate instability of the relations of control
between narrator, presented world, and implied reader as
a central technical and ideological aspect, illustrated for
example by José Donoso's 'The Obscene Bird of Night' or
Günter Grass's more recent 'Der Butt'.

Our initial question of how presentational process, presented world, and implied reader are technical and at the
same time also ideological functions of one another has
received largely intrinsic and a few extraneous answers.
Intrinsically, the term ideological refers to work ideology
(although our construction of any work ideology is of course
never purely intrinsic), ideological in general to the actual
socio-political situation of the reading act.   The immediate
and important links between fictive narrative and the
reader's society are not those seemingly one-to-one relationships between either the presented world and objects in
the world-out-there or the presentational process and communicative acts in actual society.   Rather, the significant
links are those between the narrative's work ideology as
abstracted and assembled by the reader and the dominant
ideological structures of his workaday world.   In terms of
reception as understood here, that is in terms of the
reader's construction of narrative, those links are forged
by the way in which the actual reader realizes the implied
reader. (22)   Through the realization of the implied reader
and its functions vis-a-vis presented world and presentational process, work ideology reveals itself in its quasi-
personal aspects: as implied authorial stance.

The crucial point here is the kind of identification between
actual and implied reader: whether once performed it
permanently defines the reader's stance towards the literary
construct, or whether it is a merely temporary, hermeneutic identification.   In the first instance, work ideology
becomes a positive aspect of an actual ideology, implied
authority becomes actual authority, intrinsic control
becomes actual control.   In Derrida's sense, language is
then indeed grasped as presence. (23)   In the second case,
the reader for the time being lends his consciousness to the
implied reader and so reserves his right of confrontation
with the narrative.   Thus confronted, fiction enters into a

TABLE 8.2

Type	Narrator	Presented world	Implied reader
myth	authority	dictate	minor
parable	preacher	analogue and teaching aid	believer, limited intellectual faculties
'Märchen'	artist	naive moral and presence of marvellous	naive audience
saint's legend	ecclesiastical historian	theology: process of canonization	member of medieval church
prophecy	prophet	divine vision and future truth	rebellious believer
allegorical	ideological visionary	fusion of concrete image and abstraction	naive disciple
narrative of ideas	ideologist	ideology	disciple
omniscient narration	clairvoyant	unrestricted world, especially mental processes	initiate
confession	confessor	private affairs	confidant
objective narration	observer	evidence	witness
riddle	encoder	enigma	decoder

TABLE 8.2

Type	Narrator	Presented world	Implied reader
unreliable narration	liar	false world	rebel
	insensitive speaker	misinterpreted world	moderator
joke	jester	incompatible realms of thought	bisociator, momentary
satire	satirist	distorted world	bisociator, extended, and moral judge
metafiction	player	game	playmate
innocent narration	minor	world as discovery	adult
handicapped narration	retarded person	unmanageable task	nurse
narration as cry	persecuted person	threat	rescuer and psychiatrist
dehumanized narration	dehumanized victim	inhumanity as norm	moral judge

dynamic relationship with the reader's 'construction of social reality', both qualifying one another as authorially governed systems of relations between more or less controlling communicative acts, interpreted objectivities, and more or less dependent interpreting consciousnesses.

Chapter 9

Parodic narrative

To reflect on parody from the perspective of our working definition of narrative does not mean to focus merely on a special case of literature. I am inclined to agree with the Russian Formalist view that all literature is parodic in the broadest sense of the term. But even if we look at parody in the more restricted sense of narrative parody as a deliberate distortion of previous texts, our focus will alert us to or at least consolidate our understanding of fundamental aspects of all narrative.

When we read parodic narrative and witness gestural parody we notice that the way in which we are compelled to realize each parodying transformation is identical at a certain level of structural generality. This is because narrative parody is merely a special case of literary parody which, in turn, is a special instance of parody, all of which have their roots in a parodic attitude of consciousness. Parody as an attitude of consciousness plays a prominent role in socio-cultural and historico-philosophical change in Lukács's sense. Accordingly, what is significant parody and what is sheer mimicry could be measured by the degree to which a parody is responsible for and partakes of such change.

Likewise, literary parody ought not to be viewed simply as a clever linguistic exercise addressing itself to an esoteric circle of literati, but as a mode which is present, overtly or covertly, in all literature. As such, parody is part of the study of inter-textual relations and, beyond inter-textuality, part of ideological mutation. But before we can undertake such large-scale inquiry, questions must be reaised about the hermeneutic basis of parody classification, the relationship between source object and parody,

and especially the kind and degree of modification of
sources which manifest themselves in parodies.

Generic or typological distinctions are never purely
classificatory, they are always also hermeneutic. When we
decide that a narrative like 'Johannes Baptista' by one
Adelbrecht (about 1130) is a medieval saint's legend and not
a fabliau or a biblical parable, we have or should have made
far-reaching interpretative decisions as to the overall
structural arrangement of that work. Applied to the study
of parody, classification is advantageous only if it allows
for all parodistic phenomena, if it avoids category mistakes,
if it does not exclude or impede further development in the
praxis of the form, if it leaves room for the debate of inter-
textual problems, if it addresses itself to the kind as well
as the degree of parodistic perversion, and if it does not
preclude the investigation of non-literary implications of
parody.

To be able to meet such a challenge, any literary typology
must take account of the ontological status and structure of
the literary work of art. However, there does not seem to
be much in the classification of parody which displays such
theoretical orientation. To say that parody at its best is
faithful to form and treacherous to matter, or to adopt the
widespread distinction between 'parody of form and parody
of content', as even Gilbert Highet does in his study 'The
Anatomy of Satire', (1) is to rely on one of the popular
clichés of literary criticism. It is grounded in a binary
rather than a polyphonic conception of literary works of art
(cf. Bakhtin and Ingarden). (2) Such reluctance to investigate the theoretical soundness of terminology should be a
matter of concern, especially since as early as in Russian
Formalism and the work of Roman Ingarden the traditional
dichotomy of form and content was scrutinized and rejected
at least in its loose usage.

In 'The Anatomy of Satire' Gilbert Highet also employs
another kind of categorization when he lists seven types of
literary parody: epic, romance, drama, didactic poetry,
lyric, prose: non-fiction, and prose: fiction. Evidently,
the distinctions are based on a typology of the parodied
source objects and are helpful as far as they go; but they
themselves tell us little about the kind of parodistic transformation that the didactic poem, for example, has under-
gone. But before we can proceed to suggest a fruitful way
of specifying such literary types we must briefly consider
the notion of parody as a parasitic form of literature.

In 'The Sense of an Ending' Frank Kermode tells us that
the author of 'Der Mann ohne Eigenschaften' fails because
Musil 'tries to create a new genre in which, by all manners
of dazzling devices and metaphors and stratagems, fiction
and reality can be brought together again.' (3) Musil, however, has attempted nothing of the kind; it is Kermode who
has mixed up reality and reality-as-it-appears-to-us. What
the novel does attempt, though, is to bring together fictional
narrative and interpreted reality. In this 'Der Mann ohne
Eigenschaften' is certainly successful. Applied to the
debate about literary parody, this illustrates that parasitic
here cannot mean secondary, but tertiary. All literary
parody points to the literariness, the interpretative rather
than the representational qualities of works of literature.
And perhaps it is no accident that the present trend of metafiction performs the same function; indeed, I would argue
that in metafiction literature's covert parodistic elements
have again become structure-carrying. By contrast, recent
developments in literary documentation such as the novelistic documentary (e.g., Truman Capote's 'In Cold Blood' or
Norman Mailer's 'The Armies of the Night') or the dramatic
documentary (e.g., Peter Weiss's 'The Investigation' or
'Discourse on Vietnam') aim at minimizing interpretational
inference and in so doing reduce literature's inherent
parodistic potential.
  Speaking in terms of a ladder of fictionality, the novelistic and dramatic documentary are the only literary forms
which can justly claim to rely for each of their 'items' on an
analogous source object in the world-out-there. By the
same schema, so-called realistic literature could be said to
have a purely eidetic relationship with the world-out-there,
while fantasy worlds could be argued to rest on the distortions of the eidetic bonds between familiar items. It is not
that we cannot 'understand' the pigsty, the horses, or the
patient as they are presented; we do. What we find
baffling are the combinations between those features: that
horses squeeze themselves out of a pigsty, etc. Just as in
a ladder of fictionality the interpretational distance between
the world-out-there and the literary construct widens, so
does the parodistic potential inherent in the literary
language increase on a ladder of parodic attitudes. It is
perhaps useful to say, then, that documentation in the above
sense is a primary linguistic construct in relationship to the
world-out-there (a referential interpretation), while realistic, mythic, allegorical, fantasy literature are secondary

constructs (quasi-referential interpretations or interpretations of interpretations). Literary parody then is a tertiary construct or an interpretation of an interpretation of an interpretation.

If the form-content metaphor is an inadequate device with which to approach literary works and if type distinctions based on parodied source objects are helpful only to a point, a typology ought to be designed which is related to the essential structure of literary works of art. Let us again use a stratified schema which borrows from Nicolai Hartmann and Roman Ingarden, but is modified to take into consideration the distinction between presented world and presentational process, a distinction that is particularly relevant to the discussion of parodic narrative. It seems that the parodistic impulse is always specifically aimed at one or more of the following strata: (a) print (or sound), (b) linguistic formation, (c1) the presented world and (c2) the presentational process, and (d) the stratum of high-level interpretative abstractions. In each of these strata we must distinguish artistic construction from aesthetic reconstruction or 'concretization', (4) so that in any adequate reading of parody the artistic 'reductio (or 'amplificatio') ad absurdum' is matched by an analogous aesthetic 'reductio' (or 'amplificatio'). (5)

We should further demarcate the modified stratum (or strata) which is structure-carrying in a parody from the degree of modification in each stratum. The former tells us whether print, language, presented world, acts of narrating, or world view are primarily parodied; the latter indicates whether we are dealing merely with a pastiche or an historically seminal parody. But further inquiry may well suggest that the relationship between the two contains clues which could assist in the construction of a hermeneutically fruitful typology of parody. All linguistic constructs can be said to be stratified. What is decisive in literary works of art, however, is what Ingarden calls the 'polyphony of aesthetic value qualities', the potential total aesthetic interaction of the properties of all strata. In this sense parody is always a work of art, no matter whether the source object itself be an artistic or non-artistic phenomenon. The parody of a car manual, unlike its original, has at its disposal the replete polyphony of aesthetic value qualities. (6)

(a) THE STRATUM OF PRINT

When we think of literary parody we have in mind primarily
parodied language style: and although the majority of the
better-known parodies fulfil this expectation by heightening
the characteristics of the original linguistic construct and
distort by bringing into bolder relief the salient features of
a writer's style, the linguistic stratum is only one of the
strata in which parody can manifest itself. Typographic
features, print layout and graphic design can also add to the
aesthetic value qualities of literary works.

A concrete poem by Hal Colebatch makes this point. (7)

```
THIS
t
 h
  i
   s
    is a lavatory
    people drop
     concrete
     poems
      into it from whence
                        t
                        h
                        e
                        y

                        a
                        r
                        e

                        f
                        l
                        u
                        s
                        h
                        e
                        d

                        a
                        w
                        a
                        y.
```

We may feel that the poem is a burlesque rather than

parody, since its writer 'likes low words' (8) or we may wish
to criticize it on the grounds that it does not really exploit
the genre's potential of internal cross reference and graphic
inter-relatedness. Nevertheless, it approaches the subject
from within, it functions as a form of literary criticism, it
employs subversive mimicry and can be seen as an example of
that internal check that literature keeps on itself.

But the incorporation of typographic features into literary
works of art is of course neither anything new nor restricted
to concrete poetry. Laurence Sterne in 'Tristram Shandy'
brings into play the stratum of print as one of his many parodistic devices: the black page at the end of chapter 12, volume I; the drawing of the flourish of the stick as a substitute
for a detailed description in chapter 4, volume IX; or the
whole of chapter 40, volume VI, with its interaction between
the graphic and linguistic discourse about his own technique
of constructing a story.

CHAPTER FORTY

I am now beginning to get fairly into my work; and by the
help of a vegetable diet, with a few of the cold seeds, I
make no doubt but I shall be able to go on with my uncle
Toby's story, and my own, in a tolerable straight line.
Now,

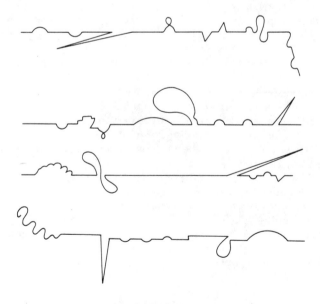

These were the four lines I moved in through my first,
second, third, and fourth volumes. - In the fifth volume
I have been very good, - the precise line I have described
in it being this:

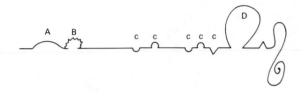

By which it appears, that except at the curve, marked A.
where I took a trip to Navarre, - and the indented curve
B. which is the short airing when I was there with the
Lady Baussiere and her page, - I have not taken the least
frisk of a digression, till John de la Casse's devils led
me the round you see marked D. - for as for ccccc they
are nothing but parentheses, and the common ins and outs
incident to the lives of the greatest ministers of state;
and when compared with what men have done, - or with my
own transgressions at the letters A B D - they vanish into
nothing.

In this last volume I have done better still - for from
the end of Le Fever's episode, to the beginning of my
uncle Toby's campaigns, - I have scarce stepped a yard
out of my way.

If I mend at this rate, it is not impossible - by the
good leave of his grace of Benevento's devils - but I may
arrive hereafter at the excellency of going on even thus;

which is a line drawn as straight as I could draw it, by a
writing-master's ruler, (borrowed for that purpose)
turning neither to the right hand or to the left.

This right line, - the path-way for Christians to walk
in! say divines -
- The emblem of moral rectitude! says Cicero-
- The best line! say cabbage planters - is the shortest
line, says Archimedes, which can be drawn from one
given point to another. -

I wish your ladyships would lay this matter to heart,
in your next birth-day suits!
- What a journey!

> Pray can you tell me, – that is, without anger, before I
> write my chapter upon straight lines – by what mistake –
> who told them so – or how it has come to pass, that your
> men of wit and genius have all along confounded this line,
> with the line of GRAVITATION?

Perhaps the key observation to make is that the parodistic
concrete poem exhausts itself largely at the level of print
which is explained and reinforced by a rather plain linguistic formation, while Sterne's eccentricities in the typographic stratum function as an integral part of all subsequent
strata, especially the narrator's scurrilous world view and,
through it, Sterne's artistic-philosophical stance. (9)

(b) THE STRATUM OF LINGUISTIC FORMATION: THE
SURFACE TEXT

Very much the same distinction can be drawn between the
pastice-parody which, even if cleverly executed, merely
captures the typical diction, sentence structure, punctuation, or rhythm of its source and parody proper which,
while parodying the linguistic stratum, at the same time
transcends language and projects a coherent world with a
recognizable philosophical-ideological commitment.   The
following parody by E.B. White is of the first kind. (10)
And although it cannot avoid permitting the reader to
construe an image chain, that image world remains
incoherent and does not result, as does Hemingway's, in a
structured 'Weltanschauung'.   This has nothing to do with
whether we think highly of the author's philosophy or not.
I am interested here only in its coherence or incoherence.

ACROSS THE STREET AND INTO THE GRILL

This is my last and best and true and only meal,
thought Mr Perley as he descended at noon and swung east
on the beat-up sidewalk of Forty-fifth Street.   Just
ahead of him was the girl from the reception desk.   I am
a little fleshed up around the crook of the elbow, thought
Perley, but I commute good.
He quickened his step to overtake her and felt the pain
again.   What a stinking trade it is, he thought.   But
after what I've done to other assistant treasurers, I

can't hate anybody.   Sixteen deads, and I don't know how
many possibles.

The girl was near enough now so he could smell her
fresh receptiveness, and the lint in her hair.   Her skin
was light blue, like the sides of horses....

'Good morning, my Assistant Treasurer,' said Botticelli, coming forward with a fiasco in each hand.   He
nodded at the girl, who he knew was from the West
Seventies and whom he desired.

'Can you drink the water here?' asked Perley.   He had
the fur trapper's eye and took in the room at a glance,
noting that there was one empty table and three pretty
waitresses.

Botticelli led the way to the table in the corner, where
Perley's flanks would be covered.

'Alexanders,' said Perley.   'Eighty-six to one.   The
way Chris mixes them.   Is this table all right, Daughter?'

Botticelli disappeared and returned soon, carrying the
old Indian blanket.

'That's the same blanket, isn't it?' asked Perley.

'Yes.   To keep the wind off,' said the Captain, smiling
from the backs of his eyes.   'It's still west.   It should
bring the ducks in tomorrow, the chef thinks.'

Mr Perley and the girl from the reception desk crawled
down under the table and pulled the Indian blanket over
them so it was solid and good and covered them right.
The girl put her hand on his wallet.   It was cracked and
old and held his commutation book.   'We are having fun,
aren't we?' she asked....

They came out from under the blanket and Perley tipped
their waitress exactly fifteen per cent minus withholding.
They left the piano in the restaurant, and when they went
down the elevator and out and turned in to the old, hard,
beat-up pavement of Fifth Avenue and headed south toward
Forty-fifth Street, where the pigeons were, the air was
as clean as your grandfather's howitzer.   The wind was
still west.   I commute good, thought Perley, looking at
his watch.   And he felt the old pain of going back to
Scarsdale again. (E.B. White)

E.B. White's parody is no doubt funny, and it is indeed
questionable whether it is at all possible to achieve anything
more profound by parodying Hemingway.   Perhaps the parodist must go beyond individual source texts and focus on a
whole genre and its enveloping ideology to achieve a major

work. This is precisely what Cervantes has done. In a
less professional manner, but with the same reliable
instinct, the precocious Jane Austen tackles the problem in
'Love and Freindship'. It addresses itself to the whole
tradition of the sentimental novel in order to replace it by
something more ambitious and complex, an aim accomplished
in Jane Austen's later novels. Although it uses the almost
formulaic vocabulary of the sentimental novel, 'Love and
Freindship' goes beyond the imitation of language style and
consciously employs typical juxtapositions of personae,
current spatial clichés, phases of action, means of characterization and, above all, a consistent artistic conception
and view of life. Together these devices expose not merely
a manner of using English, but the projection of a foul view
of the world. (11)

(c) THE STRATUM OF THE PRESENTED WORLD AND THE PRESENTATIONAL PROCESS

To treat the presented world and the presentational process
as two distinct sides of one stratum or as separate strata
does not mean that they exist independently of one another
and the linguistic phenomena; they are graspable as mental
images or schematic constructs only because their aspects
are all signified at the same time in the stratum of linguistic
formation. However, to parody a chain of events and fictive
personae or acts of telling and a narrator the parodist need
not feel bound by the linguistic formulae of his source.
And even when such formulae are transposed, they have to
play a subordinate role if the parody's main interest is to be
in either the presented world or the presentational process
or in both.

(c1) The presented world

In parodying the story of 'Pamela' and the genre of the
Gothic novel, both 'Joseph Andrews' and 'Northanger Abbey'
primarily pervert stories rather than language. This is
not to say that the surface structure of language is not
parodied; we do recognize some of Richardson's linguistic
patterns in Fielding's novel and some Gothic diction in Jane
Austen's work. They are, however, not essential; they
merely reinforce the general parodistic thrust of the deep

structure of their languages.   This relative indifference to
the imitation of a specific idiom is put to twofold use in
Thomas Mann's 'Der Erwählte' (The Holy Sinner').   Not
only is the language of the original tale 'Of the Wonderful
Dispensation of Providence and the Rise of Pope Gregory'
recast into the idiom of the narrator, the monk 'Clemens the
Irishman' (who furthermore varies his style according to
whether he is relating the old legend or addressing the
modern reader), the narrator is also made to announce this
indifference in order to underscore the mental world about
to emerge in the reader's imagination.

> For now I begin to write and address myself to tell a
> tale at once frightful and highly edifying.   But it is quite
> uncertain in what language I write, whether Latin,
> French, German, or Anglo-Saxon, and indeed it is all
> the same; ... By no means do I assert that I possess all
> the tongues; but they run all together in my writing and
> become one – in other words, language.   For the thing
> is so, that the spirit of narration is free to the point of
> abstraction, whose medium is language in and for itself,
> language itself, which sets itself as absolute and does not
> greatly care about idioms and national linguistic
> gods. (12)

While the majority of parodies are merely linguistic stabs
at more complex originals, Thomas Mann reverses this
state of affairs and illustrates the possible identity of
novelistic and parodistic amplification.   Paragraphs and
even single sentences are turned into chapters in Mann's
novel.   The sentence, 'the bells rang of their own accord'
toward the end of the legend, for instance, is expanded to
supply much of chapter I 'Who Rings?' and transformed into
the narrator's delightful justification of story-telling.
Likewise, all the other central features of the legend
undergo parodistic expansion: the incestuous union of
Gregory's parents is presented in subtle detail, the solitary
penance on the rock in the sea is accentuated by having
Gregory shrink to the size of a hedgehog.   But as in all
highly successful parody a masterly balance is maintained
between the source and the novel, so that the novel does not
destory but rather ironically complements the original.
This balance includes the 'Application', a set of interpretative clues added to the legend to guarantee its correct
ideological grasp.   Analogously, at the end of 'The Holy

Sinner', the narrator provides the reader with a similar
tongue-in-cheek admonition, a device which serves at the
same time as the functional closing part of the novel's frame.
He warns the reader to 'beware of saying to himself,'

> 'Well then, be thou a jolly sinner. If it turned out so
> well with this lot, how then shalt thou be lost?' That is
> devil's whispering. First spend seventeen years on a
> stone, reduced to a hedgehog, and bathe the afflicted for
> more than twenty, you will see if all that is a joke! But
> truly it is wise to divine in the sinner the chosen
> one. (13)

(c2) The presentational process

Apart from its many other parodic features (title, hero,
hero's birth, etc.), what is significant about 'Tristram
Shandy' in terms of presentational process is that Sterne's
emphasis is not on what is being told, but on how a novel
can be told; the author has foregrounded the presentational
process: the spatial and temporal locus of the narrator,
the various acts of telling, reader address, the 'personality' of the narrator, narrator tone, or the narrator's
'Weltanschauung'. But when we compare 'Tristram Shandy'
with the passages of 'The Oxen of the Sun' episode in
'Ulysses' in which Joyce parodies Sterne, we notice that
one of the major aspects of the presentational process,
reader address, is not exploited at all. The addressees are
personae of the presented world.

> But indeed, sir, I wander from the point. How mingled
> and imperfect are all our sublunary joys! Maledicity!
> Would to God that foresight had remembered me to take
> my cloak along! I could weep to think of it. Then,
> though it had poured seven showers, we were neither of
> us a penny the worse. But beshrew me, he cried,
> clapping hand to his forehead, tomorrow will be a new day
> and, thousand thunders, I know of a march – and de
> capotes, Monsieur Poyntz, from whom I can have for a
> livre as snug a cloak of the French fashion as ever kept
> a lady from wetting. Tut, Tut! cries le Fecandateur,
> tripping in, my friend Monsieur Moore, that most accom-
> plished traveller (I have just cracked a half bottle avec
> lui in a circle of the best wits of the town), is my

authority that in Cape Horn, ventre biche, they have a
rain that will wet through any, even the stoutest cloak.
A drenching of that violence, he tells me, sans blague,
has sent more than one luckless fellow in good earnest
posthaste to another world. Pooh! A livre! cries
Monsieur Lynch. The clumsy things are dear at a sou.
One umbrella, were it no bigger than a fairy mushroom,
is worth ten such stopgaps. No woman of any wit would
wear one. My dear Kitty told me today that she would
dance in a deluge before ever she would starve in such
an ark of salvation for, as she reminded me, (blushing
piquantly and whispering in my ear though there was none
to snap her words but giddy butterflies), dame Nature,
by the divine blessing, has implanted it in our heart and
it has become a household word that il y a deux choses
for which the innocence of our original garb, in other
circumstances a breach of the proprieties, is the fittest
nay, the only, garment. The first, said she (and here
my pretty philosopher, as I handed her to her tilbury, to
fix my attention, gently tipped with her tongue the outer
chamber of my ear), the first is a bath ... but at this
point a bell tinkling in the hall cut short a discourse which
promised so bravely for the enrichment of our store of
knowledge. (14)

While Sterne uses the stated and implied reader in a
variety of ways (as witness, sounding board, partner in a
fictive dialogue, or sensitive confidant), Joyce concen-
trates on parodying Sterne's language style, especially
diction and syntax, and the manneristic acts of telling, but
brackets the grammar of reader apostrophe. As a result,
the Sterne passage is experienced by the reader as a
partial parody only. Perhaps the reason for this restriction is that by substituting personae of the fictive Dublin for
the implied reader, none of the parody sections is able to
burst the frame of the 'Oxen of the Sun' episode; all its
parodies of English style are structurally integrated in the
one horizon of the presented world: the hospital scene.
    In the metafiction of today we recognize the same fascina-
tion with the presentational process and the same parodistic
aim in the broad sense of the term: negation as advance.
This observation does not only hold in general, but applies
as much to technical detail, so that such a formal cliché as
the traditional reader address can be transformed into
something alive, dynamic, and perhaps aggressive and
annoying.

'The reader! You dogged, uninsultable, print-oriented
bastard, it's you I'm addressing, who else, from inside
this monstrous fiction. You've read me this far, then?
Even this far? For what discreditable motive? How is
it you don't go to a movie, watch TV, stare at a wall,
play tennis with a friend, make amorous advances to the
person who comes to your mind when I speak of amorous
advances? Can nothing surfeit, saturate you, turn you
off? Where's your shame?' (15)

Offending the audience is of course only one parodistic
device of revitalizing literary conventions. In 'Pale Fire',
a poem with scholarly critical apparatus (a parody of his
own Pushkin commentary), Nabokov has invented an
intriguing game in which narrator devices and academic
approaches to literature are mocked at while at the same
time the internal coherence of the work is secured. And
Borges's work abounds in Chinese box effects, dream
structures and labyrinths. But apart from introducing
sophisticated narrative techniques which negate traditional
forms, the metafictional contributions of Nabokov, Barth,
Barthelme, Coover, William H. Gass, or Borges go further;
they demand adequate fictional equivalents for new literary
and socio-cultural conditions.

(d) The stratum of high-level interpretative abstractions

As a special case in the problematic of inter-textuality,
parody can be called significant then in terms of the relationship between the interpretative abstractions which it
makes us draw and the historical situation to which it
belongs. In this, the two aspects, the modification of a
source object and the stratum or strata in which the parody
manifests itself, are intimately linked. The former is a
measure as to whether we are dealing with mimicry, imitation, or significant negation, the latter indicates how far a
parody transcends the strata of print and linguistic formation
and to what extent it allows for a coherent world view.
Together these two aspects determine the degree to which
parody is capable of active social participation at a high
level of abstraction: at the level of ideology.
    The parodies of liturgy and biblical text in the 'Epistolae
Obscurorum Virorum' fulfil precisely these conditions.
Although they conspicuously operate in the strata of

linguistic phenomena and the presented world, at the stratum
of interpretative inference they undermine an all-powerful
and restrictive authority. It would be fruitful to investigate in which periods and for what reasons parody
flourishes, why at certain times parodistic ideological
checks are prevalent and why they are absent at other
times. 'The Praise of Folly' by Erasmus Rotterdamus or
Rabelais's 'Gargantua' and 'Pantagruel' perform this check
for scholasticism, Voltaire's 'Candide' for a popularized
Leibnizean world view. Likewise, Cervantes's 'Don
Quixote' is not merely 'una parodia de las novelas de
caballerias' (although this is of course its immediate
literary function), but because it operates at all strata of
the literary work of art it is also a critique of Christian
chivalric ideology of which that romance tradition is only a
part. Don Quixote not only replaces 'the chivalrous novel
that had succumbed to the fate of every epic that wants to
maintain and perpetuate a form by purely formal means
after the transcendental conditions for its existence have
already been condemned by the historico-philosophical
dialectic;' (16) 'Don Quixote' also transcends its formal
generic boundaries and makes ideological claims capable of
modifying that historico-philosophical dialectic itself.

With these observations in mind one could define parody
perhaps thus. Parody is always an artistic structure distorting a given structure (material objects, body communication, social conditions, conventions or institutions, music,
painting, philosophical systems, or pragmatic and artistic
language constructs) by modifying that given structure to a
certain degree, but always potentially transcending the
source object in a number of ways. Let me add an explanation to each of the items.

Parody is always an artistic structure, no matter whether
the parodied object is itself an artistic construct or not.
The parody of the instruction manual for a washing machine
is an artistic structure because the way it is put together
as to its linguistic features, signified objects and their
relations, or the implied personality of speaker and user
produces in the reading consciousness a polyphony of
aesthetic value qualities. Unlike the equivalent items in
the original text, all these features are meant to be realized
in their aesthetic and not their pragmatic function. It is
of course possible to misread both the source text and the
parody by responding to the former as to a parody (which
happens quite often as a result of linguistic incompetence on

the part of the producer) or the latter as a practical manual (as a result either of the incompetence of the parodist or the insensitivity of the reader).

Parody as an artistic structure stands in a distorting relationship over and against its source object. This is the crucial part of the general definition of parody. Two issues must be kept separate here: what is being distorted and the degree of modification that has occurred. In literary parody the question as to what has been distorted can best be answered by studying the particular stratum or strata on which the parodic attitude has concentrated. We must find out whether it is the level of print, the linguistic arrangement of the text, the signified image world, or the work's overall artistic–ideological pattern that is predominantly parodied.

Once we have identified the stratum at which the parodic distortion is most effectively aimed, we should be able, by way of comparison with the original text, to describe the degree of modification. To my mind, this is the point where the critical vocabulary of travesty, burlesque, reductive or augmentive parody has a clearly defined and useful job to do. In isolation, without a comprehensive theoretical framework of which they are functional parts, such critical terms remain arbitrary and confusing.

We cannot do full justice to parody, however, if we confine our description to its artistic status and distorting relationship with its source. We must include the fact that at least potentially parody can always transcend the structure it ridicules. Reductive or minor parody could be called the kind of parody, which, more or less cleverly, imitates in a distorting fashion the linguistic features of the source without achieving a coherent presented world and recognizable philosophical stance. By contrast, augmentive or major parody, although also recognizably distorting the linguistic features of its source, establishes a coherent parodic world and through it its own systematic pattern of artistic–ideological abstraction in the reading consciousness. (17)

What happens when we read narrative parody is that, apart from the aspects already described, we activate above all the dynamic interaction between presentational process and presented world. Moreover, we concretize not only the signified process and world of the parody itself; in a highly tentative fashion, we also concretize their shadows, process and world of the structure to which the parody is a response (see Figure 9.1).

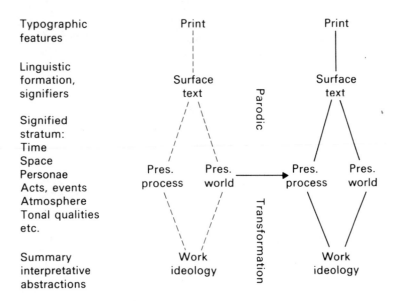

FIGURE 9.1

The fact that the structural weight in narrative is on the inter-relationship between signified process and world affects these four aspects: the polyphony of aesthetic value qualities, the question as to which stratum is most seriously distorted, the degree of modification accomplished, and the fact that parody can always transcend the original text as to complexity of structure and work ideology.

A convenient illustration of parodic narrative is James Joyce's 'Ulysses', containing as it does multiple parodies of language style (a parody of journalese in the 'Aeolus' chapter, a variety of inflated jargons in the 'Cyclops' episode, or of different historical styles of English in 'The Oxen of the Sun'), the presented world (the long brothel scene as a parody of the Homeric 'Circe' episode and also, perhaps, of Goethe's 'Walpurgisnacht' scenes, or the 'Hades' chapter as a double-edged parody of its Homeric counterpart and the clichés of modern funerals), or the presentational process (the virtuoso shifting of the narrative situation from omniscience to near objective presentation and free indirect style, the use of interior monologue in the 'Penelope' section which by far surpasses both Dujardin's 'Les Lauriers sont Coupées' and his later laboured theories, or the narrator's fast change of spatial locus in the multiply stranded chapter of 'The Wandering Rocks').

But the transcending qualities of 'Ulysses' do not lie in specific passages or techniques; indeed there is evidence, as I have pointed out in my comment on the 'Tristram Shandy' parody of the 'Oxen of the Sun' episode, that the parodic potential of the source is not always fully exploited. But the parodic links in 'Ulysses' are additional aspects rather than its core structure. Through the novel's searching language a massive world and complex presentational process emerge which stand on their own and in their interaction produce an artistic-philosophical stance of world-historical significance.

Parodic literary narrative is recognizable, then, as an artistic literary structure distorting one or more aspects of its source object, such as the stratum of print, surface text, above all its signified presentational process and presented world and, through these, also its work ideology to a certain degree, but always potentially transcending the source at any stratum as well as in the overall interplay of its strata and forward reading dimension.

Chapter 10

Narrative and the form-content metaphor

When in an everyday situation someone says, 'If only people were less aggressive,' we do not receive modality and statement in a purely propositional sense. We comprehend modality to a large extent by means of the physical manner of expression, stance, facial features, gesture, volume or intonation, the referential meaning itself by a transformation or synthesis according to our linguistic competence. By bringing together our interpretations of speech situation and proposition, we attempt to reconstruct the person's meaning intention. By contrast, when we read the pragmatic statements of the instructions for a pressure cooker, modality, we assume, is in typical accordance with 'Instructions' and does not have to be constructed carefully at each phrase or word. If it has to be, the text ceases to be instructive, it is something else, as, for example, a parody. If, on the other hand, we read the pragmatic instructions as a parody, i.e. if we change the pragmatic into an aesthetic object, we attach an alien modality, our own, to the linguistic construct.

In contradistinction to these two cases, modality in fictive statements undergoes the same complex imaginative construction on the part of the reader as does the immediate propositional meaning. It is therefore partly true that literary statements are messages oriented upon themselves; true, in as far as modality itself is experienced as a set of signified items whenever fictional narrative is read. In a statement such as 'Menard (perhaps without wanting to) has enriched, by means of a new technique, the halting and rudimentary act of reading: this new technique is that of the deliberate anachronism and the erroneous attri--bution,' (1) the immediate propositional meaning acts as one

major signified component, the presented world, to which is
added as second signified component the presentational
process: the playful, ironical, but also pensive quasi-
authorial stance of the narrator. Both signifieds must
first be constructed as imagined reality before they can be
reduced again to a set of summary interpretative propositions. But this internalized dynamic of process and world
is by no means self-sufficient; the construction of presentational process and presented world as well as the
narrative's summary meaning rely on factors outside the
text: the reader's experience of everyday reality and inter-
textuality, as well as his understanding of their ideological
structures. It is with these qualifications that we should
read the tag of literary statements as messages oriented
upon themselves. As to the focus of this chapter, the view
of fictional modality as a set of significata next to the
signified world has a number of structural consequences if
applied to the form-content dichotomy.

What in reading William Faulkner's 'As I Lay Dying' do we
declare to be the novel's form, what its content? Would it
help to say that the surface text, the given system of
signifiers, is its form, while all the activities which the
reader performs produce content, so that the construction
of the world of the narrator, the world of the fictive
personae, and the novel's overarching aesthetic-philosophical stance are elements of content? An arbitrary distinction and, more dangerously, a misleading one, especially
since all such elements are themselves structured and
consequently experienced as forms. Moreover, the
distinction is no less shaky than about a dozen others which
we can make when we attempt to cleave narrative into
aspects of form and aspects of content. And although
linguistic-structuralist and phenomenological studies have
done a good deal to clarify structural relationships, the
classical bipartition still haunts the discussion and teaching
of literature. However, to question the use of the form-
content metaphor is not the only purpose of this chapter.
There are in fact a number of structural interdependencies
in narrative texts which can be easily grasped as polarities.
So, in order to query critical terminology, those structural
relationships themselves will have to be canvassed. That
is the second aim of the chapter.

To say that we make sense of the world by means of our
typified experience is to say also that we intend our reality
by imposing structures on whatever we confront. This is

why we cannot know chaos or infinity, save as definitions;
they are purely logical asseverations, not human experience.
We are able to put our experience in array by superimpos-
ing a grid of horizons and infrastructures on phenomena;
but with chaos or infinity neither applies. The story of the
bird removing at the end of every million years a grain of
sand from a mountain until the mountain is gone suggests a
time unit: less than an instant of eternity has passed. (2)
Yet, despite the impression it makes on Stephen, what the
story really indicates is simply a very long stretch of time.
For as soon as we structure infinity or chaos into fractions,
their definitions are violated. Fortunately this compulsion
of consciousness turns out to be useful in workaday reality
as well as in the realm of reading literary works of art:
experience is always structural grasp.

Furthermore, much of that experience operates by way of
analogy or structural transfer. English-speaking boat
builders, for instance, speak of male and female moulds,
transferring the matching of bodies to the matching of other
physical objects. This works as long as the elements of
the comparison belong to the same ontological region, in
this case materiality; they fail, i.e. produce misconcep-
tions, when the analogy crosses ontological boundaries.
This is precisely what happens when we employ the form-
content trope to the literary work.

The concept of a form containing something may adequately
describe a number of material objects; it cannot do justice
to literary constructs, which are ontologically mixed, in
that their material aspects of print or sound exist simultaneously with their linguistic formations which function as do
definitions, objects of ontological ideality. From the
simple mistake of illegitimate conceptual transfer stems a
whole history of woolly terminology.

As far as I could discover, the first to explore the oris-
mological confusion was Roman Ingarden, who, in 1938,
distinguished between nine different philosophical uses of
form and content, from Aristotle to his own time. (3) There
is first Aristotle's main usage of the distinction between
'morphe' (form) and 'hyle' (matter), whereby form determines matter and matter is always formed; second, Ingarden
gives the distinction drawn in formal ontology between
matter as the sum of properties and form as its function,
designating what matter does; third, there is the distinction
according to a class conception of objects, whereby matter
or content is constituted by the elements or components of

the whole, whereas form is understood as the relationship
between the elements, the structure of components; fourth,
Ingarden finds bemuddling the distinction between how something exists, its form, and what exists, its content, since
there are at least four possible interpretations of how:
(a) its mode of existence (real, ideal, phenomenal), (b) its
mode of cognition (perception, thought), (c) its mode of
occurrence (quietly, beautifully), or (d) its mode of the
presentation of the what (system of signs, selection of
states of affairs, appearance of phenomena, etc.); fifth,
the pair form and content can be differentiated according to
the opposites constancy and mutability, whereby form is
defined as the enduring features of something, with a content
as its mutable side; a variant of this opposition is the
concept of form repeating itself continuously and content as
the unique aggregate of particular characteristics; sixth,
there is the distinction according to the kind of reception
something is given, so that form is that which is sensuously
perceived, whereas content is the mental response to the
perception; seventh, Ingarden sums up the Neo-Kantian
position which defines content as that which is immediately
given ('gegeben') and form as that which content aims at
('aufgegeben'); in this pair, achieved form becomes a new
content for further forms in an infinite process of transformation, where everything is therefore always in phases of
form and content; eighth, content and form can be
distinguished as a contrast between more or less structured
raw material; and, finally, Ingarden lists the distinction
between form as a harmonious Gestalt which is imposed on
qualitative disorganization or unshaped randomness.

I do not wish to follow Ingarden's argument any further;
he goes on to propose his own more sophisticated but as far
as my own position is concerned still dissatisfying usage of
the trope. What is important, though, is that all specific
applications of the two terms by literary critics through the
ages are recognizable variants of Ingarden's nine types.
To do the problem justice, the history of the form–content
dichotomy would have to be studied, laying bare the philosophical grounds on which the distinctions are based and
exploring their detailed applications in each epoch. (4)
But since the focus of this chapter is on showing how com-
plexly confusing the form–content polarity is when applied
to narrative structure, a few summary statements must
suffice here.

Roughly, the form–content metaphor appears to be used in

these three ways: 1, as separable components; 2, as fused into one inseparable unity; and 3, as elements in a dialectic relationship.

1 As separable items, form and content are understood as rhetorical elements facilitating the presentation of a fictive vision, as in Sir Philip Sidney's theory, where delightful poetic diction is capable of persuading the reader to accept and imitate the poet's golden world; (5) or as rhetorical and mimetic aspects of literature, as, for example, in Dryden's 'just and lively image of human nature': (6) by means of the body and soul metaphor, as in Pope's 'Essay on Criticism', where 'In some fair body thus th' informing soul, with spirit feeds, with vigour fills the whole.' (7) The Platonic-Plotinic body-soul analogy is widespread and can still be found much later, in Flaubert's observation that 'form is the flesh of the idea, just as the idea is its soul, its life.' However, Flaubert insists on the inseparability of form and content when he says that they are 'two entities which never exist without each other'. (8) But the clear deduction of a formal metrical element from content as meaning is still defended by George Saintsbury who writes: 'A feeble intellect and taste that cannot perform an easy dichotomy of metre and meaning.... You pour the poison or dishwater out; you keep and marvel at the golden cup.' (9)

A more recent view of form and content as divisible elements is held by the so-called vulgar Marxists. In 'Studies in a Dying Culture' (1938) Christopher Caudwell interprets literature as an artistic restrictive form imposed on the chaotic and dynamic content of history. (10) What this position fails to recognize is that there is no such thing as chaotic dynamic historical material, at least not as far as human consciousness experiences reality; whatever enters literary forms is already structured, is itself form. Terry Eagleton is therefore justified in accusing Caudwell of having simply reversed the bourgeois position that art organizes the raw process of life by claiming that art restricts social reality. (11) Other twentieth-century variants of this view are found among the American New Critics, especially the conception of literary form as a moral imposition of order on matter, a 'precise moral evaluation of human experience', as expounded by Yvor Winters. (12)

2 However, the majority of literary critics has favoured various kinds of fusion of form and content in the literary work of art. Without suggesting to be exhaustive, these

three kinds of coalescence appear to be dominant: 2.1, the notion of an organic unity or whole; 2.2, form as an expression of Geist shaping material; and 2.3, form as the only recognizable aspect subsuming all else.

2.1 August Wilhelm Schlegel's distinction between mechanical form as accidental addition to material and organic form unfolding from within and characterized by an inner mutual determination of the whole and the parts (13) is adopted by Coleridge, who disjoins superficial form, which does not arise from the nature of the material, from organic form as a result of man's secondary imagination and 'esemplastic power' synthesizing the parts into one inseverable unity. (14)

2.2 In Hegel's metaphysical schema art occupies a position where Geist has found expression as material image. Throughout the history of art the relationship between informing spirit and material changes in three vast stages: symbolic art is characterized by a dominance of matter over spirit; in classical art Hegel recognizes a balance between material and forming spirit; while in romantic or modern art Geist dominates material. (15) Hegel's view is certainly interesting in itself, even if we feel sympathy for Bertrand Russell's contumely:

> It is odd that a process which is represented as cosmic should all have taken place on our planet and most of it near the Mediterranean. Nor is there any reason, if reality is timeless, why the later parts of the process should embody higher categories than the earlier parts – unless one were to adopt the blasphemous supposition that the Universe was gradually learning Hegel's philosophy. (16)

But Hegel's idealistic position engages our attention also because it has influenced more recent theoreticians, notably Georg Lukács. In his early 'The Theory of the Novel' (1920) Lukács interprets classical Greek literature as an expression of a total and coherent 'Weltanschauung' as against the modern novel which is the epic of an age without an all-embracing metaphysic; the novel is the formal expression of the hero searching for lost meaning. All literary forms are thus construed as historical spiritual manifestations. (17)

2.3 In spite of his use of the body-soul metaphor Flaubert is also an early radical as far as the formal element in literary texts is concerned.   'What seems to me beautiful,' he says, 'is a book about nothing.' (18)   This is the third form of coalescence of form and content, whereby content is subsumed more and more under the formal umbrella.   From Walter Pater, to whom the 'ideal of all art is ... the point where it is impossible to distinguish form from the substance or matter' and 'art constantly aspires towards the condition of music' to Russian Formalism can be recognized an argument which increasingly favours form as the only legitimate concern of the critic. (19)   Oscar Wilde, whose artist 'gains his inspiration from form, and from form purely', (20) together with Roger Fry or Clive Bell, represents that late phase of 'l'art pour l'art' which strives towards extreme formal purity until art loses its audience for its lack of signified meaning: 'in proportion as art becomes purer, the number of people to whom it appeals gets less.' (21)   For very different reasons, the concept of form is central to Benedetto Croce's 'La Poesia'.   Apart from merely technical aspects there is an inner form ('contenuto') which is the poetic expression of feeling ('sentiento che la poesia ha espresso') and which can be recaptured by comprehensive intuition on the part of the reader ('totale e unica intuizione'). (22)

By far the most analytic discussion of the role of form and content in literature and literary criticism is found among the Russian Formalists.   And although their attitudes to the problem are anything but uniform, ranging from viewing content as non-aesthetic materials versus form as the sum of artistic devices to regarding form as the only analysable aspect, they are epitomized by Victor Shklovskij's comment that the 'Formalist method does not deny the ideology of content of art, but considers the so-called content as one of the aspects of form' (23) and Boris Ejxenbaum's statement that

> The Russian Formalists simultaneously freed themselves from the traditional correlation of 'form-content' and from the conception of form as an outer cover or as a vessel into which a liquid (the content) is poured.   The facts testified that the specificity of art is expressed not in the elements that go to make up a work but in the special way they are used.   By the same token, the concept of 'form' took on a different meaning; it no longer had to be paired with any other concept, it no longer needed correlation. (24)

3 Terry Eagleton sums up well the current Marxist position by saying that 'Marxism sees form and content as dialectically related and yet wants to assert in the end the primacy of content in determining form.' Ideologically structured content gives rise to and enters the literary work, is transformed in the process, and results in an artistic-ideological structure which stands in a dynamic relationship with the enveloping dominant ideology of the period. So Eagleton can say that any change in literary convention signifies a 'transformation in bourgeois ideology'. He also knows that literary forms have a certain degree of autonomy and therefore defines form as a 'complex unity of at least three elements: it is partly shaped by a "relatively autonomous" literary history of forms; it crystallizes out of certain dominant ideological structures'; and 'it embodies a specific set of relations between author and audience.' But that relative autonomy must be qualified by the recognition that the chosen literary forms are 'already ideologically circumscribed', that they are themselves already 'ways of seeing reality'. (25)

Eagleton's tripartition demonstrates a strength and a weakness of Marxist literary theory. It replaces autonomous conceptions of literary works by a view which fruitfully links literature with social reality or, more accurately, our literary interpretations with our interpretations of everyday life. It also allows for a structural view of literary history and hints at the structural relationships responsible for the reader's guided reception of a work. But this last point at the same time reveals a fundamental weakness, apparent also in Lukács's and more blatantly in Lucien Goldmann's approach. How, precisely, the readers of literature must ask, should we construct the work's ideological stance, beginning with the single word or sentence and concluding with the text as a whole? How, exactly, do narrative texts embody specific relations between author and audience? Are they given? Must we infer them? If so, how can we proceed? To be fair, Eagleton's position does not preclude such analysis and I hope that this study will achieve a small part of it.

Leaving aside such general possible pairs of form and content as an artistic form filled with the content of personal and social experience or a signifying form corresponding to a signified content, let us try to answer the question of which specific applications of the dichotomy offer themselves when we read a narrative text.

1 One could argue for a series of corresponding poles of form and content along a ladder starting with what strikes the reader first and finishing with what he concludes at the end of the reading process. Accordingly, the formal aspects of the print shapes could be said to be realized in the reading consciousness as the content of a narrative language which, in turn, serves as the formal aspects of its semantic content which, again, could be comprehended as a collection of formal elements giving rise to an inclusive interpretative abstraction, the story's overall content.

2 Or, one could focus more closely on each rung in the ladder of the act of reading, so that the surface text of linguistic formation is viewed as the work's formal property with distinguishable classes of understanding or content, in terms of : 2.1, the definition of words; 2.2, the reader's cumulative linguistic adquaintance; 2.3, propositional meanings as a result of the transformations of the surface text into a deep structure; or 2.4, the reader's full experiential grasp by way of his total set of typified experience, inter-textual and everyday.

3 Or, the presentational process as codified in the surface text is understood as formal property allowing the reader to compose the following different kinds of content:

3.1 As any other signified item, the presentational process is codified merely schematically, so that the process as schema may be regarded as a partly determined form inviting a number of reader concretizations of the narrative process as more or less appropriate content. When in Faulkner's 'As I Lay Dying' we witness through Darl's consciousness Jewel's attempt at rescuing his mother's coffin from the burning barn, Darl as the centre of the presentational process in this section can be concretized to a considerable degree, and far beyond the information supplied here, with the help of earlier textual clues and concretizations. We know him by the way he has experienced and interpreted the world-out-there so far. Fascinated by violent motion and rigid stasis, he is all consciousness, recording compulsively and in striking imagery the action unfolding before his eyes.

Jewel turns back into the barn. 'Here,' I say; 'Jewel!' I grasp at him; he strikes my hand down. 'You fool,' I say, 'don't you see you can't make it back younder?' The hall-way looks like a searchlight turned into rain. 'Come on,' I say, 'around this way.' When we are

through the gap he begins to run. 'Jewel,' I say,
running. He darts around the corner. When I reach it
he has almost reached the next one, running against the
glare like that figure cut from tin, Pa and Gillespie and
Mack are some distance away, watching the barn, pink
against the darkness where for the time the moonlight
has been vanquished. 'Catch him!' I cry; 'stop him!'
    When I reach the front, he is struggling with Gillespie;
the one lean in underclothes, the other stark naked.
They are like two figures in a Greek frieze, isolated out
of all reality by the red glare. Before I can reach them
he has struck Gillespie to the ground and turned and run
back into the barn. The sound of it has become quite
peaceful now, like the sound of the river did. We watch
through the dissolving proscenium of the doorway as Jewel
runs crouching to the far end of the coffin and stoops to
it. For an instant he looks up and out at us through the
rain of burning hay like a portiere of flaming beads, and
I can see his mouth shape as he calls my name.
    'Jewel!' Dewey Dell cries; 'Jewel!' It seems to me
that I now hear the accumulation of her voice through the
last five minutes, and I hear her scuffling and struggling
as Pa and Mack hold her, screaming 'Jewel! Jewel!'
But he is no longer looking at us. We see his shoulders
strain as he up-ends the coffin and slides it single-
handed from the saw-horses. It looms unbelievably tall,
hiding him: I would not have believed that Addie Bundren
would have needed that much room to lie comfortable in;
for another instant it stands upright while the sparks rain
on it in scattering bursts as though they engendered other
sparks from the contact. Then it topples forward,
gaining momentum, revealing Jewel and the sparks raining
on him too in engendering gusts, so that he appears to be
enclosed in a thin nimbus of fire. Without stopping it
overends and rears again, pauses, then crashes slowly
forward and through the curtain. This time Jewel is
riding upon it, clinging to it, until it crashes down and
flings him forward and clear and Mack leaps forward into
a thin smell of scorching meat and slaps at the widening
crimson-edged holes that bloom like flowers in his
undershirt. (26)

As in Darl's earlier experience of Jewel subduing his
horse, the dictions of dynamic action and frozen images
again characterizes his way of seeing. Words and phrases

like 'strikes ... like a searchlight turned into rain ...
run ... darts ... running against the glare ... struggling
... struck ... run back ... dissolving proscenium of the
doorway ... runs crouching ... scuffling ... struggling ...
strain ... slide ... in scattering bursts ... topples forward
... engendering gusts ... overends ... rears again ...
crashes slowly forward ... riding upon it ... crashes down
... flings him forward ... leaps ... slaps' clash with such
static images as 'like that figure cut from tin ... the barn,
pink against the darkness ... like figures in a Greek frieze
... isolated out of all reality by the red glare ... looms
unbelievably tall ... stands upright'. One may argue, as
Faulkner critics have done, that the different views of 'As
I Lay Dying' result in a 'unitary experience of people in
context' and that Darl, being detached, records most
'objectively' what is happening. (27) But this view puts the
emphasis on what can be objectively seen rather than on how
it is experienced. Instead, I would claim that the section
is above all the way Darl and nobody else subjectively
intends his world. But wherever we put the emphasis, the
reader's concretized realization of Darl as experiencing
personality stands in contrast to the text schema supplied.

3.2 A fairly common way of referring to content is to say
that modality is the formal property of a text, the way in
which a presented world or content is given. As mentioned
above, Roger Fowler accepts this usage, although he does
so unhappily. (28) In this sense, the spatial and temporal
aspects, acts, events, personae, and atmospheric qualities
of the presented world which we appresent in the act of
reading are the content of the formal mode in which the
narrative message is provided, by the spatio-temporal
position of a narrator, his acts, personality and moral
commitment. In Darl's first section we could say therefore
that the reader devises the content of Jewel and his horse
by means of the way in which Darl's reflections guide us.
Both the 'tableau savage in the sun' and the 'earthfree ...
whipping snake-limber' motion of Jewel's horse invite the
reader to project a sequence of powerful visual concretizations.

'Come here, sir,' Jewel says. He moves. Moving that
quick his coat, bunching, tongues swirling like so many
flames. With tossing mane and tail and rolling eye the
horse makes another short curveting rush and stops
again, feet bunched, watching Jewel. Jewel walks

steadily towards him, his hands at his sides. Save for
Jewel's legs they are like two figures carved for a
tableau savage in the sun.

When Jewel can almost touch him, the horse stands on
his hind legs and slashes down at Jewel. Then Jewel is
enclosed by a glittering maze of hooves as by an illusion
of wings; among them, beneath the upreared chest, he
moves with the flashing limberness of a snake. For an
instant before the jerk comes on to his arms he sees his
whole body earth-free, horizontal, whipping snake-limber,
until he finds the horse's nostrils and touches earth
again. Then they are rigid, motionless, terrific, the
horse back-thrust on stiffened, quivering legs, with
lowered head; Jewel with dug heels, shutting off the
horse's wind with one hand, with the other patting the
horse's neck in short strokes myriad and caressing,
cursing the horse with obscene ferocity.

They stand in rigid terrific hiatus, the horse trembling
and groaning. Then Jewel is on the horse's back. He
flows upward in a stooping swirl like the lash of a whip,
his body in mid-air shaped to the horse. For another
moment the horse stands spraddled, with lowered head,
before it bursts into motion. They descend the hill in a
series of spine-jolting jumps, Jewel high, leech-like on
the withers, to the fence where the horse bunches to a
scuttering halt again.

'Well,' Jewel says, 'you can quit now, if you got a-
plenty.' (29)

3.3 A narrative's work ideology has been defined as a
synthesis of the interpretative abstractions drawn from both
the presentational process and the presented world. The
fact that deductions from the presentational process play at
least as significant a role in this synthesis as those
gathered from the presented world is not always obvious in
traditional narrative; in 'As I Lay Dying' it is conspicuous.
Whichever the reader may construct as dominant, process
or world, one could make a case for regarding the presentational process as a sum of formal aspects allowing process
ideology to be inferred as a partial content. This could be
applied, first, to the individual sections of 'As I Lay Dying',
second, to the sum of one fictional persona's sections, and
third, to the entire process as a complex mosaic of ways of
seeing.

In his concluding section, Darl presents himself as a

split personality; he refers to himself at the same time as
'Darl' or 'he', to whom things happen, as 'I' or observing
consciousness, and as 'you' in his questions addressed to
himself, while in the final paragraph Darl experiences himself as being one with the rest of the family forever severed
from the mindless and foaming body, 'our brother'.

> Darl has gone to Jackson. They put him on the train,
> laughing, down the long car laughing, the heads turning
> like the heads of owls when he passed. 'What are you
> laughing at?' I said. Darl is our brother, our brother
> Darl. Our brother Darl in a cage in Jackson where, his
> grimed hands lying light in the quiet interstices, looking
> out he foams. 'Yes yes yes yes yes yes yes yes.' (30)

Having read the last one of Darl's sections, as well as
remembering the references to Darl in other passages, we
are now in a position to weave not only the fabric of a
fictive personality, but we are also able to resolve, more
tentatively, a quasi-authorial philosophical stance in
relation to Darl. When we describe Darl as a personal
medium, we do not merely repeat his acts of consciousness,
but say, for example, that as a result of his way of seeing
he cannot share the commitments of the other members of the
family, that his fascinations with the phenomenal world
prevent him from becoming involved in the affairs of the
everyday world, except for one desperate act, that he is
both privileged and handicapped by the self-sufficiency of
his consciousness and therefore is not a being-in-the-world,
that he cannot be committed even to himself and that he does
not exist in the sense in which the others do, that the price
he must pay for his clairvoyance is insanity, or that his
frantically affirmed physical separation from his family is
the outward reflection of his mental-moral segregation
throughout the novel.
  Although such observations, and more subtly perceptive
ones to be sure, do add up first of all to the reader's sense
of characterization, they also form a set of inferences
which, together with our abstractions made from the other
modes of experiencing throughout the book, impel us to
formulate such overarching thematic issues as, for instance,
man's attempt at understanding death as a permanently
present quality, as ending and renewal, the absurd acciden-
tality of the universe, the meaning of madness, the linguistic
control of our experience of reality, or the archetypal

relationships and ritual implications of the journey, water, fire, air, earth, sex, death, or marriage. Such inferences are as legitimate an aspect of the reading process, and therefore of the process of making sense of the narrative text, as a linguistic analysis of the various speech acts. The point is that, on the one hand, they are legitimate formulations by the reader of existing structural inter-dependencies rooted in the text, on the other, they stand in a contrasting relationship to the overall presentational process and therefore suggest yet another application of the form–content trope: the formal aspect of the entire signified presentational process versus the abstractable content of its philosophical meaning.
Or

4 The presented world in its temporal and spatial aspects, with its acts, events, personae, or atmospheric qualities is grasped as the central formal property, making possible the establishment of a number of different kinds of content in the act of reading.

4.1 There is first the presented world as linguistic schema with its undetermined areas to be concretized by the reader. This construction relies on three bodies of knowledge: first, our typified experience of the everyday world (codified experience and linguistic competence); second, our typifications of literary experience, or the reader's inter–textual competence; and, third, our cumulative grasp of the narrative text as we read. In criticism, we tend to take the first two kinds of knowledge for granted, and so pretend that their effects are not crucial. In fact, it is the reader's everyday experience, its ideological meaning and his sense of inter–textuality which are responsible for the radical changes in critical opinion during different epochs and in different societies. In the act of reading, this extrinsic knowledge is employed intuitively to produce an historically unique concretization of a text schema.

But the curiousest thing was Dewey Dell. It surprised me. I see all the while how folks could say he was queer, but that was the very reason couldn't nobody hold it personal. It was like he was outside of it too, same as you, and getting mad at it would be kind of like getting mad at a mud-puddle that splashed you when you stepped in it. And then I always kind of had a idea that him and Dewey Dell kind of knowed things betwixt them. If I'd 'a' said it was ere a one of us she liked better than ere a

other, I'd 'a' said it was Darl. But when we got it filled
and covered and drove out the gate and turned into the
lane where them fellows was waiting, when they come out
and come on him and he jerked back, it was Dewey Dell
that was on him before even Jewel could get at him. And
then I believed I knowed how Gillespie knowed about his
barn taken fire.

She hadn't said a word, hadn't even looked at him, but
when them fellows told him what they wanted and that they
had come to get him and he throwed back, she jumped on
him like a wild cat so that one of the fellows had to quit
and hold her and her scratching and clawing at him like a
wild cat, while the other one and pa and Jewel throwed
Darl down and held him lying on his back, looking up at
me.

The two paragraphs occur towards the end of the
novel, (31) so that the reader is able to bring to them a
considerable amount of accumulated textual information as
well as his concretizations of it made so far. It is above
all the fact that Darl has set fire to the barn which infuriates
Dewey Dell; he almost succeeded in foiling her prospects of
an abortion in Jefferson. But there are other latent feelings which mingle with her central anxiety to explode in that
final rage. By comparison, she appears much less agitated
at the end of the novel when she realizes she has been
cheated by the young chemist and that for her the journey
was indeed a failure: '"It ain't going to work," she says.
"That son of a bitch."' Two things, it seems, are responsible for the peculiarly intense relationship between brother
and sister: her realization of his clairvoyance and
especially his knowledge of her state as well as her resentment of the sexual image she feels she is to him.

And I did not think that Darl would, that sits at the table
with his eyes gone further than the food and the lamp ...

... and then I saw Darl and he knew. He said he knew
without the words like he told me that ma is going to die
without words.

The land runs out of Darl's eyes; they swim to pinpoints.
They begin at my feet and rise along my body to my face,
and then my dress is gone: I sit naked on the seat above
the unhurrying mules, above the travail.

> She sets the basket into the wagon and climbs in, her leg
> coming long from beneath her tightening dress: that lever
> which moves the world; one of that caliper which
> measures the length and breadth of life.

> Squatting, Dewey Dell's wet dress shapes for the dead
> eyes of three blind men those mammalian ludicrosities
> which are the horizons and the valleys of the earth. (32)

Darl on the ground is merely the focal point for the
release of Dewey Dell's incaged anxieties; at this moment
the desperate fears of a sensuous young trapped woman
erupt.   What is significant is that the reader must have
concretized her 'personality' in much more detail than can
be described here in order to lend full meaning to those two
paragraphs.

4.2 There is also a structural relationship between the
presented world and the presentational process in terms of
which the former is what the reader is able to construct
first, while the latter is a secondary concretization.   As
Roman Jakobson has pointed out, the relationship is the
reverse from the position of the sender of the message. (33)

> It was a fact.   It made him look a foot taller, kind of
> holding his head up, hangdog and proud too, and then we
> see her behind him, carrying the other grip - a kind of
> duck-shaped woman all dressed up, with them kind of
> hard-looking pop eyes like she was daring ere a man to
> say nothing.   And there we set watching them, with
> Dewey Dell's and Vardaman's mouth half open and half-et
> bananas in their hands and her coming around from behind
> pa, looking at us like she dared ere a man.   And then I
> see that the grip she was carrying was one of them little
> graphophones.   It was for a fact, all shut up as pretty
> as a picture, and every time a new record would come
> from the mail order and us setting in the house in the
> winter, listening to it, I would think what a shame Darl
> couldn't be to enjoy it too.   But it is better so for him.
> This world is not his world; this life his life. (34)

In isolation, the first part of the paragraph (up to 'she
dared ere a man') obstructs rather than permits the
construction of the mediating consciousness.   Before we
can infer any narrating personality, we must first
concretize the spatio-temporal and atmospheric aspects of

the presented world. Because of this structural relationship between something which is textually given and something which is a function of that given, which merely
exists as secondary inference or secondary concretization,
we could refer in this case to the presented world as the
formal element guiding the reader's fabrication of its
content, the presentational process. Conversely, the
second part of the paragraph, foregrounding as it does
Cash's consciousness with its observation ('I see'), projections ('would come ... I would think') and judgments ('But
it is better so for him.') requires the opposite reading
strategy, from realizing Cash's mediating personality to
the secondary realm of concretization, that of the fragmentary presented world as it appears through Cash's mind.

4.3 Antithetically to 3.3, the presented world of a narrative text could be regarded as the formal qualities which
permit or invite a partial ideology to be deduced as their
content. In the case of 'As I Lay Dying', where the
presentational process is foregrounded, this means to
construct first a presented world, the journey with its
events and acts, the Bundren family and their acquaintances,
and the collective world view they impart, in order then to
formulate a set of umbrella statements synthesizing that
world's ideological stance. We may not agree that this
would be a useful way of defining form and content. What
is important, though, is that such a summary abstraction is
necessary because it turns out not to be identical with what
we must assume to be the novel's work ideology. While the
ideology of the presented world has to be defined in terms
of the personae's idiosyncrasies, personal aspirations and
gratifications, material poverty, flaming human relationships, or peasant stubbornness, the novel's overall moral,
philosophical and ideological commitment subsumes these
characteristics under a more encompassing thematic
vision.

5 On a fifth theory, the tight structural relationship
between presentational process and presented world and
their dynamic interaction in the reading consciousness may
be understood as a narrative's form, with its aesthetic-
ideological position as its content. In the act of reading,
this inter-dependence can be divided into two stages: 5.1,
the concretizing transformation of the textual schema; and
5.2, the abstracting transformation of that concretization
into the narrative's meaning.

5.1 The fifteen consciousnesses and the fictive personal-

ities which are codified in the text of 'As I Lay Dying' are
personae both of the presentational process and the presented world. Darl, for example, is both viewing and viewed,
experiencing and experienced persona; or, technically
speaking, he represents both the noetic and noematic
aspects of the text. To this schematic formal interdependence of process and world could be juxtaposed the realized
content of a concretized double vision of seeing and being
in the reading consciousness.

5.2 This compound concretization may in the second stage
be considered as the formal and necessary condition for the
establishment of an encompassing work ideology, the
fabrication of which is always a retrospective exercise:
the reading dimension has contracted towards the monothetic experience of grasping the whole at the end of the novel.
In 'As I Lay Dying', gauging a likely authorial stance is
difficult for two reasons: first, because apart from selection and arrangements of parts, there is no quasi-authorial
guidance; second, traditional criticism, supported by some
structuralists, has been interested predominantly in the
presented world with its action sequences and themes. But
adequate thematic questions can be put only from a position
somewhat removed.

In narrative we should comprehend work ideology as the
product of the reciprocal action of presentational process
and presented world in the reading consciousness. Applied
to 'As I Lay Dying', what is being produced or, more
accurately, what is being constructed in the reading
consciousness is a striking contrast. On the one hand,
there is a largely down-to-earth rural reality with death,
pregnancy, burial, new teeth, a horse, cows, mules,
wagons and barns, peasant obstinacy and poverty, but also
questions about the reality of language, about the meaning
of life and death, about sanity and madness. On the other
hand, there is the highly sophisticated and complex
authorial handling of the presentational process; a technique has been employed which in its methodology as well
as philosophical message could appropriately be described
as phenomenological.

As in Husserl's view of human consciousness, there is
neither any objective nor supreme subjective guidance.
All that we are provided with is fifteen distinct consciousnesses with fifteen different worlds. As a result, there is
no 'unitary experience' as the critic with a platonic
principle of harmony in mind has us see it; (35) there is

merely an overlap of subjective experiences suggestive of
a consensus. But the consensus is wholly superficial.
Let me give three examples: first, language, the inter-
subjective tool par excellence, separates the members of
the Bundren family rather than unites them. Anse is a
stranger to Addie because of his naive dependence on words;
Addie resents language because of its power over man's
actions; Jewel, more even than his mother, despises words;
Darl finds self-sufficiency in conceptualization, so that
language sets him apart from physical reality and ultimately
from society and himself; Vardaman's symbolic usage of
words is, on the whole, as isolated as Cash's awkward but
central and balanced verbal assessment of what is happening. Language, to be sure, does little to produce a
unifying experience.

Second, the act of getting rid of Darl appears to rest on
mutual understanding, at least between Anse, Jewel, Dewey
Dell, and Cash. But this is not so. For Anse it means
that he does not have to pay for the barn, for Jewel it means
releasing his hatred against a brother who tried to stop the
journey to which Jewel is deeply committed, for Dewey Dell
it is getting rid of a consciousness which she fears as well
as taking revenge for Darl's attempt at ruining her chances
of obtaining the abortion, while for Cash it is a just
necessity and the best solution for a mentally sick brother.

Third, the journey itself, the central unifying motif,
merely underlines how much at variance, how humanly
egotistical and incongruous the reasons are for which the
family is able to make a concerted effort: affection, false
teeth, commitment to a good job, a fair, an abortion. As
a result almost the whole spectrum of human attitudes is
there, but certainly no agreement. There cannot be anything but superficial consensus, because people's reality
is identical with the way they experience themselves, the
others, and the world-out-there. That society functions
at all, the novel encourages us to conclude, is the result of
an often fortuitous overlap of human aspirations.

As in few other novels, the reader of 'As I Lay Dying'
must rely on his concretizing faculties in the fabrication
of his double vision of process and world. It is not true
that some characters are 'fully realized' (e.g., Anse),
while others remain an enigma (Addie). These are
Dickensian criteria applied to a non-Dickensian novel. (36)
Structurally, all personae are reduced to a number of
responses in their own stream of consciousness and those

of other personae. As a result, they are all highly
schematic. But the point is that Faulkner's emphasis is on
the codification of consciousness, so that we know Darl
best because we witness his consciousness most frequently.
Jewel's mastery of his horse is less a realistic image chain
of rider and horse than an exercise in seeing, Darl's way
of seeing, reminiscent of painting, freeze frame montage,
graphic design, and poetic vision. And although Cash is
fairly well established as a persona in the course of the
developing action, it is his role as experiencing and interpreting consciousness in the concluding sections which the
reader accepts as the balanced view. Likewise, Addie's
contemplation of the role of language and the meaning of her
life and death is as 'complete' a significatum as the perspective of any of the other personae. It is not the reader's
business to demand fullness of description or realism, but
to realize the structural relationships allowed for by the
text.

But 'As I Lay Dying' has an affinity with phenomenology
also in a more technical sense; in many respects it is an
exercise in phenomenological description. At the same
time that very technique could be regarded as the novel's
central message. To give the reader some assistance
Faulkner has named the many adumbrational aspects which
constitute the novel. Without question, the accumulation of
aspects is part of any act of reading; but 'As I Lay Dying'
makes the additional demands on the reader of associating
the embrangled aspects in a quasi-realistic, spatio-temporal
matrix and thematic order. Further, in a macrostructural
sense, we could conceive of the multiple consciousnesses as
the noetic aspects of the book (e.g., Darl as experiencing
consciousness) with a series of corresponding 'noemata'
(e.g., Darl as viewed by the others). Also, the novel
urges the reader to perform the following distinct acts of
consciousness: monothetic or one-rayed experience (e.g.,
the reader's experience of Vardaman's symbolic equation of
mother and fish), polythetic acts of consciousness (e.g.,
the reader's step-by-step concretization of the different
perspectives), and synthetic acts (e.g., the reader's
synthesis of the multiple views into one highly interdependent structure).

One may impugn the above list of structural relationships
suggestive of a series of form-content dichotomies on the
ground that 'As I Lay Dying' is an extreme illustration of
narrative structure. According to our definition this is

not so. The novel perfectly meets the condition of dynamic
interaction of presentational process and presented world,
both with their aspects of space, time, personae, acts and
events, atmospheric qualities and inferrable philosophical
stance; except that process and world are wholly internalized and fragmented. In first-person central narrative
the same structural relationships as catalogued can be
observed, save that there is always a temporal gap, however small, between viewing narrator and experiencing
character. As 'Moll Flanders' illustrates, the crucial
addition is memory, but, and this is important, ideologically
charged and interpreting memory. Moll's adventures and
Moll the young woman are not simply reflected, but inter-
pretatively adjusted to fit the old Moll's social role. We do
not know what the young Moll is like, except as a part of the
old narrator's ideological design. This makes the distinction between experiencing and narrating selves problematical. (37) The term suggests a quasi-objective presentation which the reader is able to reconstruct. But in fact,
the experiencing self never exists as a separate entity; it
is always the experiencing-self-as-interpreted-by-a-
narrating-self. Paradoxically, only when the two selves
collapse into one spatio-temporal unity, as is the case in
'As I Lay Dying', is the distinction accurate; what is
experienced about self and others is at the same time handed
on (though not narrated in a narrow sense) to the reader
without retrospective adjustments. Apart from this, the
formal relationships of process and world in first-person
narrative principally allow the same applications of the
form-content trope as does 'As I Lay Dying'.

Authorial narrative, third-person as well as first-person,
is defined by the horizontal separation of the presentational
process from the presented world. When, in addition,
there is also omniscience, the separation becomes an
ontological distinction: the narrating persona with its
suspension of physical laws is different in kind and mode of
existence from the personae of the presented world. In
this case the reader must pay special attention to the
possible technical-thematic value of the oscillation between
what Boris Uspensky calls the inside and outside perspective. (38) But in all authorial narrative our structural
contrasts as listed can be discovered.

A second objection to our catalogue could be to query
whether these structural relations are the same at each
rung of a ladder of fictionality, from the novelistic documen-

tary to realistic fiction, mythic-symbolic, allegorical, and
fantasy narrative. Except for the following qualifications,
the answer should be yes. In the novelistic documentary
our concretizing activity is radically channelled, since both
process and world have source objects in the world-out-
there. Strictly speaking, any adequate concretization
would have to be testable against factual evidence. At the
level of presentational process and presented world, form
and content - whichever structural relationships they are to
stand for - therefore pre-exist any reader response. In
practice, there is no novelistic documentary in the strict
sense of its definition. Even in as highly documentable a
narrative as 'In Cold Blood' fiction intrudes through the
handling of the presentational process. And as far as this
is the case, the book invites the response of a reader of
realistic narrative.

Earlier, we defined mythic-symbolic narrative as texts
in which there are secondary signifieds urging the reader
to concretize additional formal patterns over and above the
presented world, as, for example, the concentric arrangement of spatial features into thematic areas and circular
thresholds in 'Nostromo'. This kind of additional codification could again be seen as formal properties allowing a
mythic-symbolic content to be realized or, conversely, as
textual content giving rise to further thematically charged
formations in the reading consciousness.

In strictly allegorical narrative the relationship of
process and world is modified by allegorical naming with its
double aspect of abstract concept and reference to a quasi-
physical reality (e.g., Valley of Despond), so that allegorical coding could be regarded as an additional formal element
for the reader's construction of a content. Finally, fantasy
narrative, which we argued was defined above all by the
distorted eidetic relations between signified items, does not
appear to require any fundamental adjustment of our list of
structural opposites either. Both the presentation of
strange items themselves, as in the poem Jabberwocky, for
example, and the replacement of typical bonds between
items of the presented world by atypical ones prevent the
reading consciousness from responding directly by means
of typifications of the everyday world. Instead, the reader
relies on their negation and his inter-textual experience.
As a result, process and world, as well as their corresponding pairs of form and content, in, for instance, Kafka's
A Country Doctor, are constructed by the reader not

altogether differently, but merely less easily or, more precisely, with greater uneasiness.

To conclude, if we were to take the form–content metaphor seriously, i.e. if we tested it against the actual structural relations which exist whenever narrative texts are read, their application would turn out to be a laborious exercise. Also, in order to avoid any misunderstanding, as the student of literature should demand, the critic would have to justify why his form–content dichotomy signifies only one of the many possible structural contrasts – a cumbersome critical task. At the same time, those structural inter-dependencies can quite adequately be defined without reference to the form–content metaphor. I would suggest therefore, as I did in the first chapter, to drop the twins from the critical discussion of narrative.

Chapter 11

Translating narrative

To satisfy a wide range of demands, any theory of translation must be able to deal with communication in general.
On the one hand, it must be, as George Steiner says, 'an
intentionally sharpened, hermeneutically oriented way of
designating a working model of all meaningful exchanges, of
the totality of semantic communication' which 'argues the
fact that all procedures of expressive articulation and
interpretative reception are translational, whether intra-
or interlingual.' (1) On the other hand, translation theory
must have its areas of narrow precision which are able to
cater for the specific needs of, for instance, the translation of narrative. If we accept as a comprehensive framework a system of signs as stipulated by Saussure or
Peirce, we must ask how, for example in narrative texts,
the signifiers of one language are to be replaced by the
signifiers of another.

   Although the majority of traditional 'theories' of translation address themselves to poetic texts, they are often
phrased generally enough for us to ask how they can be
applied also to the structural aspects of narrative. That
most of these theories do not stand up very well to careful
structural scrutiny has to do with the fact that they are not
based on a theory either of the literary work or of language.
Certainly, the largely metaphoric use of triads as typologies of translation is too loose to suggest fruitful linguistic
tools. Such types of translation as 'metaphrase ... paraphrase ... imitation' (Dryden), 'grammatical ... modified
... mythical' (Novalis), 'paraphrase ... informative ...
emigration of foreign author' (Schleiermacher), 'informative ... adaptation, parodistic ... reproduction' (Goethe),
'formless ... in foreign style ... formal' (Mommsen), or

'literal ... idiomatic ... paraphrasical' (Protasio Maymi)
all tell us about the general results which certain attitudes
towards the translation of texts tend to produce. (2)   The
triads fail to indicate the demands which linguistic
constructs are likely to make on the translator and what
they allow him to do.

A more recent and far more useful tripartite typology is
by Roman Jakobson.   Resting as it does on an analysis of
the properties of language and the operational features of
messages, it distinguishes three kinds of translation:

> (1) Intralingual translation or rewording is an interpre-
> tation of verbal signs by means of other signs of the same
> language.   (2) Interlingual translation or translation
> proper is an interpretation of verbal signs by means of
> signs of some other language.   (3) Intersemiotic transla-
> tion or transmutation is an interpretation of verbal signs
> by means of signs of nonverbal sign systems. (3)

Jakobson's concept of translation meets two requirements:
that it relate to a larger theory of communicative transfer
and that it allow for the analysis of problems of translation
rooted in the specific linguistic arrangements of literary,
as, for instance, narrative texts.   A few other aspects of
translation, though, remain problematical.   There is the
historical dimension with, for instance, the question of when
a language is still the same language, or the fact that
Jakobson's typology is based on a specific definition of
'understanding' and 'interpretation'.   The translation into
modern Spanish of 'Don Quixote' is not so much a modern
translation as "Don Quixote"—translated-in-1978', just as
the 'intersemiotic translation or transmutation' of Fitz-
gerald's 'The Great Gatsby' into a movie with Robert
Redford is the novel's filmic version of 1974 rather than
'The Great Gatsby Movie' recapturing a past age.   The
point is neatly made by Jorge Luis Borges in his story
Pierre Menard, Author of the 'Quixote'.

> It is a revelation to compare Menard's Don Quixote with
> Cervantes's.   The latter, for example, wrote (part one,
> chapter nine):
>   ... truth, whose mother is history, rival of time,
> depository of deeds, witness of the past, exemplar and
> adviser to the present, and the future's counsellor.
>   Written in the seventeenth century, written by the 'lay

genius' Cervantes, this enumeration is a mere rhetorical
praise of history.   Menard, on the other [sic] , writes:
  ... truth, whose mother is history, rival of time,
depository of deeds, witness of the past, exemplar and
adviser to the present, and the future's counsellor.
  History, the mother of truth: the idea is astounding.
Menard, a contemporary of William James, does not
define history as an inquiry into reality but as its origin.
Historical truth, for him, is not what has happened; it is
what we judge to have happened.   The final phrases –
exemplar and adviser to the present, and the future's
counsellor – are brazenly pragmatic.
  The contrast in style is also vivid.   The archaic style
of Menard – quite foreign, after all – suffers from a
certain affectation.   Not so that of his forerunner, who
handles with ease the current Spanish of his time. (4)

Persuasive and useful as Jakobson's distinctions are,
they assume a concept of 'interpreting' and 'understanding'
which we should not accept without scrutiny.   Let me quote
his critique of an observation made by Bertrand Russell.
Russell claims that 'no one can understand the word
"cheese" unless he has a non-linguistic acquaintance with
cheese.' (5)   Jakobson's answer is that 'no one can understand the word "cheese" unless he has an acquaintance with
the meaning assigned to this word in the lexical code of
English.'   The following is a more precise definition of
Jakobson's concept of 'understanding':

  Any representative of a cheese-less culinary culture will
  understand the English word 'cheese' if he is aware that
  in this language it means 'food made of pressed curds'
  and if he has at least a linguistic acquaintance with
  'curds'.   We never consumed ambrosia or nectar and
  have only a linguistic acquaintance with the words
  'ambrosia', 'nectar', and 'gods' – the name of their
  mythical users; nonetheless we understand these words
  and know in what context each of them may be used. (6)

Jakobson's argument is valid as far as it goes.   But it
does not go far enough.   What Jakobson conceals is that
Russell may have had a different sense of understanding in
mind.   For if we look more closely at Russell's statement,
we realize that at least three different kinds of understanding are involved.   There are (a) the purely conceptual or

analytical grasp of a term, relying on our mastery of its
definition (cheese is food made of pressed curds); (b) the
cumulative linguistic understanding of a term as a result of
multiple reading experience in a variety of contexts
(ambrosia and nectar as they recur in the mythologies of
classical antiquity); and (c) our experiential understanding
in addition to definition and cumulative linguistic acquaintance (the term cheese as activated in the reading consciousness of a gourmet).

Perhaps Russell should have said that only someone who,
in addition to knowing the definition of cheese and having a
cumulative linguistic grasp of the term, has had a non-
linguistic acquaintance with cheese can understand the
word more profoundly or at more levels than someone without such experience. In the linguistic traffic of workaday
life as well as of literary production all three senses of
'understanding' are active. Function words and such cases
as 'ambrosia' or 'nectar' are understood in terms of sense
(a) and sense (b); most other language items are capable of
being grasped also in sense (c) of understanding. To
negate that the three senses interact significantly in the
reception of literary constructs would be illegitimately
restrictive. And it is this third sense of understanding
which poses such stubborn problems to the translator.

It may seem that I have merely been rephrasing the
distinction between denotation and connotation. But this
is not the case. By using common linguistic criteria one
can show that the distinctions between the three kinds of
understanding, on the one hand, and between denotation and
connotation, on the other, operate at different planes. If
we define the denotation of a word as its lexical meaning
or, more precisely, syntagmatically as a definite meaning
determined by the word's relationship with its immediate
linguistic context, then connotation should be understood as
an indefinite range of associations on a paradigmatic axis,
radiating from one linguistic item with merely a loose
relationship to its linguistic context.

Often the pragmatic sending and reception of linguistic
messages in daily life allows us to restrict our understanding to Jakobson's use of the term. When we read literary
works of art, our typified experiential understanding comes
into operation in addition to a purely analytic or cumulative
linguistic grasp of language. But what is important here
is the fact that this process of concretization can be either
denotative or connotative, or both. The denotative aspect

of concretization is simply a more precise understanding of a term, a more detailed conceptual grasp far beyond the definition given in a dictionary. The term 'late Gothic' can be concretized denotatively by a reader closely acquainted with descriptions and objects characterized by the term. The connotative side of concretization lends the term, however precisely understood, a horizonal character of additional associative meanings. Concretization in both senses may lead to visualization, but may also remain restricted to ever more detailed conceptualization, resulting in a fine linguistic mesh by means of which the reader makes sense of the more schematic construct of the literary text.

Although George Steiner prefers a wide hermeneutic concept of translation to interlingual translation involving two or more languages, (7) he has also defined 'all literature - oral or written, lyric or prosaic, archaic or modern - as language in a condition of special use'. (8) Applied to the narrower field of narrative texts this means that the translator must be aware of the special use to which language is put when stories are told. The accurate but for our purpose still too general definition of translation as 'the replacement of textual material in one language (SL)/ Source Language/ by equivalent textual material in another language (TL) /Target Language/' leaves the fundamental question unanswered as to what precisely is involved in finding, for instance, the equivalent textual material in another language for 'Humboldt's Gift'. (9) I will try, from the position of the descriptive definition of narrative given so far, to split up the problem of translating narrative texts into a number of separate issues and in so doing make a few practical suggestions.

Contrary to functional linguistic constructs which are fully designed to operate as pragmatic messages, i.e. whose deep structure and propositional meanings are more important than their surface texts, fictional narrative texts (as well as the special case of the novelistic documentary), in addition to the reader's grasp of their propositional meanings, rely on the full aesthetic realization in the reading process of all their aspects, from print to large-scale interpretative inferences. It is insignificant within the context of everyday life whether we pay attention to the fact that the notice 'Office over there' is written in Roman or Gothic, in black or red letters, so long as the immediate message is understood. The very same phrase in the context of a cartoon or story requires and, in adequate reading, receives a different response. We are called upon to construct the meaning of the words in all their adumbrational aspects, one by one, from typographic appearance to summary interpretative abstraction, and all of them together in their total aesthetic polyphony.

If we then reaffirm our concept of narrative as stratified, whereby the strata of print and linguistic formation are followed by a double stratum of presentational process and presented world, which in turn invites the realization, on the part of the reader, of an overall aesthetic ideological inference, we must claim that any adequate translation of narrative text must respond to and recreate that basic structure. Let me take each stratum in turn.

To translate a narrative text at the level of print is, strictly speaking, impossible. However, if source and target languages are closely related, a reasonable likeness can be achieved. The greater their graphological differences, the more acute will be the problem of graphological transfer. That translation at this level is none the less important is not substantiated merely by mentioning concrete poetry and its equivalent features in narrative texts. The diary entries, for example, at the end of Joyce's 'A Portrait of the Artist as a Young Man' through the shape of print alone impart a sense of restlessness, of a few last things to be observed, listed, or thrown away, as if they were items to be packed or left behind. Since narrative, unlike much concrete poetry, does not have its centre of meaning in its typographic appearance, fidelity should here be sacrificed if a close adherence to the original typographic image endangers the translation at other levels.

It is not sufficient, at the stratum of linguistic, or the surface text, to say that 'translation is an operation performed on languages: a process of substituting a text in one language for a text in another'. (10) In accordance with our definition of narrative, translation at this level must attempt to fulfil at least two requirements: (a) that both surface texts can be said to have the same deep structure, and (b) that they share the same structure of lacunae of indeterminacy. If, in addition, the linguistic shape, the way the words follow one another, can be imitated in the target language, so much the better. But, again, the imitation of syntactic arrangement should be sacrificed if it impedes requirements (a) and (b).

Since the linguistic stratum is a signifying structure

which carries two sets of signifieds, the signified process
and the signified world, its translation must be checked in
the third, double stratum as to whether it guarantees the
reader's construction of an adequate equivalent double
vision of world and process. And since, as has been
pointed out repeatedly, the dynamic interaction between
presented world and presentational process is vital to
narrative, it is here that a translation which pays attention
only to generalized deep structure and its abbreviating
propositional meaning, may be inadequate. Theodore
Savory, I think, commits this error when he says that
'"my mother" can be perfectly translated by any of the three
alternatives ... "ma mère", "meine Mutter", "mi
madre".' (11) This, certainly, is the best we can do if we
look at the words in isolation. But it should also be
obvious that the experiential understanding differs considerably if we take into consideration the readers of the
various language groups. Apart from the narrow signification of the biological child-mother relationship, 'mi
madre' means something quite different from 'my mother', as
far as the presented image with its surrounding cluster of
values as well as the narrator's stance to his statement are
concerned. No translation can ever fully solve this
problem. However, the translator who is acutely aware of
it will be able to control the linguistic context in such a way
that the Englishness of 'my mother' is reinforced and the
Spanishness of 'mi madre' undermined.

Expressed in terms of lacunae of indeterminacy this means
that the translator must seek to create a target text the
schematic nature of which invites increasingly concretizations more adequate to the English understanding of the
word than to the Spanish value system, or vice versa. The
same difficulties, though less noticeable and therefore more
deceptive, arise in the translation of historical texts
within the 'same' tongue. This is most obviously true when
we translate words which still look the same but have
changed their denotative as well as connotative meanings.

Since signified process and signified world are intricately
interlinked in the signifying structure of the surface text,
the translator will always reproduce both in some way or
other. It is crucial, however, that both are adequately
reproduced. The exception, of course, is pure process
marking, passages in which the presentational process is
foregrounded to a degree which does not allow the construction of a presented world. Then the reader's attention is

fully focused on the construction of the quasi-physical,
emotional, and ideological position of the narrator; and,
likewise, for the translator there is nothing else to
translate.

> Al otro, a Borges, es a quien le ocurren las cosas.   Yo
> camino por Buenos Aires y me demoro, acaso ya
> mécanicamente, para mirar el arco de un zaguán y la
> puerta cancel; de Borges tengo noticias por el correo y
> veo su nombre en una terna de profesores o en un
> diccionario biográfico.   Me gustan los relojes de arena,
> los mapas, la tipografia del siglo XVIII, el sabor del
> café y la prosa de Stevenson; el otro comparte esas
> preferencias, pero de un modo vanidoso que las convierte
> en atributos de un actor. (Jorge Luis Borges, 'Borges y
> yo')

> The other one, the one called Borges, is the one things
> happen to.   I walk through the streets of Buenos Aires
> and stop for a moment, perhaps mechanically now, to
> look at the arch of an entrance hall and the grillwork on
> the gate; I know of Borges from the mail and see his
> name on a list of professors or in a biographical
> dictionary.   I like hourglasses, maps, eighteenth-
> century typography, the taste of coffee and the prose of
> Stevenson; he shares these preferences, but in a vain
> way that turns them into the attributes of an actor.
> ('Borges and I') (12)

But it is when the presentational process is submerged
that the translator must be sensitive to its reconstruction.
Take as an example the Penguin modern English translation
of the opening of 'Sir Gawain and the Green Knight', where
the translator has foregrounded the presentational process
by means of parentheses, a feature not found in the original.
I suggest that this translator's introduction of an 'aside', a
turning to the reader to provide information in addition to
the presented world, is an illegitimate shift of narrative
meaning.

> Siþen þe sege and þe assaut watȝ sesed at
> Troye, þe borg brittened and brent to
> brondeȝ and askeȝ, þe tulk þat þe trammes of
> tresoun þer wrogt
> Watz tried for his tricherie, þe trewest
> on erthe:

...
...

(The treacherous trickster whose treasons there
flourished was famed afar for malfeasance, falsehoods
unrivalled)

or
...
...
The warrior who wove there the web of his treachery
Tried was for treason, the truest on earth. (13)

If the relationship between presentational process and
presented world is radically altered, an altogether
different kind of story telling and a completely different
story are the result. As an illustration, let me juxtapose
to an oral, recorded narrative an English literary attempt
at translating and at the same time 'civilizing' Australian
Aboriginal story material.

[Tunnel Creek] was once the hiding-place, and the last-
ditch stand, of Sandemara, also called Pigeon. In one
way, Pigeon was a kind of black William Wallace. He
tried to drive the white invader from the land.
   Pigeon was a 'black-tracker' in the employ of the
Western Australian police in the 'nineties of the last
century. On patrol with Constable Richardson he
personally captured the notorious Ellemara, a tribal
outlaw and cattle spearer of the Kimberleys. But before
Pigeon got Ellemara back to Richardson's camp, the
captive had persuaded him that black should not be in
league with white, and that Pigeon should join Ellemara
in a struggle against all Europeans. That night,
Pigeon, and another tracker, Captain, murdered the
sleeping Richardson. They liberated the prisoners and
took to the bush with the guns and ammunition that the
white men had taught them to use. They hoped that every
aboriginal in the territory would join the movement, and
that the white man would be erased from the landscape.
   Of course it did not happen that way. By and large,
the white men who settled in the area had treated the
natives fairly. Pigeon found relatively few volunteers.
Worse, other aborigines who were smarting under injus-
tices inflicted by Pigeon (concerned, as usual, with
women) joined the whites. Soon, however, Pigeon,

Captain and Ellemara ambushed and slaughtered two more
white men in Winjana Gorge. These were Burke and
Gibbs, who, confident in their long friendship with the
local tribes, had refused to arm themselves even after
hearing of the death of Richardson.

Today this country breathes peace and serenity. (From
'Journey among Men')

Compare this with the Aboriginal material:

alright he took all the ammunition ...
take-im down the cave.
put it all his ammunition there, guns and all.
he might a been train (laughs)
oh yes he was still fighting.
oh no chance. he was keep fighting.
Pigeon was still fighting.
he had a ostrich inside his paddock (laughs)
he had his lil' paddock you know.
you know and er Pigeon home.
oh he was a real bushman that fella. real
real bushman.
used to be on a mountain.
they can't hardly find 'cos they can't see-im.
he's having the leaves front him and all the
long leaf an' he right behind the leaf.
used to be in the rock you know (SM:men)
had a few trick that fella (laughs)
(SM: How'd he finish up?)
eh?
(SM: How'd he finish up?)
he was finished ah un ah ...
that was good while he keep that fighting
goin'
'till um places were getting more bigger
and bigger see?
then he finished then ...
but we was still frightened of him you
know (laughs)
(SM: they killed him in the end didn't they?)
yeah killed him after (from transcript of orally presented
tale) (14)

It is evident that the first quotation is not a translation
of quotation two; rather, both are versions of the same

story paradigm. Or, one could say that example one is an intralingual translation or rewording in Jakobson's sense of story material as the white settlers grasped and ordered the local historical events, while example two is an interlingual translation of an Aboriginal version or versions into Pidgin English by an Aboriginal story teller. All this rather complicates the matter. One observation, though, which is crucial to my argument can be made without extravagant speculation: in the English version the narrative structure is dedramatized as a result largely of the suppression of the presentational process in favour of a controlled presented world. But the technical difference has ideological implications: unlike Aboriginal versions, our English example indeed 'breathes peace and serenity'.

By contrast, even in Pidgin English the Aboriginal story teller is stressing the dynamic presence of a narrator who caters for the joyful involvement of an audience. Story telling, no doubt, is here a communal activity. But to say that the difference between the two versions is the common one between oral and written narrative is not very helpful. It is essential to Aboriginal secular and, to a lesser degree, religious narrative that the presentational process be preserved as an integral structural element. The suppression of the multiple aspects of telling produces a falsification of Aboriginal literature. Unfortunately, as far as the treatment of narrative process is concerned, the quoted English example is fairly representative of the way in which the Australian English-speaking public receives Aboriginal narrative. Since the stories are made palatable, the reader is bound to construct a fictional world which is more his own view of Aboriginal culture than that culture revealing itself to him.

Unlike presentational process and presented world which are grasped by the reader by means of propositional and concretizing transformations, work ideology comes into existence at a further remove. It operates at a level of deep structure at which partly given (i.e. stated in the surface text) and largely inferred abstractions are combined into a set. Work ideology should be understood as the partly stated but largely derived structure of interpretative abstractions which serve the reader to characterize the work's artistic and ideological commitment. Since it is inferred to a high degree, work ideology cannot be translated in the sense in which typographic shape can be imitated or the linguistic stratum matched. However, the translator must feel obliged to allow the reader to construct, through the translation, a work ideology which, if not exactly the same, is at least closely related to the one the reader would be likely to abstract from the source text.

The matter, though, is further complicated by the fact that in the establishment of a story's work ideology the reader's own cultural and especially philosophical background play an even more decisive role than in the construction of any other part of narrative structure. For this reason I believe an additional source of information to be necessary. Especially when the historical and/or cultural gap between source and target text, between the sender and the receiver of the narrative message is considerable, the following items should be part of the introduction or the Translator's Note: a sketch of the history of ideas and socio-economic conditions from which the source text comes; special references to issues which are likely to be misinterpreted, i.e. are likely to be read in terms of the target culture rather than in terms of the philosophical background of the source text; and perhaps also a warning that such adequate reading will of necessity result in a relativization of the reader's own position.

Well-known cases in point are the translations into English of Sartre's 'La Nausée', Camus's 'L'Etranger', or Kafka's narratives, all of which have enjoyed a wide readership in the English-speaking world. It was only after existentialist thought in its Danish, German, and French variations was taught and debated in English that the novels' and stories' artistic-ideological commitments began to be constructed with some adequacy. Of course, this problem is not restricted to the reading of narrative. Brecht's epic-dialectic theatre has suffered a worse fate. The difference is that in narrative the reader concretizes both presentational process and presented world before he is able to derive an adequate set of interpretative umbrella propositions. As has been pointed out several times, in staged drama the presentational process is given immediately in physical shape and movement.

To discuss some of the many pitfalls of translation from the viewpoint of its reception is not to query the translator's business. On the contrary; it is, as Ortega y Gasset says, 'para que fuese resorte balistico que nos lanzase hacia el possible esplendor del arte de traducir.' (15) Translations play a vital role in the cultural life of any nation; they are a measure of how far it is in touch with the

rest of the world, how far it dares or seeks to encourage
foreign codes and visions to modify its own.   In this sense
translations are an instance of 'parole' placed in a dialec-
tical relationship with 'langue'.   Sometimes a translation
becomes fully integrated, so that it is understood as a part
of 'langue'.   'Sein oder Nichtsein', just as 'To be or not
to be', is a heading, an abbreviation, a cliché.   But when
this happens, the translation's active ingredient is lost,
its challenge to the existing norm of language and thought
has vanished;   there is no dialectic but mere identity.   In
translation, it is the ongoing process of new works and
their visions confronting 'langue' in the reading process
that counts.

Chapter 12

Fictional modality: a challenge to linguistics

The manners of speaking in a literary narrative comprise more than narrational speech acts, or the presentational process. Just as the speech acts of presented personae are ultimately subsumed under the reader's construction of presentational process, so the presentational process is in the end seen as a function of the narrative's overall implied authorial manner of speaking. To say therefore that a novel is a statement is an example once more of our habitual emphasis on the propositional and referential side of language. If we wish to make such generalizations at all we should at least say: a novel is a statement made in a certain manner (whereby manner is understood in the widest possible sense).

Language is always at least as much a structure for persuasion as it is a matrix for referential orientation. This is obviously true of social discourse but I would claim this is even more so of artistic uses of language. But the discussion of persuasion leads of necessity to considerations of modality, the speaker's overall stance to what he is saying. From this perspective literary art can be seen as the discourse which, certainly potentially, is more fully determined by modal operations than other forms of utterance.

If this is so, why is it that literary criticism has received so little help from the disciplines professionally concerned with modality: modal logic and linguistics? The summary answer is that the gap between interpretational demand and the tools of logic and linguistics is vast. In order for the concept of modality to be a valuable aid to literary art it must be sufficiently comprehensive to include the overall conditions and implications of the speech act in

its three narrative instances: presented speech, presentational discourse, and implied authorial stance.   Unfortunately, however, modal logic and, to a lesser degree,
linguistics have tended to restrict seriously the notion of
modality.   Consequently, both disciplines have achieved a
high degree of accuracy and, from the viewpoint of literary
studies, an equally high degree of triviality.

At best, modal logic has restricted modality to those
overt items of propositions that indicate necessity, impos-
sibility, contingency, non-necessity, possibility, non-
contingency.   Indeed, some philosophers, as for instance
W.V. Quine, go so far as to oppose the notion of modality
altogether. (1)   According to Nicholas Rescher, author of
'Studies in Modality', the major blame for impeding the
development of modal logic must be placed squarely at
Bertrand Russell's door.

> The distaste for modal logic in Anglo-American philos-
> ophy during the interim between the two World Wars was
> virtually initiated by Russell and largely propagated by
> his great influence.... Russell's philosophically
> inspired attitudes propagated a negative view of modal
> logic and helped to produce that disinclination to take
> modality seriously which can still be seen at work among
> our own contemporaries of the older generation (e.g.,
> W.V. Quine and N. Goodman).   The very success of
> Russell's work in the more mathematically oriented
> sectors of logic gave authority and impact to his antag-
> onistic stance towards the logic of modality.   For the
> development of this area of logic, at any rate, Russell's
> work represented a distinctly baneful influence. (2)

With its traditional emphasis on modal auxiliaries,
linguistics has had a similarly hampering influence on the
discussion of modality, since it must therefore ignore the
extensive range of implicit or covert indications of
modality. (3)   This strikes me as an astonishing phenomenon since, without also including covert modal operations in
the debate about language exchange, we are not describing
what is actually taking place.   Indeed, if we negate the
covert modality, our constructed meaning may even be the
very opposite of the meaning intended by the sender of the
message.   Some recent publications in linguistics have increasingly acknowledged the necessity of approaching the
question of modality as part of literary message in the broadest

possible sense.   Halliday's functional approach, for
example, sees the interpersonal function as a pervasive
aspect of language use, realized primarily but not exclusively through the system of modality. (4)   Summing up an
analysis of an interview transcript Gunter Kress and
Robert Hodge observe that: 'The major content of an
utterance is often found in the modal operations rather than
in the ostensible content', and further that:

> There are a large number of ways of realising modality:
> non-verbal and verbal, through non-deliberate features
> (hesitations, ums, ers, etc.) and deliberate systematic
> features, which include fillers (sort of), adverbs
> (probably, quite, better), modal auxiliaries (can, must),
> and mental-process verbs (think, understand, feel), and
> intonation. (5)

In reading a narrative text, the range of sources of
immediate information about modality which we have available is narrowed down to the total of printed (or spoken)
words.   But paradoxically this reduction in the basis for
information makes for more complex rather than simpler
operations in the reading consciousness.   Umberto Eco's
semiotic definition of aesthetic texts gives a useful
'structural model for the unstructured process of communicative interplay'.

> In the interpretive reading a dialectic between fidelity
> and inventive freedom is established.   On the one hand
> the addressee seeks to draw excitement from the
> ambiguity of the message and to fill out an ambiguous text
> with suitable codes; on the other, he is induced by
> contextual relationships to see the message exactly as it
> was intended, in an act of fidelity to the author and to the
> historical environment in which the message was
> emitted....
> A responsible collaboration is demanded of the
> addressee.   He must intervene to fill up semantic gaps,
> to reduce or to further complicate the multiple readings
> proposed, to choose his own preferred paths of interpre-
> tation, to consider several of them at once (even if they
> are mutually incompatible), to re-read the same text many
> times, each time testing out different and contradictory
> presuppositions.
> Thus the aesthetic text becomes a multiple source of

unpredictable 'speech acts' whose real author remains
undetermined, sometimes being the sender of the message,
at others the addressee who collaborates in its development. (6)

This applies fully to the literary narrative text, which has
a tripartite structure of modality, in that the multiple
variants of the linear arrangement of the text are complicated by the hierarchy of speech acts from presented and
presentational discourse to implied authorial modal stance.
Viewed in this way the construction of narrative meaning
relies on a vast matrix of possible modal transformations.
And if this is so, then literary narrative, more than any
other form of discourse, tends to be characterized by a
relatively high degree of modal instability.

The very possibility of ironic reversal suggests not only
two opposites but the full spectrum or circle of modal
modifications between these extremes. Further, because
of the mutual qualification of the three levels of speech act
in fictive narrative by what is said as well as by what is not
said, the possible combinations of modal operations in the
reading consciousness are potentially unlimited. It is this
formal complexity of the literary text rather than any
material 'content' (especially not eternal values) which
makes the construction of meaning not only and simply
enjoyable but also socially significant.

Isn't it surprising, then, that while specific readings and
criticisms have taken account of modal phenomena, literary
theory itself has remained insensitive to the problem?
Although certain aspects of fictive modality have been
studied in detail by some research from Bakhtin's discourse
typology to Chatman's 'Story and Discourse' (1978), the
full range and significance of modal operations in narrative
remains a project for the future. Chatman, for instance,
rightly places his discussion of discourse (presentational
process) and story (presented world) in the larger
assumption that the 'real author and audience ... communi-
cate ... through their implied counterparts'. But instead
of seeing discourse and story as two equally complex,
indeed, parallel systems, Chatman in the end resorts to a
disappointingly traditional discussion of the speech-act side
of narrative. (7)

This relative insensitivity to narrative modal operations
in the methodological discussion can be demonstrated also
by looking at the relationship between Barthes the reader/

critic and theorist of the reading process and Barthes the
theorist of literary codes in 'S/Z'. Barthes the reader/
critic in The Casuistry of Discourse says of a passage of
Balzac's story Sarrasine, it 'shows us that the discourse
is trying to lie as little as possible', (8) thus making it
clear that he is aware of the overt/covert modal aspects of
the text, their role in his construction of the presented
world, and the function of this relationship in his inferences
of the implied authorial stance.

By contrast, Barthes the theorist who imposes a five-code
structure on what happens when we read narrative is blind
to modal operations. His hermeneutic, semic, symbolic,
proairetic and referential codes are defined as to their
function mainly in the reader's establishment of the signified world. And summing up Barthes's schema Jonathan
Culler sees the 'absence of any code relating to narration'
as a 'major flaw'. (9) Culler is obviously right in pointing
out the absence of the narrative transmission in Barthes's
theory, but he does not go quite far enough, I believe, in
suggesting as a solution that we add discourse (or the
aspects of the presentational process) as a further code.
The modal side of speech is not an additional code at all,
but one of the 'two ever present aspects' of utterance, as
Todorov observes (10) or, in Halliday's terms, the
speaker's 'assessment of the validity of what he is
saying'. (11) Therefore, in order to match Barthes the
reader/critic with Barthes the theorist of codes each of his
five codes has to be amended to accommodate also a modal
aspect.

I argued at the beginning that literary theories which
approached the literary work of art from an extrinsic system
of inquiry were more likely to discover aspects of that
system in literary texts than features peculiar to fictive
literature. The discussion of a number of aspects of the
performance of narrative texts in the reading consciousness lead me to show how the presentational process as a
major aspect of fictional modality must be granted special
emphasis in literary theory if we are to come to grips
systematically with what we do when we read. Although an
essential part of all speech, modality finds its most complex
expression in fictional narrative. For its systematic study
two broad avenues of research appear to offer themselves:
the one which Wolfgang Iser proposes towards the end of
his 'The Act of Reading' (1979; German edn, 1976), and
the other, inquiries of the kind initiated by Lacan and continued, for example, by Francesco Orlando. (12)

Towards the end of his study Iser distinguishes
'Leerstellen' (blanks) along the syntagmatic axis of reading
from 'negation' which consists of the unformulated but
implied alternatives on the paradigmatic axis.   In the activities of reading 'Leerstellen' and negation are combined to
form a peculiar condensation of the fictional text.   The
bringing together of formulated and unformulated text items
thus results in what Iser calls doubling effect or 'negativity'. (13)   Expressed in terms of fictional modality, the
full spectrum of modal transformations of the text lies
between that which is quasi-referentially given and its unformulated, implied negative alternatives.

The total sphere of unformulated text alternatives (syntagmatic as well as paradigmatic, along the forward reading
dimension as well as through all the strata of meaning
construction, and at all three levels of narrative speech
acts – presented, presentational, and implied authorial)
functions as a potential set of modal qualifiers of a text.
How much of that modal sphere is activated in the individual
reading event depends on a number of inter-related factors,
such as the reader's linguistic competence, stock-piled
inter-textual and everyday typifications and ideological
position.   But in any performance of narrative the reader
must begin with the data of the text and his/her typified
inter-textual and everyday knowledge-at-hand and proceed
towards increasingly inferential acts of consciousness,
part of which are covert modal operations.   One kind of
text alternatives is formulatable but not formulated; there
is another kind which consists of the reader's construction
of the speaker's (presented, presentational, and implied
authorial) subconscious and repressed text alternatives.
They too appear to me to be legitimate forms of modality.
However, their study requires a definition of meaning construction different from and beyond the one underlying the
present study.   Fictional modality in this sense challenges
literary theory and especially linguistics to include a
psychoanalytic approach.

Notes

PREFACE

1 Cf. also Robert Magliola, Parisian Structuralism
   Confronts Phenomenology: the Ongoing Debate,
   'Language and Style', VI (1973), pp. 237-48.
2 Especially Mikel Dufrenne, Critique littéraire et
   Phénoménologie, 'Revue Internationale de Philosophie',
   68/69 (1964), pp. 173-208; 'The Phenomenology of
   Aesthetic Experience', tr. Edward S. Casey et al.
   (Evanston, Ill.: Northwestern University Press, 1973);
   Nicolai Hartmann, 'Aesthetik' (Berlin: Walter de
   Gruyter, 1955); Wolfgang Iser, 'The Implied Reader'
   (Baltimore: Johns Hopkins University Press, 1974) and
   'The Act of Reading' (London: Routledge & Kegan Paul,
   1979); Michael Murray, 'Modern Critical Theory' (The
   Hague: Martinus Nijhoff, 1975); Maurice Natanson,
   'Literature, Philosophy and the Social Sciences' (The
   Hague: Martinus Nijhoff, 1962); Georges Poulet,
   Phenomenology of Reading, 'New Literary History', 1
   (1969), pp. 53-68; Paul Ricoeur, 'Le Conflit des
   interprétations: essais d'herméneutique' (Paris:
   Editions du Seuil, 1969); Peter Berger, The Problem
   of Multiple Realities: Alfred Schutz and Robert Musil,
   'Phenomenology and Social Reality: Essays in Memory
   of Alfred Schutz', ed. Maurice Natanson (The Hague:
   Martinus Nijhoff, 1970), pp. 213-33; Paul Brodtkorb,
   'Ishmael's White World' (New Haven, Conn.: Yale
   University Press, 1965); R. Swaeringen, 'Reflexivity
   in Tristram Shandy: A Phenomenological Analysis' (New
   Haven, Conn.: Yale University Press, 1977).
3 'Struktur der Entwicklung' (Munich: Wilhelm Fink,
   1975), pp. 93ff.

4 Tzvetan Todorov, La lecture et reconstruction du texte, 'Poétique', 6 (1975), p. 417.
5 Gerald Prince, 'A Grammar of Stories' (The Hague: Mouton, 1973).
6 'Journal of Literary Semantics', 5 (1976), pp. 5-14.
7 'Literatur als System und Prozess', ed. and tr. Rolf Fieguth (Munich: Nymphenburger, 1975), pp. 81-109; especially pp. 102-4.
8 See John L. Austin, 'How to do Things with Words' (London: Oxford University Press, 1962); J.R. Searle, 'Speech Acts' (Cambridge University Press, 1969).
9 See Stanley Fish, Literature in the Reader: Affective Stylistics, 'New Literary History', 1 (1970), pp. 123-62; Erwin Wolff, Der intendierte Leser, 'Poetica', 4 (1971), pp. 140-66; Wayne C. Booth, 'The Rhetoric of Fiction' (Chicago: University of Chicago Press, 1963), pp. 137f.; Michael Riffaterre, Criteria for Style Analysis, 'Word', 15 (1960), pp. 154-74.
10 Formen Narrativer Identitätskonstitution im Höfischen Roman, 'Identität' (Munich: Wilhelm Fink, 1979), pp. 553-89; especially pp. 553-7.
11 Terry Eagleton, 'Criticism and Ideology: A Study in Marxist Literary Theory' (London: New Left Books, 1976), p. 80.

1 WHAT HAPPENS WHEN WE READ A NARRATIVE TEXT?

1 E.g., the seminal works of Wayne C. Booth, 'The Rhetoric of Fiction' (Chicago: University of Chicago Press, 1961), and Robert Scholes and Robert Kellogg, 'The Nature of Narrative' (New York: Oxford University Press, 1966).
2 E.g., Robert Champigny, 'The Ontology of Narrative' (The Hague: Mouton, 1972); Roger Fowler (ed.), 'The Languages of Literature: Papers on Some Linguistic Contributions to Criticism' (London: Routledge & Kegan Paul, 1971); Roger Fowler, 'Linguistics and the Novel' (London: Methuen, 1977); Ingrid Hantsch, 'Die Semiotik des Erzählens' (Munich: Fink, 1975); Teun van Dijk (ed.),'Text Grammar and Narrative Structure' ('Poetics', No. 3, The Hague: Mouton, 1972), which contains papers given by linguists at the Fourth International Symposium on Narrative Structures at Constance, Western Germany, 13-17 April 1971; or John Woods, 'The Logic of Fiction' (The Hague: Mouton, 1974).

3 The general principles of this approach were explored between the late 1920s and late 1960s by the Polish philosopher Roman Ingarden; see the English translations of his two seminal German works on literary theory, 'The Literary Work of Art' and 'The Cognition of the Literary Work of Art', both published in the USA (Evanston, Ill.: Northwestern University Press, 1973); I shall comment critically on his approach in more detail at a later stage.

4 'Horizons of expectations' is a Husserlian term employed by Hans Robert Jauss in 'Literaturgeschichte als Provokation der Literaturwissenschaft' (Constance: Druckerei und Verlagsanstalt, 1969), e.g. especially pp. 33f., 36, 39, 43, or 64.

5 For the concepts 'typification' and 'stock-of-knowledge-at-hand' see Alfred Schutz, e.g., 'Collected Papers I: The Problem of Social Reality', ed. Maurice Natanson (The Hague: Martinus Nijhoff, 1962).

6 Franz Stanzel, 'Narrative Situations in the Novel' (Bloomington: Indiana University Press, 1971); the German edition of Stanzel's book precedes Wayne C. Booth's 'The Rhetoric of Fiction' by six years. It has had considerable influence at German universities, but less so in the USA and the UK, where its central types are often rejected as categories too rigid to be useful. Nevertheless, the book does deserve careful consideration not only on the grounds of its theory, but also because it contains some excellent analyses of narrative texts. Seymour Chatman resumes Stanzel's concern with narrative speech situations as well as the sentiments of Stanzel's earlier critics in The Structure of Narrative Transmission, in Roger Fowler (ed.), 'Style and Structure in Literature: Essays in the New Stylistics' (Oxford: Blackwell, 1975), pp. 213-57; he, too, finds Stanzel's schema somewhat 'taxonomic' and prefers a 'feature kind of analysis', p. 237.

7 For a detailed discussion of implied readers and the way we construct them from texts see Wolfgang Iser, 'The Implied Reader' (Baltimore: Johns Hopkins University Press, 1974). In chapter 2 below the implied/stated reader is given a separate column.

8 Stanzel, 'Narrative Situations in the Novel', p. 61.

9 An intelligent (but as far as the first-person novel is concerned misled) discussion of 'statement subject' and 'I-origo' can be found in Käte Hamburger, 'Die Logik

der Dichtung' (Stuttgart: Ernst Klett, 1957), pp. 29ff.;
see also the English edition, 'The Logic of Literature',
tr. M.J. Rose (Bloomington: Indiana University Press,
1973), pp. 28ff.

10 In order to avoid the confusion of foregrounded narrative process and discourse as part of the presented
world, I shall refer to the former as 'process markers'
and to the latter as 'discourse within the presented
world'.

11 Fowler, 'Linguistics and the Novel', p. 44.

12 In Jurij M. Lotman, 'Aufsätze zur Theorie und Metho-
dologie der Literatur und Kunst', ed. Karl Eimermacher
(Kronberg: Scriptor, 1974), pp. 21-9.

13 A.J. Greimas, 'Sémantique Structurale' (Paris:
Larousse, 1966), 'Du Sense' (Paris: Editions du
Seuil, 1970); cf. also his 'Sign, Language, Culture'
(The Hague: Mouton, 1970) and 'Essais de Sémiotique
Poétique' (Paris: Larousse, 1971), of which Greimas
is editor.

14 Tzvetan Todorov, 'Grammaire du Décaméron' (The
Hague: Mouton, 1969), especially pp. 27-48.

15 Teun van Dijk, Jens Ihwe, Janos S. Petöfi and Hannes
Rieser, 'Zur Bestimmung narrativer Strukturen auf der
Grundlage von Textgrammatiken' (Hamburg: Helmut
Buske, 1974), p. 16.

16 Fowler, 'Linguistics and the Novel', p. 45.

17 Ibid., p. 47.

18 'The Westminster Study Edition of the Holy Bible'
(Philadelphia: Westminster Press), pp. 23-6; Robert
Coover, 'Pricksongs and Descants' (New York: Plume
Books, 1970), pp. 20-45.

19 Fowler, 'Linguistics and the Novel', p. 126.

20 Jurij M. Lotman, 'Die Struktur des künstlerischen
Textes', ed. Rainer Grübe (Frankfurt: Suhrkamp,
1973), p. 415.

21 Roman Jakobson and Morris Halle, 'Fundamentals of
Language' (The Hague: Mouton, 1956), pp. 81f.

22 Roman Jakobson, Closing Statement: Linguistics and
Poetics, in Thomas A. Sebeok (ed.), 'Style in
Language' (Cambridge, Mass.: MIT Press, 1966),
p. 370.

2   PRESENTATIONAL PROCESS AND 'NARRATIVE TRANSGRESSION'

1 Roland Barthes, Action Sequences, in 'Patterns of
   Literary Style', ed. Joseph Strelka (University Park:
   Pennsylvania State University Press, 1971), pp. 13f.
2 Roland Barthes, An Introduction to the Structural
   Analysis of Narrative, 'New Literary History', 6 (1975),
   pp. 263f.
3 Teun A.J. van Dijk, Philosophy of Action and Theory of
   Narratives, 'Poetics', 5 (1976), pp. 323ff.; cf. also
   his paper Action, Action Description and Narrative,
   'New Literary History', 6 (1975), p. 291; and John
   Searle, The Logical Status of Fictional Discourse,
   ibid., pp. 319-32.
4 Roland Barthes, Action Sequences, in Barthes,
   'Patterns of Literary Style', pp. 7 and 9.
5 A.J. Greimas and J. Courtès, The Cognitive Dimension
   of Narrative Discourse, 'New Literary History', 7
   (1976), p. 440.
6 Teun A.J. van Dijk, Action, Action Description and
   Narrative, 'New Literary History', 6 (1975), p. 291.
7 Teun A.J. van Dijk, Philosophy of Action and Theory of
   Narrative, 'Poetics', 5 (1976), p. 323.
8 Roman Ingarden, 'The Cognition of the Literary Work of
   Art' (Evanston, Ill.: Northwestern University Press,
   1973); e.g., p. 13.
9 Barthes, An Introduction to the Structural Analysis of
   Narrative, p. 245.
10 Robert Scholes and Robert Kellogg, 'The Nature of
   Narrative' (New York: Oxford University Press, 1966),
   p. 4.
11 E.g., by Bachelard, Butor, Raleigh, Spanos, Spencer,
   et al.
12 E.g., by Bronzwaer, Butor, Church, Gross, Kumar,
   Melchiori, Mendilow, Müller, Pascal or Weinrich.
13 E.g., by Blankenburg (1774), Galsworthy, Harvey,
   McCarthy, Mudvick, Walcutt, Zabel or Ziolkowsky.
14 E.g., by Barthes, Jolles, Lämmert, Propp, Todorov,
   or Van Dijk.
15 E.g., by Crane, Goldmann, Lukács, or Trilling.
16 E.g., by Bourneuf and Quellet, Booth, Frey, Friedemann, Friedman, Kayser, Koskimies, Leisi, Neuhaus,
   Romberg, Spitzer, Stanzel, Weimann, Uspensky or
   Chatman.

17 Especially by Fish, Iser, Jauss, Vodička, Warning.
18 W.J.M. Bronzwaer, 'Tense in the Novel: An Investigation of Some Potentialities of Linguistic Criticism'
   (Groningen: Wolters-Noordhoff, 1970), p. 84.
19 Franz Stanzel, 'Narrative Situations in the Novel'
   (Bloomington: Indiana University Press, 1971).
20 Lubomír Doležel, Toward a Structural Theory of
   Content in Prose Fiction, 'Literary Style: A
   Symposium', ed. Seymour Chatman (London: Oxford
   University Press, 1971), p. 97.
21 Mixail Baxtin, Discourse Typology in Prose, in
   'Readings in Russian Poetics: Formalist and Struc-
   turalist Views', ed. Ladislav Matejka and Krystyna
   Pomorska (Cambridge, Mass.: MIT Press, 1971),
   p. 193.
22 Erich Kahler, 'The Inward Turn of Narrative', tr.
   R.C. Winston (Princeton, N.J.: Princeton University
   Press, 1973).

3 NARRATIVE LANGUAGE

1 Michel Butor, 'Inventory', tr. and ed. Richard Howard
   (New York: Simon & Schuster, 1969), p. 26.
2 'Novel: A Forum on Fiction', II (Fall, 1968), pp. 5f.
3 This agrees with the observation made by Robert
   Kellogg that 'for writing to be narrative no more and no
   less than a tale and a teller are required': 'The Nature
   of Narrative' (New York: Oxford University Press,
   1966), p. 4. However, the processes of telling are
   much more complex than this laconic statement may
   suggest, and require special attention.
4 'Towards a Poetics of Fiction', 'Novel: A Forum on
   Fiction', II (Fall, 1968), p. 5.
5 Käte Hamburger, 'The Logic of Literature', 2nd rev.
   edn, tr. M.J. Rose (Bloomington: Indiana University
   Press, 1973), pp. 8ff.
6 N.W. Visser, 'The Novelistic Documentary: A Study of
   the Non-Fictional Novel', unpubl. doct. diss., Rhodes
   University, South Africa, 1972.
7 David Lodge, 'Language of Fiction: Essays in Criticism
   and Verbal Analysis of The English Novel' (London:
   Routledge & Kegan Paul, 1966), and 'The Novelist at the
   Crossroads and Other Essays on Fiction and Criticism'
   (London: Routledge & Kegan Paul, 1971).

8 This, I am afraid, applies also to Tzvetan Todorov who, no doubt, is convincing in 'cerner les manifestations les plus évidentes d'une catégorie linguistique dans le récit littéraire.'   But other areas such as 'le temps, la personne, l'aspect, la voix en littérature' remain problematical: 'Poétique de la prose' (Paris: Editions du Seuil, 1971), p. 41.

9 'The Languages of Literature: Papers on Some Linguistic Contributions to Criticism' (London: Routledge & Kegan Paul, 1971), p. 52.

10 Ibid., p. 54.

11 F.W. Bateson, Linguistics and Literary Criticism, in 'The Disciplines of Criticism: Essays in Literary Theory, Interpretation, and History', ed. Peter Demetz, Thomas Greene, and Lowry Nelson, Jr (New Haven, Conn.:   Yale University Press, 1968), p. 16.

12 E. Stankiewicz, Poetic and Non-Poetic Language in Their Relation, 'Poetics', by Donald Davie, Roman Jakobson, et al. (The Hague: Mouton, 1961), p. 23.

13 Roman Jakobson, Linguistics and Poetics, in 'Style in Language', ed. Thomas A. Sebeok (Cambridge, Mass.: MIT Press, 1966), p. 377.

14 Parts and Wholes, in 'Selected Writings II: Word and Language' (The Hague: Mouton, 1971), p. 280.

15 Visual and Auditory Signs, in ibid., p. 336.

16 Parts and Wholes, p. 284.   Cf. S. Saporta, who concedes that there may be something else besides language in poetry when he says that 'the application of linguistics to poetry must assume that poetry is language and disregard whatever else poetry may be': The Application of Linguistics to the Study of Poetic Language, in 'Style in Language', p. 93.

17 Parts and Wholes, p. 284.

18 Roman Jakobson, Zeichen und System der Sprache, in 'Selected Writings', pp. 277f.

19 See, e.g., Simon O. Lesser, 'Fiction and the Unconscious' (New York: Random House, 1957), and Norman N. Holland, 'The Dynamics of Literary Response' (New York: Oxford University Press, 1968); cf. also the work of M.D. Faber.

20 The Language Animal, 'Encounter', 33 (August 1969), p. 19.

21 Max Rieser, Roman Ingarden and His Time, 'Journal of Aesthetics and Art Criticism', 29 (1971), pp. 448.

22 Stankiewicz, Poetic and Non-Poetic Language in Their Relation, pp. 13ff.

23 S.L. Bethell, 'Essays on Literary Criticism and the English Tradition' (London: Dennis Obson, 1969), p. 45.
24 Poetik und Sprachwissenschaft, in 'Poetics', ed. Donald Davie, Roman Jakobson, et al. (The Hague: Mouton, 1961), pp. 3-9.
25 Lodge, 'Language of Fiction: Essays in Criticism and Verbal Analysis of the English Novel', p. 46.
26 Lodge, 'The Novelist at the Crossroads and Other Essays on Fiction and Criticism', p. 59.
27 Ibid., p. 60.
28 Ibid., p. 58.
29 'Language of Fiction', p. 78.
30 Ibid., p. 79.
31 Standard Language and Poetic Language, in 'Linguistics and Literary Style', ed. Donald C. Freeman (New York: Holt, Rinehart & Winston, 1970), p. 29.
32 'The Short Stories of Ernest Hemingway' (New York: Charles Scribner's Sons, 1953), pp. 91-5.
33 In the edition quoted.
34 Hemingway, 'Short Stories', p. 89.
35 Alfred Schutz, 'Collected Papers I: The Problem of Social Reality', ed. Maurice Natanson (The Hague: Martinus Nijhoff, 1962), pp. 9, 18, 76f.

4 NARRATIVE STRATIFICATION AND THE DIALECTIC OF READING

1 Quoted by Roland Barthes, An Introduction to the Structural Analysis of Narrative, 'New Literary History', 6 (1975), p. 245.
2 An essential feature which is neglected by René Wellek in 'Theory of Literature' (New York: Harcourt, 1947), p. 157; cf. Roman Ingarden's indignation at this error in his Preface to the third edition of 'Das literarische Kunstwerk' (Tübingen: Max Niemeyer, 1965), pp. xx–xxiv.
3 Cf. his Artistic and Aesthetic Values, 'The British Journal of Aesthetics', 4 (1964), pp. 198-213.
4 Cf. Alfred Schutz, 'Collected Papers I: The Problems of Social Reality', ed. Maurice Natanson (The Hague: Martinus Nijhoff, 1962), pp. 9, 18, 76.
5 Roman Ingarden, 'Vom Erkennen des literarischen Kunstwerks' (Darmstadt: Wissenschaftliche Buchgesellschaft, 1968), pp. 10ff. See the English edition, 'The

Cognition of the Literary Work of Art' (Evanston, Ill.: Northwestern University Press, 1973), pp. 12ff.

6 An attempt is thus being made to render more precise such general notions as 'the problem of point of view is narrative art's own problem, one that it does not share with lyric or dramatic literature', Robert Scholes and Robert Kellogg, 'The Nature of Narrative' (New York: Oxford University Press, 1966), p. 240, as well as Franz Stanzel's general position as expounded in 'Narrative Situations in the Novel', tr. James J. Pusack (Bloomington: Indiana University Press, 1971).

7 Stanzel, 'Narrative Situations in the Novel', pp. 92ff. Originally published in German in 1955, Stanzel's work must still be regarded as a major contribution to a descriptive approach to the presentational features in narrative. From my special angle, however, one shortcoming is the central term 'narrative situation', in that it suggests stasis rather than process.

8 Cf. Stanzel's typology in 'Narrative Situations in the Novel', pp. 158ff. By comparison, Käte Hamburger's separation of first-person narration from fiction seem far-fetched. Cf. also Text Structure Against the Background of Language, by Wojciech Górny, who distinguishes between three levels of narration: a central level or 'main narration'; a 'lower level' or 'direct quoted speech' (one could add thoughts); and a 'superstructure' consisting of 'remarks on the text': 'Poetics', ed. Donald Davis, Roman Jakobson et al. (The Hague: Mouton, 1961), p. 36.

9 Modes of Interior Monologue, A Formal Definition, 'Modern Language Quarterly', 28 (1967), p. 238.

10 For a further detailed analysis of the relationship between presentational process and presented world, see chapter 10 below.

11 Malcolm Bradbury, 'Possibilities: Essays on the State of the Novel' (London: Oxford University Press, 1973), p. 23.

12 Cf. Maurice Natanson, 'Literature, Philosophy and the Social Sciences' (The Hague: Martinus Nijhoff, 1962), pp. 84ff., or Jean-Paul Sartre's view that 'the literary object has no other substance than the reader's subjectivity': 'What is Literature?' tr. Bernard Frechtman (New York: Harper & Row, 1965), p. 39. See also the more recent work of Wolfgang Iser, especially Indeterminacy and the Reader Response in Prose Fiction, in

'Aspects of Narrative: Selected Papers from the English
Institute', ed. J. Hillis Miller (New York: Columbia
University Press, 1971), pp. 1-45; and The Reading
Process: A Phenomenological Approach, 'New Literary
History', 3 (1972), pp. 279-99.
13 Bradbury, 'Possibilities', p. 12.
14 See, e.g., Joseph Frank, Spatial Form in Modern
Literature, 'Sewanee Review', 53 (Spring, Summer
and Autumn 1945), pp. 221-40; 433-56; 643-53.
15 Poetics and Linguistics, in 'Linguistics and Literary
Style', ed. Donald C. Freeman (New York: Holt,
Rinehart & Winston, 1970), pp. 112ff.
16 Iser, The Reading Process, pp. 279f., 293, 299.
17 In 'A Walk in the Night' (London: Heinemann, 1972),
pp. 121-4.
18 'Reflections on the Problem of Relevance', ed. Richard
M. Zaner (New Haven, Conn.: Yale University Press,
1970), pp. 26, 35f., 46, 50; for Schutz's concept of
'stock of knowledge at hand' see 'Collected Papers I',
e.g., pp. 7ff.
19 'Ideen zu einer reinen Phänomenologie und phänomenol-
ogischen Philosophie, Buch I, Allgemeine Einführung in
die reine Phänomenologie', Husserliana v. III (The
Hague: Martinus Nijhoff, 1950), pp. 216ff.

5 LADDERS OF FICTIONALITY

1 Cf. Käte Hamburger's 'experience-field of the lyric I'
in 'The Logic of Literature', tr. M.J. Rose, 2nd rev.
edn (Bloomington: Indiana University Press, 1973),
p. 292; but unlike Hamburger's, my study does not
exclude first-person narrative from the realm of
fictional narrative.
2 Cf. Robert Champigny, 'The Ontology of Narrative: An
Analysis' (The Hague: Mouton, 1972), pp. 9ff.
3 This schema is in part Roman Ingarden's, partly Nicolai
Hartmann's, and partly my own.
4 Cf. Maurice Natanson's 'artistic reduction' and
'reflexive reconstruction' in 'Literature, Philosophy,and
the Social Sciences' (The Hague: Martinus Nijhoff,
1962), pp. 81ff. These aspects are discussed also in
some detail in my paper Reading Works of Literary Art,
'The Journal of Aesthetic Education', 8 (1974), pp. 75-
90.

5 R.G. Collingwood, 'The Idea of History' (Oxford: Clarendon Press, 1967), pp. 235ff.; cf. also A.J.P. Taylor's comment that the historian is 'writing to shape into a version a tangle of events that was not designed as a pattern', in 'Times Literary Supplement', 23 March 1973), p. 327. See also Warner Berthoff, Fiction, History, Myth: Notes Towards the Discrimination of Narrative Forms, in 'The Interpretation of Narrative: Theory and Practice', ed. Morton W. Bloomfield (Cambridge, Mass.: Harvard University Press, 1970), pp. 263–87; Leo Braudy, 'Narrative Form in History and Fiction' (Princeton, N.J.: Princeton University Press, 1970); Russell B. Nye, History and Literature: Branches of the Same Tree, in 'Essays on History and Literature', ed. Robert H. Bremner (Columbus: Ohio State University Press, 1966), pp. 123–57; or Maurice Mandelbaum, A Note on History as Narrative, 'History and Theory', 6 (1967), pp. 413–19.

6 Edmund Husserl, 'Ideas: General Introduction to Pure Phenomenology', tr. W.R. Boyce Gibson (London: Allen & Unwin, 1958), pp. 71f.

7 Cf. Roman Ingarden's concepts of 'lacunae of indeterminacy' and 'concretization'.

8 Cf. Husserl's Fifth Meditation in 'Cartesian Meditations: An Introduction to Phenomenology', tr. Dorian Cairns (The Hague: Martinus Nijhoff, 1960), especially pp. 112f.

9 See the letter of 8 March 1866, in which Trollope recalls that 'the house which I had chiefly in my mind's eye when I described Mr Thornes house in Barchester Towers was a place called, I think, Montacute House, belonging to Mr Phelips – not far from Yeovil in Somersetshire,' in 'The Letters of Anthony Trollope', ed. B.A. Booth (London: Oxford University Press, 1951), p. 179.

10 A term used by Ronald Beck in Art and Life in the Novel, 'Journal of Aesthetics and Art Criticism', 31 (1972), pp. 63–6, to attack such positions as David J. Schneider's in Techniques of Composition in Modern Fiction, 'Journal of Aesthetics and Art Criticism', 26 (1968), pp. 317–28, or David Madden's in Form and Life in the Novel: Towards a Freer Approach to an Elastic Genre, 'Journal of Aesthetics and Art Criticism', 25 (1967), pp. 323–33; I would add also much of Mary McCarthy's The Fact in Fiction, 'Partisan Review', 27 (1960), pp. 438–58.

11 E.M.W. Tillyard, 'The Epic Strain in the English Novel' (London: Chatto & Windus, 1958), p. 200
12 Ernst Cassirer, 'The Philosophy of Symbolic Forms', vol. 2, 'Mythical Thought', tr. Ralph Manheim (New Haven, Conn.: Yale University Press, 1955), p. 100.
13 E.g., Angus Fletcher's idea of allegory as presenting 'an aesthetic surface which implies an authoritative, thematic, "correct" reading,' 'Allegory, The Theory of a Symbolic Mode' (Ithaca, N.Y.: Cornell University Press, 1965), p. 305. Cf. also Michael Murvin's claim that 'allegory is intimately associated with the society in which the poet writes; it demands human participation and must be explicable in social terms, 'The Veil of Allegory: Some Notes Toward a Theory of Allegorical Rhetoric in the English Renaissance' (Chicago: University of Chicago Press, 1969), p. 74; or, more narrowly, Edwin Honig's suggestion that allegory is 'a rhetorical instrument used by strategists of all sorts in their struggle to gain power or to maintain a system of beliefs,' 'Dark Conceit: The Making of Allegory' (Evanston, Ill.: Northwestern University Press, 1959), p. 179.
14 Volker Neuhaus, 'Typen Multiperspektivischen Erzählens' (Cologne: Böhlau, 1971), pp. 78ff.
15 Natanson, 'Literature, Philosophy and the Social Sciences', p. 82.
16 Ibid., p. 91.
17 Helmut R. Wagner (ed.), 'Alfred Schutz on Phenomenology and Social Relations: Selection Writings' (Chicago: University of Chicago Press, 1970), p. 256.
18 See chapter 10 for a more detailed discussion of the relation between world and process in 'As I Lay Dying'.
19 Erich Auerbach, 'Mimesis: The Representation of Reality in Western Literature', tr. Willard R. Trask (Princeton, N.J.: Princeton University Press, 1953), p. 27.
20 As a result of such multiple dialectic, 'objective interpretation' which is 'founded on a self-critical reconstruction of textual meaning' must remain a purely theoretical claim: E.D. Hirsch, Objective Interpretation, 'PMLA', 75 (1960), p. 463.

6 BRACKETED WORLD AND READER CONSTRUCTION IN THE MODERN SHORT STORY

1 Bret Harte, The Rise of the Short Story, 'Cornhill Magazine', 7 (July 1899), p. 1; Frederick B. Perkins, 'Devil-Puzzlers and Other Stories' (New York: Putnam's Sons, 1877), Preface, p. xviii; Danforth Ross, 'The American Short Story', Pamphlets on American Writers, 14 (Minneapolis: University of Minnesota Press, 1963), p. 35; Robert W. Neal, 'Short Stories in the Making' (New York: Oxford University Press, 1914), p. 15; Norman Friedman, What Makes the Short Story Short?, 'Modern Fiction Studies', 4 (1958), pp. 103-17.

2 Frank O'Connor, 'The Lonely Voice: A Study of the Short Story' (London: Macmillan, 1965), pp. 15, 39; Bonaro Overstreet, Little Story, What Now?, 'Saturday Review of Literature', 24 (22 November 1941), p. 4; Theodor Wolpers, Kürze im Erzählen, in 'Die Amerikanische Short Story: Theorie und Entwicklung', ed. Hans Bungert (Darmstadt: Wissenschaftliche Buchgesellschaft, 1972), pp. 388-426; Vladimir Propp, 'Morphology of the Folktale' (Austin: University of Texas Press, 1975), especially pp. 20f. for the definition of 'functions'; H.S. Canby, 'The Short Story in English' (New York: Henry Holt, 1909), p. 301.

3 Ruth J. Kilchemann is quite wrong, I think, in seeing a modern open ending in the anecdote; see her 'Die Kurzgeschichte: Form und Entwicklung' (Stuttgart: Kohlhammer, 1967), p. 23; Kafka's indebtedness to Hebel is pointed out, for instance, by Hans Bender in Ortsbestimmung der Kurzgeschichte, 'Akzente', 3 (June 1962), pp. 205-25.

4 Cf. chapter 8; A.L. Bader presents a similar argument when he says that the surprise ending merely 'contributes a new understanding', in The Structure of the Modern Short Story, 'College English', 7 (1945), p. 86.

5 Cf. Howard C. Brasher's typology of Western novels in The Cowboy Story from Stereotype to Art, 'Moderna Sprak', 56 (1963), pp. 290-9. On the use of character formulae, cf. Howard Baker, The Contemporary Short Story, 'Southern Review', 3 (1938), p. 581; cf. also Theodore Stroud's definition of the popular love story in A Critical Approach to the Short Story, 'Journal of General Education', 9 (1956), p. 93. See above all Robert Scholes, 'Structural Fabulation: An Essay on

Fiction of the Future' (Notre Dame, Ind.: University of
Notre Dame Press, 1975).

6 Especially since the publication of Lance in Vladimir
Nabokov, 'Nabokov's Dozen' (New York: Books for
Libraries Press, 1958), pp. 197-212.

7 Baker, The Contemporary Short Story, p. 577; Warren
Beck, Art and Formula in the Short Story, 'College
English', 5 (1943), pp. 61 and 58.

8 In Roman Jakobson's sense.

9 'The Complete Works of Edgar Allan Poe', ed. James A.
Harrison (New York: Thomas Y. Crowell, 1902),
especially 11, pp. 106-8; 14, pp. 193f. Such later
theories as those by Brander Matthews, 'The Philosophy
of the Short Story' (New York: Longman's, 1901) or
J.B. Esenwein, 'Writing the Short Story' (New York:
Hinds, Noble & Elredge, 1909), do not add significantly
to Poe's observations.

10 Chekhov, 'Letters on the Short Story, the Drama, and
Other Literary Topics', ed. Louis S. Friedland, tr.
Constance Garnett (New York: Minton, Balch, 1924),
pp. 11f., 69-71, 82f., 106. Chekhov's suggestions
about reader concretization are paraphrased later, for
example, by L.A.G. Strong in The Short Story: Notes
at Random, 'Lovat Dickson's Magazine', 2 (March 1934),
p. 281.

11 'The Art of the Novel: Critical Prefaces by Henry
James', ed. Richard P. Blackmur (New York: Charles
Scribner's Sons, 1935), pp. 278, 239f.

12 Henry James, 'Critical Prefaces', p. 220.

13 Tr. John Macquarrie and E. Robinson (London: SCM
Press, 1962), p. 298, note XII.

14 'Philosophie II: Existenzerhellung' (Berlin: Springer,
1956), pp. 201-54; especially 220-49.

15 Chekhov, 'Letters', p. 69.

16 On the belated recognition even in Latin America of
Borges's work, cf. José Donoso, 'The Boom in Spanish
American Literature, A Personal History' (New York:
Columbia University Press, 1977), pp. 19, 21.

17 Cf. Robert Scholes, Metafiction, 'Iowa Review', 1
(1970), pp. 100-15; Philip Stevick, Scheherazade runs
out of plots, goes on talking; the king, puzzled, listens:
an essay on new fiction, 'Tri Quarterly', 26 (1973), pp.
332-62; Arlen J. Hansen, The Celebration of Solipsism:
A New Trend in American Fiction, 'Modern Fiction
Studies', 19 (1973), pp. 5-15; or Charles I. Glicksberg,

Experimental Fiction: Innovation Versus Form, 'Centennial Review', 18 (1974), pp. 127-50.

7 NARRATIVE STRANDS: PRESENTED AND PRESENTATIONAL

1 The little attention which narrative strands have received has been focused on presented strands; and although most of my observations concerning presentational strands have been made outside any comprehensive terminology, the structural interdependence of both kinds of strands appears to make their related discussion logically cogent. Cf., e.g., Eberhard Lämmert, 'Bauformen des Erzählens' (Stuttgart: Metzlersche, 1912), pp. 43-67.
2 My emphasis.
3 Joseph W. Reed, Jr, 'Faulkner's Narrative' (New Haven, Conn.: Yale University Press, 1974), p. 112.
4 Ibid., p. 113.
5 Olga W. Vickery, 'The Novels of William Faulkner' (Baton Rouge: Louisiana State University Press, 1961), p. 66.

8 ACTS OF NARRATING: TRANSFORMATIONS OF PRESENTATIONAL CONTROL

1 Cf. Edmund Husserl, throughout his works; for a brief introduction to intentionality see Aron Gurwitsch, On the Intentionality of Consciousness, in 'Philosophical Essays in Memory of Edmund Husserl', ed. Marvin Farber (New York: Greenwood Press, 1968), pp. 65-83.
2 See especially Wolfgang Iser, 'The Implied Reader' (Baltimore: Johns Hopkins University Press, 1974).
3 The relationship between the structural system of process-world-implied/stated reader and the actual reader is explained satisfactorily neither by autotelic theories (e.g., New Criticism) nor by those stressing the extraneous message of narrative (e.g., Terry Eagleton's notion of signification and ideology).
4 Käte Friedemann, 'Die Rolle des Erzählers in der Epik' (Darmstadt: Wissenschaftliche Buchgesellschaft, 1965; 1910); Norman Friedman, Point of View in Fiction: The Development of a Critical Concept,

'PMLA', 70 (1955), pp. 1160-84; Wayne C. Booth, 'The Rhetoric of Fiction' (Chicago: University of Chicago Press, 1961); Franz Stanzel, 'Narrative Situations in the Novel' (Bloomington: Indiana University Press, 1971; 1955); Derek Bickerton, Modes of Interior Monologue: a Formal Definition, 'Modern Language Quarterly', 28 (1967), p. 238; Käte Hamburger, 'The Logic of Literature' (Bloomington: Indiana University Press, 1973); Seymour Chatman, The Structure of Narrative Transmission, in 'Style and Structure in Literature: Essays in the New Stylistics' ed. Roger Fowler (Oxford: Blackwell, 1975), pp. 213-57.

5 Boris Uspensky, 'A Poetics of Composition' (Berkeley: University of California Press, 1973).

6 See chapter 1, above.

7 Jean Piaget, 'Structuralism' (London: Routledge & Kegan Paul, 1971), pp. 5-16.

8 Matthew 13:11; cf. the 'mystery of the Kingdom of God' in Mark 4:11, or also Luke 8:10.

9 Cf. André Jolles, 'Einfache Formen', 2nd edn (Tübingen: Max Niemeyer, 1958), on 'Märchen', myth, joke, riddle, Saint's legend, and other rudimentary forms of narrative.

10 For an exhuastive study of the English saint's legend see Theodor Wolpers, 'Die englische Heiligenlegende des Mittelalters' (Tübingen: Max Niemeyer, 1964); see also Klaus Sperk (ed.) 'Medieval English Saints' Legends' (Tübingen: Max Niemeyer, 1970).

11 E.g., 'in the days of Uzziah, Jotham, Ahaz, and Hezekia, kings of Juda' (Isaiah); or 'in the eighth month, in the second year of Darius' (Zechariah).

12 This is certainly the case in such confessions proper as St Augustine's, Rousseau's, De Quincey's, Alfred de Musset's, Chateaubriand's, or George Moore's; the fictional confession, as for example Camus's 'La Chute', requires the additional construction by the reader of the relationship between narrator and implied author.

13 Alain Robbe-Grillet, La Plage, in 'Instantanés' (Paris: Editions de Minuit, 1962), pp. 63-73.

14 If there is no solution, the reader at the end of the narrative anuls the narrator's seeming advantage.

15 Cf. Wayne C. Booth's classic comments on the story in 'The Rhetoric of Fiction', pp. 347-54.

16 Arthur Koestler, 'The Act of Creation' (London: Picador Books, 1977), pp. 32-8.

17 Ibid., pp. 72-4.
18 José Donoso, 'The Obscene Bird of Night' (New York:
    Alfred A. Knopf, 1973), p. 67.
19 Tadeusz Borovsky, Supper, in 'Polen Erzählt:
    Zweiundzwanzig Erzählungen', ed. Gerda Hagenau
    (Frankfurt: Fischer, 1963), pp. 22-5.
20 Mixail Baxtin, Discourse Typology in Prose, in
    'Readings in Russian Poetics: Formalist and Structura-
    list Views', ed. Ladislav Matejka and Krystyna
    Pomorska (Cambridge, Mass.: MIT Press, 1971), p.
    193.
21 Apuleius, 'Metamorphosen oder Der Goldene Esel', in
    Latin and German by Rudolf Helm (Berlin: Akademie
    Verlag, 1961), p. 28.
22 The links established by way of literary production are
    not the focus of this study, but see chapter 5, above.
23 Jaques Derrida, 'L'Ecriture et la Différence' (Paris:
    Editions du Seuil, 1967), pp. 41-4.

9 PARODIC NARRATIVE

1 Gilbert Highet, 'The Anatomy of Satire' (Princeton,
    N.J.: Princeton University Press, 1962), pp. 80ff.
2 Mikhail Bakhtin, 'Problems of Dostoevsky's Poetics'
    (1929), tr. R.W. Rotsel (Ann Arbor, Mich.: Ardis,
    1973); Roman Ingarden, e.g., in 'The Cognition of the
    Literary Work of Art', tr. R.A. Crowley and K.R.
    Olson (Evanston, Ill.: Northwestern University
    Press, 1973).   See chapter 10, below, for a discussion
    of the application to narrative structure of the form-
    content metaphor.
3 (London: Oxford University Press, 1970), p. 127.
4 Cf. Roman Ingarden, 'The Literary Work of Art'
    (Evanston, Ill.: Northwestern University Press, 1973);
    and 'The Cognition of the Literary Work of Art'; W. Iser,
    The Reading Process: A Phenomenological Approach,
    'New Literary History', 3 (1972), pp. 279-99; H.G.
    Ruthrof, Reading Works of Literary Art, 'The Journal of
    Aesthetic Education', 8 (1974), pp. 75-90; F.V.
    Vodička, 'Struktur der Entwicklung' (Munich: Fink,
    1975), especially pp. 63, 65, 66, 69ff., 87ff., 103ff.,
    120f., 124f.
5 Ingarden's two studies, 'The Literary Work of Art' and
    'The Cognition of the Literary Work of Art' are designed

to clarify the more general aspects of this distinction.

6 Ingarden, 'The Cognition of the Literary Work of Art',
   'polyphony of aesthetically valent qualities', p. 13;
   'polyphony of aesthetically relevant qualities', p. 225;
   'harmony of aesthetically relevant qualities', p. 369.
   I am leaving aside here Ingarden's other criterion, the
   quasi-proposition of works of literature versus proper
   propositions in, e.g., a scientific report.

7 First published in 'Westerly', December 1969.

8 Highet, 'The Anatomy of Satire', p. 103.

9 Cf. Viktor Šklovskij, Der parodistische Roman:
   Sterne's 'Tristram Shandy', in 'Russischer Formalis-
   mus', ed. with an introduction by Jurij Striedter
   (Munich: Fink, 1971), pp. 245–99.

10 Dwight Macdonald, 'Parodies' (London: Faber & Faber,
   1960), pp. 251–4.

11 Ibid., pp. 43, 44, 47.

12 Thomas Mann, 'The Holy Sinner' (Harmondsworth:
   Penguin, 1961), pp. 5f.

13 Ibid., pp. 227f.

14 James Joyce, 'Ulysses' (Harmondsworth: Penguin,
   1976), pp. 402f.

15 John Barth, Life-Story, in 'Lost in the Funhouse' (New
   York: Doubleday, 1968), p. 127.

16 George Lukács, 'The Theory of the Novel' (Cambridge,
   Mass.: MIT Press, 1971), p. 101.

17 The terms 'reductive' and 'augmentive' parody were proposed at a Conference on Parody held at the Australian
   National University in Canberra, 1976.

10 NARRATIVE AND THE FORM-CONTENT METAPHOR

1 Jorge Luis Borges, Pierre Menard, Author of the
   Quixote, in 'Labyrinths: Selected Stories and Other
   Writings', ed. Donald A. Yates and James E. Irby
   (Harmondsworth: Penguin, 1976), p. 71.

2 James Joyce, 'A Portrait of the Artist as a Young Man'
   (New York: Viking Press, 1968), p. 132.

3 Roman Ingarden, Das Form-Inhalt Problem in
   literarischen Kunstwerk, 'Helicon', 1 (1938), pp. 51–67;
   see also his The General Question of the Essence of
   Form and Content, 'Journal of Philosophy', 57 (1960),
   pp. 222–33.

4 See René Wellek's paper, Concepts of Form and

Structure in Twentieth Century Criticism, 'Neophilo-
logus', 42 (1958), pp. 1-11.

5 Sir Philip Sidney, An Apology for Poetry, in 'English
Critical Texts', ed. D.J. Enright and Ernst de
Chickera (London: Oxford University Press, 1962),
pp. 19f.

6 John Dryden, An Essay of Dramatic Poesy, in 'English
Critical Texts', p. 55.

7 Alexander Pope, Essay on Criticism, 11, p. 76f. in
'The Poems of Alexander Pope: vol. I, Pastoral Poetry
and An Essay on Criticism', ed. E. Audra and A.
Williams (London: Methuen, 1961), p. 247; cf. their
explanation of 'informing' as 'endowing with a form of
essential character; permeating as an animating and
characterizing quality', suggestive of an outer and
inner form.

8 Gustave Flaubert, 'Correspondence', Nouvelle Edition
Augmentée, vol. 3 (1853), p. 141: 'La forme est la
chair même de la pensée, come la pensée en est l'âme,
la vie,' quoted in René Wellek, 'A History of Modern
Criticism 1750-1950', vol. 4 (New Haven, Conn.: Yale
University Press, 1965), p. 10 and notes, p. 477.

9 George Saintsbury, 'The History of English Prosody'
(London: Macmillan, 1906), quoted in Wellek, 'A History
of Modern Criticism', vol. 4, p. 418 and note on
Saintsbury, p. 624.

10 Christopher Caudwell, Studies in a Dying Culture
(1938), in 'Studies and Further Studies in a Dying
Culture' (New York: Monthly Review Press, 1971),
pp. 1-228.

11 Terry Eagleton, 'Marxism and Literary Criticism'
(London: Methuen, 1976), p. 24.

12 Yvor Winters, 'In Defense of Reason' (New York:
Swallow Press, 1947), p. 464; cf. also his 'fallacy of
expressive, or imitative form' which 'succumbs to the
raw material of the poem', p. 41, or his attack on Joyce
and other modern writers who behave 'like Whitman
trying to express a loose American by writing loose
poetry', p. 62; they all fail to impose moral artistic
form on 'crude experience', p. 464. But even Wimsatt
and Brooks adopt the critical cliché:

Our exposition has preferred to make use of the
readily definable and widely understood convention
that 'matter' is the content or message of literary

works, so far as that may be extricated from their
dense formality, and 'form' is all that complication and
stylization which in past ages has in one way or
another been looked on as extraneous to matter – a
kind of ornament, recommendation, fortification,
dress, or the like. ('Literary Criticism, A Short
History' (New York: Alfred Knopf, 1957), p. 748)

13 August Wilhelm Schlegel, 'A Course of Lectures on
Dramatic Art and Literature', 2nd edn, 2 vols (London:
J. Templeman and J.R. Smith, 1840).
14 Samuel Taylor Coleridge, 'Biographia Literaria', ed.
J. Shawcross, vol. 1 (London: Oxford University
Press, 1949), pp. 107 and 249.   See also his definition
of primary and secondary imagination and fancy, p. 202,
as well as his statement, 'the idea which puts the form
together cannot itself be the form', vol. 2, p. 259.
15 Georg Wilhelm Friedrich Hegel, 'Vorlesung über
Ästhetik' (Stuttgart: Reclam, 1971), pp. 449–682; see
especially the Introduction to Part II; cf. also Part
III, 'Die Poesie'.   Hegel's view is related to
Friedrich Schlegel's idea of early art being characterized by receptivity, later art by spontaneity, so that
to begin with material is the dominating force, while
formal principles gradually become the decisive factor
as art advances through history: 'Schriften und
Fragmente' (Stuttgart: Kroner, 1956), pp. 2–153.
16 Bertrand Russell, 'History of Western Philosophy'
(London: Allen & Unwin, 1975), pp. 705f.
17 George Lukács, Die Theorie des Romans, in
'Zeitschrift für Ästhetik und Allgemeine Kunstwissen-
schaft', 2 (1916), pp. 225–71, 390–431; English
version: 'The Theory of the Novel' (Cambridge, Mass.:
MIT Press, 1971).
18 Gustave Flaubert, 'Correspondence' (1852): 'Ce qui me
semble beau ... c'est un livre sur rien,' quoted from
Wellek, 'A History of Modern Criticism', vol. 4, p. 10
and note 29 on Flaubert, p. 477.
19 Walter Pater, 'The Renaissance: Studies in Art and
Poetry' (London: Library Edition, 1910), p. 134; to
quote the passage in context:

All art constantly aspires towards the condition of
music....   That the mere matter of a poem, for
instance, its subject, namely, its given incidents or

situation – that the mere matter of a picture, the
actual circumstances of an event, the actual
topographie of a landscape – should be nothing without
the form, the spirit of the handling, that this form,
this mode of handling, should become an end in itself,
should penetrate every part of the matter: this is what
all art constantly strives after.

20 Oscar Wilde, The Critic as Artist, in 'Intentions'
(London: Osgood, McIvaine, 1881), p. 197. In this
fictive dialogue between Ernest and Gilbert, Wilde has
Gilbert make the central observation: 'The repetitions
of patterns give us rest. The marvels of design stir
the imagination' (p. 196); 'Yes: Form is everything.
It is the secret of life' (p. 198); or, 'Start with the
worship of form, and there is no secret in art that will
not be revealed to you' (p. 198).
21 Roger Fry, 'Vision and Design' (London: Chatto &
Windus, 1920), p. 10.
22 Benedetto Croce, 'La Poesia' (Bari: Laterza and Sons,
1936), p. 124.
23 Victor Shklovskij, in 'Readings in Russian Poetics:
Formalist and Structuralist Views', ed. Ladislav
Matejka and Krystyna Pomorska (Cambridge, Mass.:
MIT Press, 1971), p. 12.
24 Boris Ejxenbaum, The Theory of the Formal Method,
in ibid., p. 12.
25 Terry Eagleton, 'Marxism and Literary Criticism', pp.
23 and 26. See also his 'Criticism and Ideology'
(London: New Left Press, 1976).
26 William Faulkner, 'As I Lay Dying', in 'The Sound and
the Fury and As I Lay Dying' (New York: Random House,
1946), pp. 500f.
27 Hyatt Waggoner, 'William Faulkner: From Jefferson to
the World' (Lexington: University Press of Kentucky,
1959), pp. 76 and 71.
28 Roger Fowler, 'Linguistics and the Novel' (London:
Methuen, 1977), pp. 45f., 54.
29 Faulkner, 'As I Lay Dying', pp. 345f.
30 Ibid., pp. 526f.
31 Ibid., pp. 513f.
32 Ibid.: Dewey Dell's sections, pp. 355f.; Darl's
sections, pp. 422, 458.
33 Roman Jakobson, Zeichen und System der Sprache, in
'Selected Writings II: Word and Language' (The Hague:
Mouton, 1971), pp. 277f.

34 'As I Lay Dying', pp. 531f.
35 Waggoner, 'William Faulkner', p. 76.
36 Ibid., p. 77.
37 Franz Stanzel, 'Narrative Situations in the Novel' (Bloomington: Indiana University Press, 1971; 1955): 'In the future a distinction will thus be made between the experiencing self and the narrating self,' p. 61.
38 Boris Uspensky, 'A Poetics of Composition' (Berkeley: University of California Press, 1973), especially pp. 81-100.

11 TRANSLATING NARRATIVE

1 George Steiner, 'After Babel: Aspects of Language and Translation' (London: Oxford University Press, 1975), p. 279.
2 Quoted in the Bibliography in R.A. Brower, 'On Translation' (New York: Oxford University Press, 1966).
3 Roman Jakobson, On Linguistic Aspects of Translation, in 'On Translation', p. 233; cf. also Steiner's discussion of Jakobson's schema in 'After Babel', pp. 260f.
4 In Jorge Luis Borges, 'Labyrinths: Selected Stories and Other Writings', ed. Donald A. Yates and James E. Irby (Harmondsworth: Penguin, 1976), pp. 62-71.
5 Bertrand Russell, Logical Positivism, 'Revue Internationale de Philosophie', 4 (1950), p. 18.
6 Jakobson, On Linguistic Aspects of Translation, p. 233.
7 Steiner, 'After Babel', p. 279.
8 George Steiner, Linguistics and Poetics, in 'Extraterritorial: Papers on Literature and the Language Revolution' (New York: Atheneum, 1971), pp. 126-54; cf. Boris Ejxenbaum's statement as quoted in chapter 10.
9 J.C. Catford, 'A Linguistic Theory of Translation' (London: Oxford University Press, 1974), p. 20.
10 Ibid., p. 1.
11 Theodore Savory, 'The Art of Translation' (Boston: Mass.: Writer, Inc., 1968), p. 14.
12 Jorge Luis Borges, 'El Hacedor' (Madrid: El Libro de Bolsillo, 1975), p. 69; the English translation is quoted from 'Labyrinths', p. 282.
13 'Sir Gawain and the Green Knight', ed. J.R.R. Tolkien and E.V. Gordon (Oxford: Clarendon Press, 1960), p. 1; 'Sir Gawain and the Green Knight', tr. with an Introduction by Brian Stone (Harmondsworth: Penguin,

1965), p. 23; 'Sir Gawain and the Green Knight', tr. Theodore Howard Banks, Jr (New York: Appleton-Century-Crofts, 1957), p. 11.

14 The excerpts are taken from a draft of a PhD thesis presently being prepared by Stephen Muecke (SM) in the Department of Anthropology at the University of Western Australia; the English quotation is from Jock Marshall and Russell Drysdale, 'Journey among Men' (London: Hodder & Stoughton, 1962), p. 126; the excerpt in Pidgin English is part of the transcription by Stephen Muecke of his tape recording of 'Pigeon Story' told by Sam Woolagoodja.

15 Ortega y Gasset, 'Miseria y Esplendor de la Traduccion', tr. into German as 'Elend und Glanz der Übersetzung' by Katharina Reiss (Munich: Deutscher Taschenbuch Verlag, 1976), p. 22.

12 FICTIONAL MODALITY: A CHALLENGE TO LINGUISTICS

1 Cf. the discussion of modal logic in 'Readings in Semantics', ed. F. Zabeeh, E.D. Klemke, and A. Jacobson (Urbana: University of Illinois Press, 1974), pp. 761-853, including papers by Carnap and Quine.

2 Nicholas Rescher, 'Studies in Modality', American Philosophical Quarterly Monograph Series (Oxford: Basil Blackwell, 1973), p. 96.

3 Even Lubomír Doležel's Narrative Modalities, 'Journal of Literary Semantics', 5 (1976), pp. 5-14, seems to me to curtail the field of fictional modality far too rigorously.

4 Cf. 'System and Function in Language: Selected Papers', ed. G. Kress (London: Oxford University press, 1976).

5 Gunther Kress and Robert Hodge, 'Language as Ideology' (London: Routledge & Kegan Paul, 1979), p. 127; cf. also R. Fowler, R. Hodge, G. Kress and T. Treu, 'Language and Control' (London: Routledge & Kegan Paul, 1979).

6 Umberto Eco, 'A Theory of Semiotics' (London: Macmillan, 1977), p. 276.

7 Seymour Chatman, 'Story and Discourse' (Ithaca, N.Y.: Cornell University Press, 1978), pp. 31 and 267; the chart on p. 267 does not do full schematic justic to the author's detailed argument between pp. 147 and 262.

8 Roland Barthes, 'S/Z' (New York: Hill & Wang, 1974),
   p. 141.
9 Jonathan Culler, 'Structuralist Poetics' (London:
   Routledge & Kegan Paul, 1975), p. 203.
10 Tzvetan Todorov, 'The Poetics of Prose' (Oxford:
   Basil Blackwell, 1977), p. 26.
11 M.A.K. Halliday, 'Language as Social Semiotic'
   (London: Edward Arnold, 1978), p. 223.
12 Cf. Francesco Orlando, 'Towards a Freudian Theory of
   Literature' (Baltimore: Johns Hopkins University
   Press, 1979; Italian edn, 1973).
13 'Der Akt des Lesens' (Munich: Wilhelm Fink, 1976), pp.
   283-355; modal transformations of text affirmations by
   their implied opposites constitute a special area of
   meaning construction as part of the much wider concept
   of negativity of art as argued by Adorno and analysed by
   Hans Robert Jauss in 'Ästhetische Erfahrung und
   literarische Hermeneutik 1' (Munich: Wilhelm Fink,
   1977), pp. 37ff.

Subject index

action sequence, viii, 10;
  emphasis on, 110; gram-
  mars of, x
acts of narrating, xiii;
  kinds of, 122
acts of splicing, 121
acts of synthesizing, vii, 121
adumbrational aspects, xii
aesthetic object, viii
'amplificatio' and 'brevitas',
  97; artistic and aesthetic,
  143
appresentation, vii, 79ff.
artistic object, viii

boundary situation story,
  103ff.; circular structure
  in, 106f.; focal structure
  in, 107; linear structure
  in, 105ff.; reader 'epoche'
  in, 107f.
bracketing, xii, 96ff.

classical narrative as norm,
  23f.
concretization, vii; combinations of, 28ff.; compulsory, ix; connotative and
  denotative, 184f.; differ-

ent kinds of, ix; imaginative, ix; linguistic, ix;
  variable, 55f.
connotation and denotation,
  184f.
control relations, xiii, 122ff.

dialectic of reading, xii;
  and narrative, 76

Eco's semiotic definition of
  aesthetic texts, 196f.
eidetic vs mimetic, 26

fictionality, ladders of, xii,
  79ff.
form-content metaphor, xiii,
  158ff.; kinds of, 160ff.;
  in narrative, 166-80
formalization-deformaliza-
  tion, vii, ix, 83
forward reading dimension,
  viii; in Blankets, 69ff.

horizon of expectations, x,
  2; formally empty, 6
horizons, vii; in 'Alice',

Name index

Adorno, T.W., 223
Aichinger, I., 104, 106
Aldrich, T.B., 100
Apuleius, 135f., 216
Aristotle, 160
Audra, E., 218
Auerbach, E., 95, 211
Austen, J., 149
Austin, J.L., x, 201

Bachelard, G., 204
Bachmann, I., 29
Bader, A.L., 212
Baker, H., 212f.
Balzac, H. de, 198
Barth, J., 10, 29f., 108, 132, 217
Barthelme, D., 31, 153
Barthes, R., x, xii, 23, 197f., 204, 207, 223
Bateson, F.W., 36, 206
Baxtin (Bakhtin), M., 32, 135, 141, 205, 216
Beck, R., 210
Beck, W., 213
Beckett, S., 10
Bell, C., 164
Bellow, S., 28, 128
Bender, H., 212
Berger, P., viii, 200

Berthoff, W., 210
Bethell, S.L., 38, 207
Bickerton, D., 64, 122, 215
Bierce, A., 99f., 106
Bierwisch, M., 68
Blackmur, R.P., 213
Bloomfield, M.W., 210
Böll, H., 104
Booth, B.A., 210
Booth, W.C., xi, 201, 204, 215
Borchert, W., 106
Borges, J.L., 10, 107, 132, 153, 182, 188, 217, 221
Borovsky, T., 135, 216
Bradbury, M., 40, 67, 208f.
Brasher, H.C., 212
Braudy, L., 210
Brecht, B., 192
Bremner, R.H., 210
Brodtkorb, P., viii, 200
Brontë, C., 90
Bronzwaer, W.J.M., 25, 204f.
Brower, R.A., 221
Bungert, H., 212
Butor, M., 34, 204f.

Camus, A., 103, 130
Canby, H.S., 98, 212